Sams **Teach Yourself**

Microsoft®

Dynamics CRM 4

in
24 Hours

SAMS   800 East 96th Street, Indianapolis, Indiana, 46240 USA

Sams Teach Yourself Microsoft® Dynamics CRM 4 in 24 Hours

Copyright© 2010 by Pearson Education, Inc.

ISBN-13: 978-0-672-33067-4

ISBN-10: 0-672-33067-9

Library of Congress Cataloging-in-Publication Data

Stanton, Anne A.
  Sams teach yourself Microsoft Dynamics CRM 4 in 24 hours / Anne Stanton.
     p. cm.
  Includes index.
  ISBN-13: 978-0-672-33067-4
  ISBN-10: 0-672-33067-9
  1. Microsoft CRM. 2. Customer relations--Data processing. 3. Relationship marketing. 4. Management information systems. I. Title. II. Title: Teach yourself Microsoft Dynamics CRM 4 in 24 hours.
  HF5415.5.S7345 2010
  658.8'12028553--dc22
                                            2009039573

Printed in the United States of America

First Printing October 2009

Trademarks

All terms mentioned in this book that are known to be trademarks or service marks have been appropriately capitalized. Sams Publishing cannot attest to the accuracy of this information. Use of a term in this book should not be regarded as affecting the validity of any trademark or service mark.

Warning and Disclaimer

Every effort has been made to make this book as complete and as accurate as possible, but no warranty or fitness is implied. The information provided is on an "as is" basis. The author and the publisher shall have neither liability nor responsibility to any person or entity with respect to any loss or damages arising from the information contained in this book.

Bulk Sales

Sams Publishing offers excellent discounts on this book when ordered in quantity for bulk purchases or special sales. For more information, please contact

U.S. Corporate and Government Sales
1-800-382-3419
corpsales@pearsontechgroup.com

For sales outside of the U.S., please contact

International Sales
international@pearsoned.com

Associate Publisher
Greg Wiegand

Acquisitions Editor
Loretta Yates

Development Editor
Kevin Howard

Managing Editor
Patrick Kanouse

Project Editor
Mandie Frank

Copy Editor
Keith Cline

Indexer
Ken Johnson

Proofreader
Sheri Cain

Technical Editor
Irene Pasternack

Publishing Coordinator
Cindy Teeters

Designer
Gary Adair

Compositor
Mark Shirar

Contents at a Glance

Table of Contents

About the Author

Anne Stanton, Certified Microsoft Dynamics CRM professional and CRM MVP alumni, has been working with line-of-business software for professional service companies for more than 20 years. A passionate technologist with a degree in computer science and a master's degree in business administration, Anne has been known as The CRM Lady on her blog at www.crmlady.com for the past 5 years. She has held such positions as Vice President of Commercial Logic, Inc.; Director of Microsoft Dynamics CRM Practice at The Rand Group, LLC; and President and Owner of The Norwich Group. Anne has also been a national speaker for such events as Microsoft Convergence, SMB Nation, Information Technology Alliance, and the Association of Accounting Marketers.

Dedication

This book is dedicated to my patient and loving husband, who has spent a significant amount of time encouraging me to pursue personal and family goals, sometimes at his own great personal sacrifice. It is also dedicated to my daughter, stepdaughter, and stepson, who have been tackling college and young adulthood and of whom I am extremely proud!

I also want to dedicate this book to the community of passionate people who, for no other reason than to help continue to participate in the online forums, post incredibly helpful knowledge on various blogs, keep Twitter updated in real time, and share their personal lives on Facebook and other social media platforms. This includes peers, friends, and family who have been there in one form or another through some crazy times.

Acknowledgments

My deepest thanks to the following contributing writers, who, through their writing, taught me even more about the inner details of Microsoft Dynamics CRM: Irene Pasternack (Hours 20 and 21), Darren Liu (Hour 9), Curt Spanburgh (Hour 14), Guy Riddle (Hour 5), and Scott Head (Hour 23).

An extra thank you to the people at Pearson Education, a great team to work with and whose contributions were extremely valuable.

We Want to Hear from You!

As the reader of this book, you are our most important critic and commentator. We value your opinion and want to know what we're doing right, what we could do better, what areas you'd like to see us publish in, and any other words of wisdom you're willing to pass our way.

You can email or write me directly to let me know what you did or didn't like about this book—as well as what we can do to make our books stronger.

Please note that I cannot help you with technical problems related to the topic of this book, and that due to the high volume of mail I receive, I might not be able to reply to every message.

When you write, please be sure to include this book's title and author as well as your name and phone or email address. I will carefully review your comments and share them with the author and editors who worked on the book.

Email: networking@samspublishing.com

Mail: Greg Wiegand
         Associate Publisher
         Sams Publishing
         800 East 96th Street
         Indianapolis, IN 46240 USA

Reader Services

Visit our website and register this book at www.informit.com/title/9780672330674 for convenient access to any updates, downloads, or errata that might be available for this book.

Introduction

Microsoft Dynamics CRM, a product of great depth and versatility, is a customer-relationship management application, a salesforce automation application, a customer-service application, a platform and framework for software development, and an application that you can configure to meet a variety of relationship management needs. In this book, we cover the sales, service, and reporting functionality of Microsoft Dynamics CRM, as well as the core building blocks of the product and the extensibility. We also touch on the CRM industry and how customer-relationship management business needs align with CRM technology. Finally, we discuss the concept of using CRM as an *xRM* development platform.

Who Should Read This Book?

All direct users of Microsoft Dynamics CRM and Microsoft Dynamics CRM Online will find this book helpful, as will Microsoft partners expanding into the Microsoft Dynamics CRM space, software developers, and others interested in learning more about the product.

If you are already working with Microsoft Dynamics CRM, you will still find helpful information in this book that will expand your understanding of the product (and perhaps put your experience with it into fuller perspective). And, if you have never worked with Microsoft Dynamics CRM, this book provides the foundational knowledge to get you started and upon which you can expand as you learn to exploit the software's full potential.

Microsoft Dynamics CRM has changed dramatically since it inception, with many of those changes emanating from user suggestions. Now that Microsoft Dynamics CRM has matured to version 4.0 R6, the product is rich with functionality, backed by a powerful community, and built for myriad uses, as you will learn throughout this book.

How This Book Is Organized

This book is divided into six parts that will get you up to speed quickly with Microsoft Dynamics CRM:

Part I: Introduction to the Business Use of Microsoft Dynamics CRM

Part II: The Structure of Microsoft Dynamics CRM

Part III: Getting Started Using the Software

Part IV: The Support Department

Part V: Reporting

Part VI: Expanding the Application

Special Features

This book includes the following special features:

- ▶ **Hour roadmaps:** At the beginning of each hour, you will find a list of what the hour covers.

- ▶ **Did You Know?:** Throughout the hours, these notes and tips provide further information and clarification about items of interest that are just beyond the range of the regular text.

- ▶ **Watch Out!:** Throughout the hours, you'll find these warnings, which it will behoove you to note, remember, and respect.

- ▶ **Tasks:** Delineated in numbered lists so that you can easily follow the steps and thus easily complete each task.

- ▶ **Workshop:** Each hour has a "Workshop" section, where you find a "CRM in use" example and a case study that relates to the material covered in the hour.

- ▶ **Q&A:** At the end of each hour is a "Q&A" section that considers frequently asked questions about material covered in that hour.

- ▶ **Quiz:** These quizzes (and answers), at the end of each hour, test you on what you learned during the hour.

- ▶ **Exercises:** To reinforce what you learned each hour, you should complete the recommended exercises at the very end of the hour.

HOUR 1

What Is Microsoft Dynamics CRM?

What You'll Learn in This Hour:

▶ Overview of the CRM Industry

▶ Multiple Dimensions of CRM Software

▶ Department Roles: Different Perspectives

▶ Business Applications and Functions

▶ Executive Summary

This hour focuses on opening the mind to a potential new world: the world of customer relationship management (CRM). This world did not start with the invention of technology nor does it end with a specific application. This world has long been researched, studied, documented, debated, and discussed. The goal of this hour is to build a foundation of understanding that will leave a few doors open. Doors that answer your questions and allow you to master Microsoft Dynamics CRM.

Overview of the CRM Industry

The list of customer relationship management (CRM) line-of-business applications was long prior to Microsoft Dynamics CRM coming to market five years ago. In fact, CRM software is one of the oldest applications available and has been released in numerous flavors by many vendors over the years. When solving the CRM business need with CRM technology, we are talking about a well-researched subject. A simple search will open the door to the CRM industry, which includes industry-specific magazines, generic and product-specific white papers, articles, books, debates, blogs and wikis, and a long list of successes and failures at all company levels. In this chapter, we peek into this broad world.

When it comes to technology, CRM software is often the heart and soul of a company. CRM software often crosses all departments, offices, and niches within a company, and is both a corporate and a personally needed toolset. The product can support an individual in his efforts to organize his day and to-do list, and it can aggregate data from many individuals for corporate analysis and decision making. It can automate a process to enhance and support corporate standards, and it can automate a process to support an individual's interest in efficiency. CRM software not only has to be successful for the corporation, it must also empower the individual.

Watch Out!

Thoughts on Process

If automation speeds up processes, what happens when the processes are incorrect?

CRM Software Is Multidimensional

CRM software is multidimensional and has a number of core areas within it (see Figure 1.1). These include corporate interests and personal interests. Let's dive into a number of these areas.

FIGURE 1.1
CRM is multidimensional.

CRM Software Is Extremely Personal

We each have our own style for getting things done, managing our relationships, and reminding ourselves of what we have to do. Technology focused on the CRM space must be flexible enough to support individual styles and yet structured enough to promote corporate standards. If we consider applying this technology to an audience of salespeople, we also have unique audience-specific considerations. Many times, salespeople have become successful because of their own talent, habits, style, and connections. These factors are often unique and come from a salesperson's experiences, trainings, and focus. When rolling out CRM software, changes are inevitable, but asking any salesperson to change a successful style is often an uphill battle. Unlike other audiences, an additional element to the salesperson audience is that a salesperson's success usually contributes and pays a part of his salary. To get a high level of adoption in this market, the CRM application must offer something to salespeople that they want and something that meets a need that can not be met without the tool.

Common CRM marketing touts include *faster access to information* and *more personal efficiency*, but this is often not enough when talking to an established and successful salesperson. However, technology continues to break down barriers and offer more. It can increase success and support efforts to maintain success in an increasingly fast-paced world. Offering key features, such as integration to mapping data (GeoData) with an easily reachable map to the contact's office or capturing instant customer-specific information from the Internet and feeding it up in the customer summary, can be very powerful.

Another powerful option is increasing the functionality of already much loved and well-used tools through enhancement and integration with other applications. Taking existing habits and tools and bringing them to the next level can speed and increase adoption while also creating loyal users. This is one reason why Microsoft Dynamics CRM functions through the email client, Microsoft Outlook, and it works closely with other Microsoft applications, such as Microsoft Word, Microsoft Excel, and Microsoft Office SharePoint Service.

We have talked about the mindset of a successful salesperson, but what about a salesperson who is not doing so well? We can attribute this to any number of variables, but how would an offer of or improvement to CRM software be considered in this situation? When the pressure is on from management and the "rope is short," having powerful tools to get the job done quickly, smoothly, and efficiently can help. These tools, if already existing prior to a failure, can also be blamed for an individual's lack of success. As the heart and soul of a firm and of individual productivity, CRM software sits in a very volatile space.

CRM Software Helps Individuals Move Past Limitations

How many people can you keep track of without using technology or a piece of paper? Perhaps you have a special gift and can keep track of hundreds of people, but what about all the specific details? We all have our crutches. Perhaps this is a small black book, a manila file on each client, or a bit of technology (from a computer to mobile device), but the small details are often captured in more places than just memory. CRM software enables us to capture and store more information.

CRM also helps automate processes, and when it comes to individual's habits and tasks, automation can reduce redundancy. If someone is spending time doing the same tasks over and over again for different clients, for example, CRM software can automate this mundane process and free her up to do more advanced and unique tasks, tasks that require more intelligence or careful thinking or the unique skills of a human. Take the process of sending out a follow-up package when a new prospect inquires about a company (a rather repetitive process). Instead of the salesperson redoing the entire process over again, he can customize the letter to a specific inquirer and let the system automatically compile standard electronic material to include for new prospects. CRM software can also customize the material for this specific prospect based on other criteria, such as industry, location, or interest.

CRM Software Collects Firm Wide Data

In this information age, one of the biggest assets for a company is the data captured and retained and the intellectual capital that this represents. This idea of captured information when it comes to relationships is a controversial one, and yet much of a corporation's success in marketing and customer service is based on knowledge about the customer and the relationship the corporation has with the customer. As staff turnover becomes more common, the retention of this critical data becomes even more difficult. Customer information can be captured. The size, location, industry, products purchased, purchasing habits, and preferred service variables are all data oriented, but what about the relationship? A relationship is often between two people or a small group of people and another group of people. A customer has a point person who regularly calls and places orders. The person taking the order might be the same person, the same one or two people, or always someone new. In the first scenario, a relationship exists between the point person at the customer site and the point person taking the orders. After an order is placed, these two people might share more information (a laugh, a question about the weather on the other side of the country, or more personal information). If either one of these people leaves, the customer still gets service, but the service level changes. In the second scenario, we have one specific point person, but when he calls to place an order, he talks to two or three different people. In this scenario, the risk of reducing the connection to the customer is slightly lower.

Increasingly, companies are trying to reduce the risk of compromising customer service when key staff people leave or when contacts within the customer change positions. When looking to capture some of the details needed to reduce this risk, CRM software is called upon. A customer service point person, who adds a note indicating that her customer always calls on a Friday morning and that recently her daughter was married, helps the next customer service person to offer that much more personal service.

CRM Offers Various Returns on Investment

Let's now consider a corporation's return on investment (ROI) from the adoption of a CRM solution. There is a primary ROI, which is enhanced customer service or a shorter sales cycle based on already captured knowledge. However, the adoption of CRM software creates multiple ROIs depending on which audience is accessing or working with the product. The board of directors of a corporation might be interested in the financial returns or the long-term predictive analysis of the data captured within the core line-of-business CRM application, but a manager might have a totally different need. A manager might use CRM software as a coaching tool, standardizing his much loved and much tested best practices into the toolset used by his direct reports. A manager might also use CRM software for compliance and managing of the human resources he or she is responsible for. The ROI for a manager does not necessarily have to be the same ROI as a chief financial officer or a customer support representative. In addition, the success or failure of a CRM application can be contradictive. One department can experience great success, while another experiences frustration and limitations and time-consuming extra data entry. No other application crosses so many different audiences in so many different ways. And, no other application brings with it such great risk from failed adoption and such great benefits from true corporate understanding and mastery.

CRM Software Helps Retain Intellectual Capital

Twenty years ago, employer/employee loyalty was pervasive, but that has changed. So, what happens when someone leaves your firm? How does this relate to the use of a CRM application? Every person who works within a company retains a certain amount of knowledge about the firm, their specific job, and the people they work with (internal staff and customer contacts). This knowledge is often overlooked but sometimes critical to the success of a business. The combined knowledge of all staff is also the single most unique difference between two companies offering the same product or service, a real competitive differentiator. A CRM application can help to capture some of this knowledge. It also supports company efforts to standardize, document, and automate company-specific processes. After these processes have been captured, they are not forgotten when key staff leave. Figure 1.2 shows the three critical areas that need to be put together to have a successful CRM environment.

FIGURE 1.2
Putting it all together.

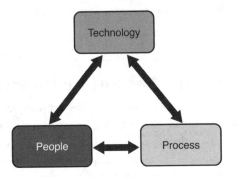

Successful CRM Projects

It is easy to focus only on purchasing a software package and the actual install, but companies considering the whole project, including the level of involvement of people, the design of process, and the actual technology footprint to support the new solution, are focused on success and are wise to do so. One of the key goals of Microsoft Dynamics CRM is to be a product that is extremely flexible and that can be reconfigured or changed as a company environment changes. These changes can include the people using the software, technology revolutions as the world of technology matures, and the processes that a company either change or refines. CRM is not just an application or a technology it is a methodology, a culture and a philosophy, and because of this wide-reaching paradigm, Microsoft Dynamics CRM requires management decisions about configuration and use.

People

Every human is unique. Some are masters at math, some are passionate about software, and others are incredible writers or excel at sports. Some are masters of all. The key is that human talent can impact the success of a project or application.

A core team may be critical to efficient adoption and change management; however, each person is unique, and core teams rarely represent 100% of all unique needs. When considering applying technology to the CRM space, consider the various levels of people who could be involved. There will be a variety of different individuals, and as mentioned, each individual has his or her own specific habits and technology in use.

There are a variety of different departments, and each department has different people and different needs and focuses, and there are a variety of different personalities. Some will make excellent champions, whereas others will be incredible users. You might find that an administrator is a role best accomplished by a person who is a master of software, a depth of understanding about the business, and a passion for learning. These skills might not be needed by the user champion. A user champion would have an outgoing personality, a likable demeanor, and an ability to put people at ease. They would also need understanding and skill in the CRM software, and an understanding about how the new software impacts their world.

You also have management, and management buy-in is the biggest single factor to success.

Process

If you are diving into the new world of Dynamics CRM, a helpful exercise is to document existing processes. These processes can be extremely small, or they can be large and complex. Process documentation can start at a very high level and then have supporting documents at a more detailed level, or it can be at a very detailed level from the start. Changing processes is not required for the successful adoption of Dynamics CRM.

When considering change in an existing firm, a person first outlines and documents existing processes and then chooses areas of inefficiency or poor workflow to improve and correct. Process modification generally requires change; change requires a broad spectrum of initiative.

Before we consider making changes before rolling out Dynamics CRM, we must also consider that within three to six months of Microsoft Dynamics CRM adoption, there will be options for additional change or process modification (as the technology opens new doors).

If your primary mode of transportation is a horse and buggy, for example, your process will have to include the care and feeding of the horse and the total number of hours a day that the horse could be used. You must also consider the conditioning of the leather components and the impact of weather on these components and the wear and tear of daily use. When you replace that horse and buggy with a car, the variables change so significantly that your processes change. You no longer have to consider the number of hours that you have available in any given day for transportation; after all, a car does not care whether it is used for 24 hours or for 1. However, you must continue to care about the wear and tear of daily use. Some processes do not change, but others do.

When considering processes associated with specific tools, such as a CRM application, you can be sure that certain functions and features available can improve or change your process.

Making initial decisions about process when first installing Dynamics CRM is important, but considering change after use is just as critical. Features don't change, but user knowledge and mastery of these features does. This knowledge motivates adoption of more functionality.

The key with process in the CRM space is continual learning by the teams involved and the leveraging of Microsoft Dynamics CRM's powerful flexibility when it comes to change and design.

As a last note on processes, always consider this: If your processes do not work, what happens when automation speeds up those processes?

Technology

Technology includes the well-tested CRM software applications, the changes these applications will mean for your company, and the environment in which the new software will live. New technology always involves new choices, which may push people into uncomfortable decision-making positions.

Microsoft Dynamics CRM is both a foundation for development (often referred to as xRM) and a powerful line-of-business application focused on CRM features and functionality (a CRM application). The product is built on a solid foundation (Microsoft .NET Framework and Microsoft SQL Server, for example) and can be easily extended, configured, and modified into a unique fit for each business where it is deployed. The product is flexible, but it also comes with a number of standard features and functionalities that can be used without extra effort. Think of the product as having standard features, requested by almost all clients, and you can add unique features and functionalities specific for your company or project.

Department Roles: Different Perspectives

Depending on your responsibilities and focus, CRM can offer different benefits. Let's look at a few roles.

Board of Directors

If a Board of Directors (BOD) could choose one word when thinking of the company it oversees, that word would be *transparency*. Members of a BOD do not want surprises from either the press or from the CxO team. The financials of a company are transparent. The G/L is available to the board, the financial statements are available to the board, but what is often missing is insight and perspective as to corporate culture and application of such to relationships with customers. In addition, board members often lack insight into the sales funnel, which offers a wide range of support from the extensive experience often found within a BOD. Board members have industry expertise and knowledge, but without something to compare this to from the company they oversee, their ability and contribution may be limited. Microsoft Dynamics CRM offers some of this insight from two perspectives. First, it is extremely good at capturing more data. Second, it is extremely good at offering this data in a user-friendly manner to people who do not necessarily use the application every day. Graphical reporting and dashboard analysis with a common Microsoft Office interface eliminates a number of barriers present in other vendor offerings.

Chief Executive Officer

Microsoft Dynamics CRM offers the chief executive officer (CEO) insight into the company and management variables via access to management teams, departmental decisions, and other "pure" data. It also provides analysis and integration points to other core applications running within a firm. A CEO who appropriately leverages CRM technology can more easily implement his vision with Microsoft Dynamics CRM. Microsoft Dynamics CRM software can help cutting-edge CEOs refine, change, and position the company. CRM represents a pool of wisdom for the CEO.

Chief Financial Officer

Chief financial offers (CFO) are tasked with reducing risk, lowering costs, and managing company financial investments. They also organize and classify corporate assets and work with managers to ensure efficiency. A CFO significantly benefits from the adoption of Microsoft Dynamics CRM. CFOs benefit from the additional available data, from the increased standardization of processes (which thus reduces risk and lowers costs), and from the analysis and predictive potential of this tool that captures the corporate asset known as data.

Chief Information Officer and Chief Technology Officer

Microsoft Dynamics CRM results in key benefits for the chief information officer (CIO) and chief technology officer (CTO) because of the product's flexibility. The product's available source code and core building blocks are standard Microsoft tools. With these tools, technical staff can leverage the power of the platform without extensive extra training, and long-term support is available from multiple resources. Microsoft Dynamics CRM actually becomes a bridge between technology departments and the business. The software is a tool that technology departments can use to meet their own internal business needs (customer service or knowledge-base management, for instance), and it is a tool that can help meet corporate goals, such as automation of the sales process and prospect management.

Sales Manager

Meeting numbers, setting expectations, and reporting realistic goals to management and the BOD, the sales manager is well served with a tool that can capture processes and then communicate them to his superiors. If a sales manager has defined, refined, and implemented best practice sales processes, these processes are transparent within the world of Dynamics CRM.

Microsoft Dynamics CRM also helps a sales manager coach, mentor, and encourage team members to perform at a higher level through applicable experience applied to areas that Microsoft Dynamics CRM indicate need fine-tuning. Just as football coaches classify their players and then review their skills so that the appropriate weight training, running drills, and practices can be designed, so must a sales manager gain insight into who needs training, mentoring, and support.

Microsoft Dynamics CRM can capture skill sets, but it can also offer transparency into prospect interaction and completion of process. Instead of a sales manager having to pull teeth to get numbers for analysis and management reporting, asking the sales team to do painful week-end or month-end data entry or updating of Excel spreadsheets, daily capturing of activities and status changes can be used to see what is going on. This shift moves from a monthly re-active reporting model to an any-time pro-active management paradigm.

Salesperson or Sales Executive

A sales executive's resistance to sharing data is well founded. Sales executives either have a well-practiced and much coveted technique that they do not want to share with their peers or they are vulnerable to judgment and correction. Even in a team-oriented culture, style is individual, and success is important.

In addition, the features and functions available to the salesperson can be significant. I have yet to see a salesperson choose to drive a horse and buggy over a well-tuned race car. If the well-tuned race car helps the salesperson get the job done with more ease and more quickly, the decision is a no-brainer. The key is to give the salesperson the race car with the features and functions and clean simplicity that they need to do their job as he or she sees fit.

Customer Service Manager

The customer service manager strives to help his team meet a certain level of measurable statistics: total number of completed calls, number of cases successfully closed, happy customers, customer success stories, and more. Additionally, the customer service manager must quickly respond to any cases that escalate from any level within the team. The manager must receive alerts so that he can quickly resolve problems and have visibility into the tone and traffic coming across the wires. Usage of Microsoft Dynamics CRM generates these much loved statistics. Integration of Microsoft Dynamics CRM into social media applications, such as Twitter, means that management can measure and track unregistered complaints and the organization of all activities associated with a tracked case.

Customer Service Representative

Customer service representatives are often on the phone all day. They need to quickly capture the notes from one call, often while they are talking, so that they can transition to the next call. Often times, customer service representatives will make promises during these calls, and they must follow-up and remember these promises. Microsoft Dynamics CRM can easily remember promises and individual or team obligations. It can also automatically meet promises by having a workflow that kicks off on the closing of a Case or Activity.

Marketing Manager

Marketing managers often have a specific budget or a set number of marketing dollars. They are also often focused on the return of investment associated with the use of these marketing dollars. They do not have many tools available to them that can capture this black and white data in a world of a lot of grey, but Microsoft Dynamics CRM's marketing campaign feature not only captures return on investment, it also helps organize all the planning tasks and campaign activities associated with the use of that investment.

Marketing Professional

Marketing professionals are often interested in slicing and dicing a wide variety of information. They need a tool that can encourage company staff members to collect as much data as possible on prospects, contacts, clients, opportunities, and campaigns as they happen. The marketing professional is interested in mailing to subsets of prospects and needs to have the details to create marketing lists of these subsets. Microsoft Dynamics CRM supports an almost unlimited number of details and the creation of marketing lists. A marketing professional might want to send out a mailing to all clients who have purchased a certain product in the last year or they might want to setup a telemarketing campaign for all prospects with a certain SIC code.

As you work through the next 23 hours, keep in mind that this is a whole new world of technology.

Executive Summary: Key Points to Remember

▶ "An essential requirement for a CRM system meeting a CRM philosophy is the ability to extract the information you need to understand your customers. Therefore, it is essential you understand what information you want about your customers." (Tribe, 2009)[1]

▶ Microsoft Dynamics CRM becomes the core heart and soul of many companies, and it is an application that is impacted by your design decisions, business process decisions, country philosophy, corporate culture, and style and pure individual impact and adoption.

▶ Microsoft Dynamics CRM is extremely flexible and requires management decisions about configuration and use.

▶ There is an entire CRM industry packed with a wealth of magazines, white papers, and CRM successes above and beyond a specific CRM technology. The CRM industry offers magazines, articles, blogs, wikis, podcasts, and case studies.

▶ If automation speeds up processes, what happens when the processes are incorrect?

▶ Microsoft Dynamics CRM is built using standard Microsoft technologies, such as Microsoft .NET Framework and Microsoft SQL Server.

▶ The Microsoft Dynamics CRM Software Developer's Kit (SDK) is available for download and is regularly updated.

▶ The Microsoft Dynamics CRM Help files are regularly updated and are available for download.

▶ The need for good Customer Relationship Management is not new, and CRM software is not a new technology.

Workshop

A large professional services company focused on offering technology services has various offerings, including selling, supporting, and recommending software and hardware technologies to other businesses. It also has internal personnel with various skills and certifications in each of these technologies. The company sells software, hardware, and consulting services.

From a business perspective, this professional services company has many needs for CRM software as a core piece of heart and soul for their company. It has a product catalog that includes software, hardware, and service items. Hardware includes servers, workstations, laptops, routers, cables, network cards, fax devices, repair components, and other devices. Software includes security suites, antivirus software, Office suites, word processing, spreadsheets, databases, utilities, desktop publishing, and accounting applications. Services include the unique consulting skills that it delivers with these various products. The company has a Microsoft Certified engineer who can install Windows Server and a database expert who is a master of Oracle and Microsoft SQL. Microsoft Dynamics CRM captures and organizes the hardware, the software, and the services as sellable items. It also organizes the clients and prospects that this company works with and captures every contact related to each prospect and client. Microsoft Dynamics CRM is used to track the stage where a particular prospect is with regard to when they will actually buy and the probability that this will occur. It is used to capture specifically which products and services this prospect is interested in. The company also uses CRM to schedule their resources so that the right talent is used on the right projects. It does not want to send its database expert on a sales call if the prospect is not interested in the database technology.

After a product is sold, the company offers support services. When a customer calls, the technician who answers the service call creates a case in Dynamics CRM. This case is then scheduled or assigned to the appropriate service technician, and each activity associated with this case is captured. This might include a phone call, a specific task, such as researching a problem, or a site visit. When the case is closed, the system also captures that the case was closed and on what date this was accomplished.

Q&A

Q. *How can I increase adoption of our new Microsoft Dynamics CRM project?*

A. Management involvement is an important factor for high company adoption of any CRM application.

Q. *What do you mean when you indicate that Microsoft Dynamics CRM can capture corporate assets?*

A. In today's information age, details on client and prospect interactions can be a valuable corporate asset.

Q. *What benefit is there in reading some of the CRM industry magazines? I have my solution. What more do I need to know?*

A. CRM industry magazines have some great articles on topics such as getting management buy in, improving business process with the help of technology, and lists of ways to improve efficiency. These subjects are not technology specific, but they can be huge differentiators.

Quiz

1. What are two benefits to an individual staff member if a company roles out Microsoft Dynamics CRM successfully?

2. What are the three components of a successful CRM project?

3. Why might a CxO (where x can be different letters) be interested in Microsoft Dynamics CRM?

4. Why is documenting processes so important to CRM adoption?

5. Why might salespeople be resistant to CRM software?

Answers

1. Everything that is done today in Microsoft Outlook can be communicated to corporate without having to retype anything into Excel, Word, or a summary email.

2. People, technology and process.

3. Organization of data, efficiency, a common environment that the entire organization is working within.

4. Microsoft Dynamics CRM offers so much choice that it is important to understand the processes that you want to support with the Microsoft Dynamics CRM toolset.

5. Salespeople are often on the move and capturing information within a technical tool does not lend itself to face-to-face conversations and travel time.

Exercise

Using a flowchart or diagrams, document one of the business processes that is part of your working world. You can do this using Microsoft Office Visio or you can leverage the power of paper and pen. If you have not done flowchart diagramming before, approach this exercise from the concept of pictures. Figure 1.3 and Figure 1.4 provide examples.

FIGURE 1.3
Documented
business
process flow-
chart.

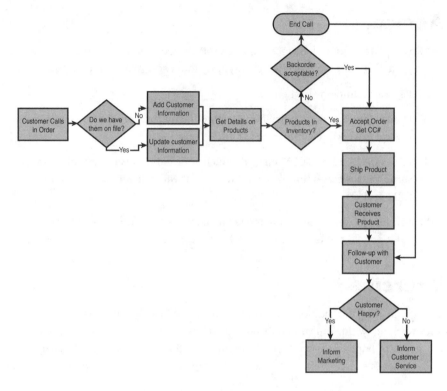

FIGURE 1.4
Documented
business
process with pic-
tures.

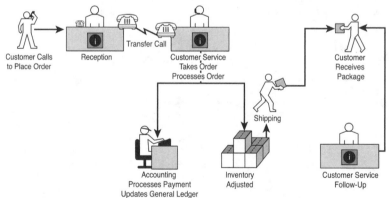

HOUR 2

The Basics: The CRM Functionality Vocabulary

What You'll Learn in This Hour:

▶ Key Building Blocks of Microsoft Dynamics CRM

▶ Record Type Concept

In this hour, the building blocks of Microsoft Dynamics CRM are explored. The core entities (record types), or building blocks, make up the Microsoft Dynamics CRM system. Building blocks include items such as an Account, Contact, and Opportunity. Additionally, some building blocks might not be used by every company as Cases, Orders, and Invoices. Within each of these sections, I have also added insight into areas around each building block that might be less obvious.

Key Building Blocks of Microsoft Dynamics CRM

If we compare Microsoft Dynamics CRM to a brick house, the entities (record types) within Microsoft Dynamics CRM are the bricks or building blocks. Each block can stand on its own and represents a specific thing (in this example, a brick). When put together, these bricks enable us to create a completely different structure, a house, tower, fireplace, or school. Microsoft Dynamics CRM is also built of "bricks" or "building blocks," and you can take a variety of these different blocks and literally create different structures. Microsoft Dynamics CRM is both a Customer Relationship Management (CRM) application prebuilt and designed as well as an xRM platform that can be designed and shaped into different applications. Let's look at a number of these specific building blocks, as outlined in Figure 2.1, starting with the Account entity (record type).

FIGURE 2.1
Building blocks.

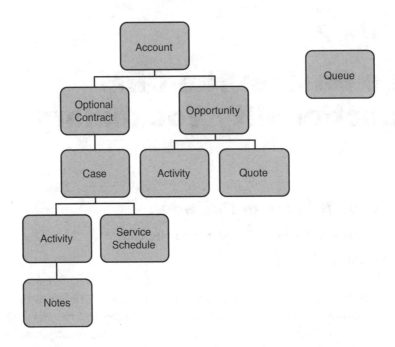

What Is an Account?

At first glance, an Account entity (record type) is a company, but the automatic assumptions about an Account entity are not always correct. So, we will specifically look at the use of *Account* within the world of Microsoft Dynamics CRM. A first assumption is that an Account is a corporation or client. Although this may be correct, an Account entity is so much more. For instance, an Account entity can also represent a vendor, prospect, contracting company, location, division headquarters, a legal firm that represents a client, a shared bank, and the various locations of the bank, and more.

An Account entity can also be changed to mean something unique for your business niche. Take, for instance, a dairy farm that wants to track all the relationships of the various cows that it has at its location. In this particular example, the farm might use the Account entity as the originating location of where a specific cow was born. This then helps the farm track ancestry or track strains of a particular genetic disease. Microsoft Dynamics CRM supports this customizability by allowing you to name the Account entity something that's more meaningful to your business. In my example, we might find that our farm renames the Account entity to Farm.

In other examples, companies often want to rename the Account entity to Corporation or Client. However, if you do this, you create a conflict with an Account type of

Prospect, Vendor, or Supplier. You might also want to track a client's bank or the common accounting firms (Firm). Account is a wonderfully generic term that covers a variety of Account entities (record types).

What Is a Contact?

A Contact entity is slightly easier to explain. In most examples, a Contact entity represents a specific person and all the associated information as it relates to that specific person. (Using the previous example, the Contact entity might be a specific cow.) I have also seen a Contact entity represented as a specific individual thing (for instance, a specific plant that relates to a specific Account location or family of plants). The idea is that, although Microsoft Dynamics CRM is a powerful CRM system, it is also a system that you can configure to track any kind of relationship. The Contact entities have a relationship to the Account entities. You can have an unlimited number of contacts associated with a given account, and each Contact entity has a number of details that can be tracked. In most cases, you will see that contacts can be any number of different employees in a specific company. Later in this book, we examine what makes up a contact. Figure 2.2 shows a tree structure and where contacts fall with regards to some of the relationships a contact has to other entities.

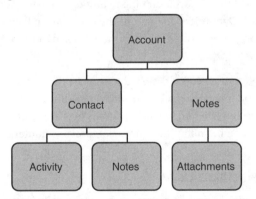

FIGURE 2.2
Related building blocks within Microsoft Dynamics CRM.

What Is a Lead?

A Lead is an area where there can be a number of different thoughts. In Microsoft Dynamics CRM, a lead is a flat unqualified business card or an unqualified contact obtained from a purchased list of contacts. Once a lead is qualified, it can be converted to a hierarchical structure of account, contact, and opportunity offering the ability to add more contacts and related building blocks (contract, quote, order, case).

Additionally, all the history that has been done to qualify the lead is stored with the lead and related to the new account, contact, and/or opportunity. For instance, suppose you attend a trade show, obtain a list of all the attendees, and you want to follow up with these attendees to see whether any might make future clients. In this case, the Lead is the person who you might (or might not) have met at the show. This lead is unqualified with regard to if he truly is a potential new client for your company. Microsoft Dynamics CRM has a special place for "Leads" in the system; after all, you would probably not want to purchase a list of 50,000 names and immediately have these names mixed with all of your qualified and existing information. You may, however, want to have access to these 50,000 names as you continue to market and qualify information. In the true sense of the world of sales, a Lead is an unqualified prospect who has the potential, with some qualification effort, to become a new client. One of the most common misconceptions (and therefore frustrations) that can occur is when a company uses a lead as a qualified prospect. It enters large amounts of data, notes, and activities to its leads, but when a lead is ready to have an associated opportunity, or more contacts, the system is not ready to serve that up until the lead is converted. You convert the lead, but all the captured history and activities do not get copied to the Account and Contact record. For instance, how would the system copy activities? Would these be copied to the account or the contact or both and, if copied to both, wouldn't the redundancy be just as confusing? Needless to say, Microsoft Dynamics CRM retains the relationship between a lead and the new contact, but only moves a certain amount of information to the new qualified account and contact.

Again, let me stress that a Lead is designed to capture that large list of unqualified Contacts, and the brief history associated with the qualification process is filed with the Lead when it is converted and associated to its new Account, Contact, and Opportunity. We talk more about the conversion process in later chapters.

What Is a Prospect?

A prospect is a potential client or customer who has usually been qualified through at least one conversation or a salesperson's researched effort. A Prospect is a type of Account and is generally created when a lead has been converted to an Account, Contact, and optionally an Opportunity. (We will talk more about Opportunity later in this chapter.) One of the key concepts to grasp is that a Lead and a Prospect are different in terms of how the system thinks about them. They both represent a company and, most likely, a primary contact, but a Lead is often a name that might or might not be real, and a Prospect is a name with an associated company, a salesperson's understanding, other key data, and even an expressed specific interest in the salesperson's products or services behind it. In linear terms, you start with a Lead, you qualify the Lead, and then once qualified you convert and create a Prospect and you sell the Prospect product or services (and thus create a Customer).

The goal of every salesperson is to close deals by first qualifying leads to the point that they become a sales prospect. Of the numerous configurations of Microsoft Dynamics CRM that are deployed, you will find that not every sales process uses the concepts of Leads and Prospects in this manner; however, it helps to understand the concepts behind the design of the system. It has been noted that, at any given company, you might not want to have all your Leads configured as robust Prospects in this system. The Microsoft Dynamics CRM Lead and Prospect concept allows for a pool of many leads that does not interfere with or muddy the waters for the core data within the system. This allows a company elbow room for importing large lists of Leads without showing numerous unqualified Leads on Sales Funnel and Prospect reports. Figure 2.3 shows how a lead might flow from lead to prospect to client.

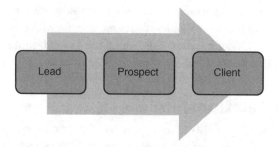

FIGURE 2.3
A lead moves from Lead to Prospect to Client.

What Are More Addresses?

The Account entity (record type) in Microsoft Dynamics CRM has two addresses directly associated with it. However, Microsoft Dynamics CRM offers you the option of adding even more addresses. If you have ever ordered something online, you understand why customers might want an unlimited number of addresses that they can provide and associate with any given Account entity. For instance, you might want to have more than one shipping address or you might find that a specific Contact resides in two locations. Each Account entity within the system and each Contact in the system can have an unlimited number of associated addresses. They each have a primary address, but they each can also have more addresses.

What Is an Activity?

An Activity entity is something that you are most likely familiar with; although each Activity entity is really a set of different types of entities in Microsoft Dynamics CRM. Each type has unique qualities and can stand on its own. We will discuss Activities as one entity (record type) as they work and act like one entity within the system and from a usage perspective they are generally considered an "Activity." For those more technically oriented, each activity type is actually its own entity (record type) and activity is an Activity Pointer. An Activity has seven different types within Microsoft Dynamics CRM. These types include a phone call, a task, an email, a service activity, an appointment, a campaign activity, and a campaign response. In Microsoft Dynamics CRM, you cannot add other Activity types to the core list just outlined; however, Activities can be further categorized. One of the key functionalities of an Activity is that it can be scheduled and pending, or another way to think about them is that they can be completed. Activities also have a special relationship to Microsoft Outlook, the email application included within the Microsoft Office suite. For instance, a Microsoft Dynamics CRM Activity with an activity type of task can optionally (based on user configuration) synchronize in real time with a Microsoft Outlook task. If you complete, check off, or close a task in Outlook, this task will also be shown as a completed Activity in Microsoft Dynamics CRM. If you take it one thought further, imagine someone who completes a task on his mobile device, which then flows through Microsoft Outlook, which synchronizes with the corporate Microsoft Dynamics CRM databases. This behind-the-scenes technique eliminates the need for anyone to send email asking whether a certain task has been completed.

What Is a Relationship?

Although a "relationship" exists in many forms within Microsoft Dynamics CRM, it helps to point out that a feature in Microsoft Dynamics CRM, called Relationship entity, includes associated relationship roles. Relationship roles can be defined by the user through system configuration and might consist of items such as association member and association, banker and customer, or other relationships that differ from your standard Contact entity as it relates to an Account that Contact might work for. Relationships can be tracked between two contacts: Contact and Contact, between Account and Contact, or reversed Contact and Account. Additionally, relationships can be represented between an Opportunity and Contact and an Opportunity and Account. Figure 2.4 shows a list of relationships. When you set up a relationship, you choose the Account, Contact, or Opportunity and their role as it relates to a different Account, Contact, or Opportunity.

What Is an Opportunity?

An Opportunity entity is sometimes a new concept for people learning about Microsoft Dynamics CRM. The first thing to remember is that an Opportunity entity is not a person or a company. An Opportunity entity is the "potential sale," which relates to an Account entity, and it often contains the estimated dollar value, the estimated close date, the sales stage, and the probability percentage of closing. An

Opportunity entity is used for forecasting and sales funnel analysis. Yes, an Opportunity entity is associated with an Account entity, but it is not necessarily defined as an Account. For some companies, this works extremely well because they have many Opportunities for any given Account. For others, however, the concept is a bit more difficult because they only ever focus on one sale per Account. Consider this: If you make a sale to a prospective Account and that prospective Account then becomes a Client, you potentially have a new Opportunity to resell, upsell, or even renew that relationship through a new Opportunity.

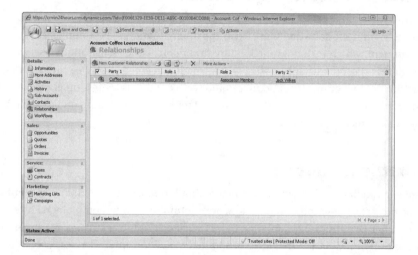

FIGURE 2.4
Relationships.

What Is a Case?

A Case is also referred to as a ticket in some businesses and, when using Microsoft Dynamics CRM, it can be renamed. A Case captures all the details related to a problem or request. In most examples, a Case is associated with a customer service department that has incoming reported issues that need tracking, activities, notes, and resolutions. A Case can have an unlimited number of associated activities and can be related to a specific Account or Contact and an annual or monthly service contract. A Case can also accumulate total number of hours or minutes invested in working the Case, and this accumulation can offset a standard number of purchased hours defined in a service contract. A Case also has a case resolution entity associated with it when the Case is closed through the Dynamics CRM close case function.

What Is a Contract?

The Contract feature of Microsoft Dynamics CRM can be configured to track many different details. A Contract is associated with an Account and is an optional feature.

The Contract functionality was designed in association with a Case. The concept is that an Account might have purchased a certain number of service hours or service tickets, and the Contract captures the details of this agreement. The Contract also has an ongoing relationship with the total number of Cases used or hours of service provided. A Contract not only captures the specific details making up a contract, but also the relationship of that contract to the services provided and tracked.

What Is a Service Schedule?

Microsoft Dynamics CRM is not just about sales, it is also about serving existing clients. Within the software, there exists the ability to manage a complex service department, which includes functionality to support service scheduling. A service schedule is specific tracking of who, what, when, and where a service will occur, with additional functionality around managing service conflicts. This is different than the standard appointment activity, which is used for simple scheduling and as such doesn't include tracking available sites and service personnel.

What Is a Queue?

A queue is a first in, first out data structure that organizes specific data in a "waiting to be processed" method. A queue does not contain its own building blocks; it contains other Dynamics CRM building blocks, such as Cases or activities. Examples of a queue in Dynamics CRM include a configured queue to capture service cases or a queue to manage incoming activity requests that need to be processed by a specific department. Microsoft Dynamics CRM enables users to create different queues with associated tasks or business process. A queue is similar to a line of people waiting to be serviced, but the line is made up of something other than people (see Figure 2.5).

FIGURE 2.5
Queue.

What Is a Campaign?

A campaign in Microsoft Dynamics CRM has many parts and comes in two versions. The first version is called a quick campaign and is designed for use by a salesperson.

A quick campaign has an associated marketing list or subset of specific contacts. It is also usually used once to announce a month-end special or to send out one quick email blast of information. A full campaign, the second version of a campaign, is more detailed, and it includes the ability to budget for a specific event, to compose or plan a long list of activities associated with a marketing event, and to capture results and costs when the marketing event is completed. Many CRM systems do not have campaign tracking and, therefore, you will find that the concept of tracking all the details of a campaign is new to most users. The full campaign is designed to be used by the marketing department as a tool to empower them to organize and track the efforts surrounding a specific marketing event. A full campaign includes campaign activities and campaign results as associated items.

What Is a User?

A user is a staff person for the Microsoft Dynamics CRM organization who is assigned a CRM license and who is using Microsoft Dynamics CRM to capture specific information. A user has relationships to the Account (she can be the owner of the Account) and to specific activities and service scheduling items. Microsoft Dynamics CRM leverages the user in many of its automatic system functionality. A user is tied directly to a specific person as that person is listed in Microsoft Server Active Directory. It is also assigned a Microsoft Dynamics CRM security role for other CRM functionality-specific security. For instance, a user may be assigned to the salesperson role, and the salesperson role may be limited to sales functionality only, preventing this user from creating service tickets or marketing campaigns.

Record Types

All the items that we just reviewed are classified as record types within the world of Dynamics CRM. Record types are the building blocks of Microsoft Dynamics CRM, and, from a structural design perspective, a record type is a Microsoft SQL database table. Entities can have relationships to other entities from many different perspectives. They can have a parental relationship where there is a key connection to the two entities, or they can have other types of relationships such as referential (they refer to each other), or for any given one record type there are many other related entities such as the relationship between Account and Contact. For any given one Account, you can have many Contacts. The relationship can also go the other way. For instance, for any given Opportunity, you can only have one Account, but your choice of which Account is unlimited. If you consider all the different ways that entities can relate to other entities, you start to see the full picture of Microsoft Dynamics CRM being a foundation of any "relationship management" need. In this way, Microsoft Dynamics CRM is not only a CRM software application and a sales force automation application, it is also an "any Relationship" (xRM) development platform, which is a term you will see and hear much more as you delve deeper into Microsoft Dynamics CRM.

Workshop

A small alternative medicine clinic is using Microsoft Dynamics CRM to organize and run its practice. The clinic uses the CRM scheduling features to keep track of its patient appointments. Each staff member is set up as a CRM user, and each one can access Microsoft Dynamics CRM from his or her main office machine or from any other available machine in the clinic upon individual login. The clinic also schedules appointment follow-up telephone calls, and it leverages the mailing features of Dynamics CRM to send out regular appointment postcard reminders.

The clinic also uses a sophisticated medical billing line-of-business application. This application handles the insurance company management and billing compliance. The clinic has integrated Microsoft Dynamics CRM with its medical insurance billing software so that data can be shared.

During the winter, the clinic gets a high number of incoming telephone calls that require a return call from a doctor or specialist. One feature important to the clinic was the ability to manage the priority of the necessary follow-up calls using queues. The clinic uses Microsoft Dynamics CRM to schedule appointments, send out mailings, track the contact details of their patients, and manage the many relationships that it has with the pharmaceutical representatives.

Q&A

Q. *What if I do not want to use one of these described entities? Can I ignore it?*

A. You can ignore an entity and not use it. You can also delete it, although that is not recommended, because you might want to use it later.

Q. *I rely on the Tasks feature in Microsoft Outlook. How do these tasks associate to activities in Microsoft Dynamics CRM?*

A. An Outlook task synchronizes to a Microsoft Dynamics CRM activity of type task. You can manage your activities/tasks from either Outlook Tasks or Microsoft Dynamics CRM activities.

Q. What are the disadvantages of renaming Account to Customer and using leads for all prospects?

A. Although the system supports your ability to do this, you will significantly limit your ability to associate other powerful built-in functions to your prospects, including Opportunities, Quotes, Orders, Invoices, Relationships, and more. Additionally you might want to use Accounts to track vendors, suppliers, and other companies.

Quiz

1. The building blocks of Microsoft Dynamics CRM are referred to as record types. Name some of these record types.

2. What is Opportunity?

3. Do record types have relationships? What are some of these relationships?

4. How does the term record type relate to the Microsoft SQL Server database foundation upon which Microsoft Dynamics CRM is built?

Answers

1. Account, Contact, Activity, Opportunity.

2. An entity that tracks the details of a potential sale, including estimated premium, estimated close date, and probability of closing.

3. Yes, the relationship between Account and Contact is a good example.

4. An Entity represents a Microsoft SQL Server Table.

Exercise

Using paper or Microsoft Word, create a list of the record types that you consider as the core building blocks for your firm. For this exercise, do not worry about the names. Instead, focus on the specific entities as you define them. How do these record types map to the record types listed in this chapter? How would have you defined the Account record type, or how would you define the Account record type? What are the advantages and disadvantages of this design? Will this design cause issues for your firm in two or three years? What would be some of those issues?

Using paper or Microsoft Office Visio or any of the family tree applications, create a sample of what and how you would organize some of the record types within your firm and how they relate to other record types.

Figure 2.6 shows an example of the exercise.

FIGURE 2.6
Some of the Farm entities.

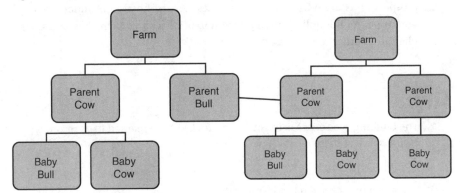

HOUR 3

The Business Roadmap

What You'll Learn in This Hour:

▶ Fundamentals

▶ Deeper Look at Business Process

▶ Capturing Processes

▶ Practical Considerations

In this hour, we will dive into the concept of business processes and the capturing and matching of business processes to the technology application Microsoft Dynamics CRM. Taking a deeper look at business processes supports the ultimate goal of getting the highest level of utilization from the application.

Fundamentals

Fundamental changes need to take place in a company for CRM to be a success, and some companies have an advantage. They have made many of these changes. They have management that gets how technology and process impact each other, and they have synergy between business and technology expertise. They also have the people who balance out the total formula. Most likely, they also have had at least one failed CRM attempt and are perhaps looking for more success, or maybe they are pushing the innovation envelope and understand some of the new paradigm shifts in communication. The companies without the advantage can also find success.

The world of CRM taps into the world of data flow within a company. A call comes in, and then what happens? A problem occurs. How does the company respond? What roles are affected? Who is responsible? What is happening with a prospect? What about a client? Who understands what is happening? Is this information stored so that others can have insight into the situation if that person is not available? What about the data on the available skills and knowledge that can be used to solve a problem or meet a request or accomplish a goal?

How is a contact related to a specific company? How is that same contact related to us? Does that contact have other relationships that would be beneficial to know about? What about a building? How is a building related to another building? Or how is a building related to a management company?

When we consider process as it relates to Microsoft Dynamics CRM, we are looking at the processes surrounding the flow of data within a company, the handling of that data, and the desired results of handling that data effectively to produce a desired end result.

Deeper Look at Business Process

A business process is a series of activities or tasks that lead to a specific completed service or defined product. These activities can also be bundled into a specific step within the process, with the process made up of a series of steps or stages.

A business process can be thought of as something that serves a particular goal for a particular prospect, customer, or customers. The automation of process keeps promises and tasks from falling between the cracks and helps to organize and systemize particular business best practices. The automation of process also supports the effort of a corporation to standardize process within certain groups of users.

One of the first excitements when initially purchasing Microsoft Dynamics CRM is the power of using the software to automate processes. The risk with this approach is that, if there is no understanding of items that are automatically created, then the world gets very noisy. Emails get automatically created or activities get automatically generated and a to-do list gets overwhelmed or inbox gets full without comprehension of where these items are going from. Ultimately, the goal is to make any given process more efficient and less complex. Automating can create more complexity, more noise, and more data in more places. When you automate based on a practiced and well loved process you gain more success. Needless to say, manually mastering a process at a variety of levels before automating is recommended.

When it comes to the concept of learning more about business process, there are as many additional resources available. You can find books, articles, and magazines on business process by industry, by type of work, and by role (such as management processes, operational processes, and supporting processes). You can even find some good fiction, such as the 1948 book Cheaper by the Dozen by Frank Gilbreth Jr. and Ernestine Gilbreth Carey.

Despite all this, one thing to keep in mind is that if you can capture the processes that are in practice today, you can complement them, replace them, and fine-tune them as you roll out Microsoft Dynamics CRM.

One of the first tasks to do when learning to master Microsoft Dynamics CRM is to understand and learn your own processes and how these processes can either fit or change within your company as you adopt or increase your usage of Microsoft Dynamics CRM. It is extremely difficult to use a software package that supports a process without clarity and understanding of the process to begin with.

Capturing process does not have to be difficult. In fact, it can be quite fun. Grab a white board or notepad and a set of appropriate markers. For those technically inclined (yes, you Mr. Developer and Mrs. Infrastructure Specialist), open Microsoft Visio. The point is to diagram both the high-level process and the lower-level details. You can even go so far as to think of some of the lower level details as related sub processes.

Now, depending on a role such as a salesperson, administrator, financial officer, marketing expert, business engineer, software developer, or network administrator, put a hat on and start drawing. Feel free to whip up a set of paper hats and make this a fun team exercise. If you are struggling with picking a role or thinking of all the roles that might be considered, check out this great Microsoft web page called "Microsoft Dynamics Is Familiar to Your People" (www.microsoft.com/dynamics/product/familiartoyourpeople.mspx). The graphic is enough to get the exercise kick started.

With a specific role hat on, what do you do in a given week? What about on a given day? What systems do you currently use? What decisions do you have to make? I know you know the details, but write them down and capture each decision and every step using pictures. Pictures communicate a thousand words, so you might as well make it easy on yourself.

Remember that paper you had to write in, perhaps, seventh grade? The one where the teacher told you to document how you do something and then made someone else do it by only using the instructions on the paper? It was difficult to explain how to drink a glass of water, particularly when you forgot to include how to turn on the faucet, or perhaps you chose how to open your desk and forgot to include that the person had to first walk over to the desk to reach it. Documenting processes at work are not necessarily as difficult, but it can be just as eye opening.

Pretend you are talking to someone who is going to fill in for you, or even to your 12-year-old son or perhaps your 20-year-old daughter who is considering careers. You can even think about telling your spouse, your mother, or a patient sibling. The concept is to really document the big picture and the specific details within that big picture.

Figures 3.1, 3.2, and 3.3 show a few sample business processes diagrammed using different formats. Figure 3.1 uses flowchart boxes and outlines the handling of a list of leads received from a trade show.

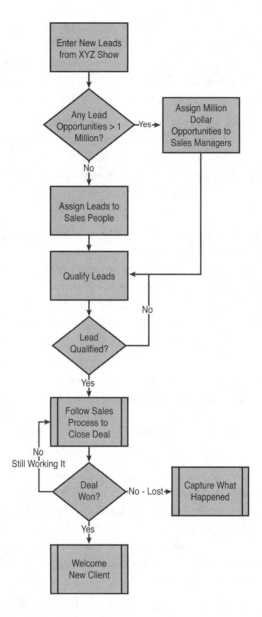

Figure 3.2 uses a different format and shows a general process of a vendor bill arriving through the mail and being received by the receptionist at a specific company.

Figure 3.3 is more of a general, big-picture diagram of a process that shows the marketing department starting a process that flows through sales to order to delivery. It also includes a small process surrounding manufacturing feeding inventory.

How Vendor Bills Are Handled

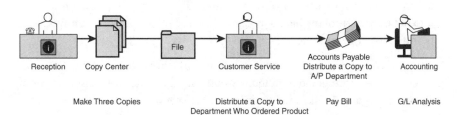

Reception   Copy Center   File   Customer Service   Accounts Payable   Accounting
                                                                        Distribute a Copy to
                                                                        A/P Department

Make Three Copies   Distribute a Copy to   Pay Bill   G/L Analysis
                           Department Who Ordered Product

FIGURE 3.2
A vendor bill arrives.

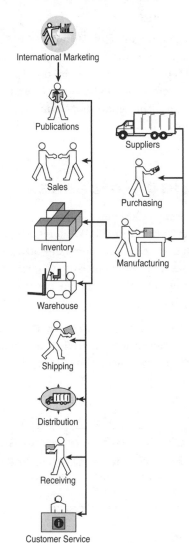

International Marketing

Publications

Suppliers

Sales

Purchasing

Inventory

Manufacturing

Warehouse

Shipping

Distribution

Receiving

Customer Service

FIGURE 3.3
General overview from sales to delivery.

Another way to capture process is by using a swim lane document. A *swim lane* is a horizontal or vertical format of a process flow diagram which offers you a way of showing what or who is associated with a particular sub process. Swim lanes allow you to not only capture the big picture, but they also offer a smooth transition to capturing the related sub processes.

As much as capturing process is critical, it is also critical to realize that in office environments process changes, and in today's world, many of these processes are continually being tweaked. Unlike manufacturing, where certain items are built and the steps to build those rarely change, in the world of data, adaptability and riding the waves of change are key to success.

One of the benefits of Microsoft Dynamics CRM is that adding automated process does not require a programmer or advanced programming skills. The ability to automate process is achieved with the workflow functionality which is part of the Microsoft Dynamics CRM application. Mastering the workflow feature allows a company to continually automate and change processes built into the technology as its world changes.

Capturing Processes

Microsoft Dynamics CRM helps automate processes in a few different ways. The first is that Microsoft Dynamics CRM captures, stores, and organizes data. The second is that, through the use of automation of workflow, Microsoft Dynamics CRM automates processes that would otherwise be done manually. In fact, beginners to workflow automation can take something as simple as a small business rule and apply it to something that happens in Microsoft Dynamics CRM.

Let's say that every time someone closes a new opportunity as a win, the sales manager wants an email sent to him. Without workflow, the salesperson could manually create an email every time he closes a deal. With workflow, the system can send the email for him.

Masters of Microsoft Dynamics CRM

Masters of Microsoft Dynamics CRM tend to get away from the system sending email alerts, preferring to just look at a variety of views, but this makes a good example.

Microsoft Dynamics CRM can kick off an email when a new opportunity is closed with a status of win. This email can also include a link that enables the sales manager to quickly click and see all the details of this win, or the email can be set up to include the details that are of interest. The power of Microsoft Windows Workflow Foundation is part of Microsoft Dynamics CRM. Workflow can be scary and complicated (some even have advanced degrees in the concept), or it can be extremely simple. I encourage you to set up a few simple workflows as you are learning about them in Hour 16, "Workflow: Creating Simple Workflow," and then use them for a week or so to get familiar with how not only your process, but your entire team's processes, are impacted.

Other examples of automating process based on data entered into the system could include the following:

1. When a new opportunity is created, automatically generate all the activities associated with the first step of the sales process (if the first step is defined as a set of activities that need to be completed).

2. You can further extend this to include the second step, third, fourth, and final step so when all the activities associated with the first step in the sales process are completed, automatically update the probability percentage of close on the opportunity, and create the second set of activities that need to be completed, and this can continue until you close the deal.

You can also apply automation to services:

1. When a user creates a new service case in the system and that service case is of type "Fix Broken X," automatically create a set of activities that result in fixing the broken X, and close the case.

2. When a user creates a new service case, automatically send an email to the client indicating that a service technician is working on their case.

   A common manual process, the assignment of leads, can be automated.

3. When a new lead is entered in the system, check the zip code, associate the territory, and assign to the sales manager for that territory.

We know that workflow can take business rules and apply or automate processes based on those rules, but what about other process impacts from a CRM system?

Practical Considerations

Given that Microsoft Dynamics CRM captures, organizes, and manages data, a key consideration is to configure Microsoft Dynamics CRM so that it makes it extremely easy for users to enter data. You have the power to add new fields to Microsoft Dynamics CRM. You have the power to remove data fields from the forms in Microsoft Dynamics CRM. And you have the power to organize how data fields are displayed within a structured offering in Microsoft Dynamics CRM.

Much can be learned from a popular search engine in use today. It offers you one box for data entry. The screen is not cluttered with distracting information that is perhaps not of interest. In addition, no training is needed until you get into more advanced concepts.

This key concept is of particular importance when people are starting to use Microsoft Dynamics CRM. The "Keep it Simple" concept is well married to mastery, usability, and adoptability.

Remember that Microsoft Dynamics CRM is a robust system that can take years to master, but even in the first few hours of using it, much can make sense. Start slow, dive into a subset of your business processes, apply these to Microsoft Dynamics CRM, and then grow with the software or let the software grow on you. Your understanding of Microsoft Dynamics CRM will continue to increase, and this understanding will open doors for you. You might find that a process you captured and defined in the early weeks of use does not even apply anymore because of how you use Microsoft Dynamics CRM.

Another helpful habit is to visit the Microsoft Dynamics CRM Resource Center and read how others use the system or peek into a few of the Microsoft Dynamics CRM blogs or podcasts. You might find a helpful tip, a snippet of code, or a learning technique. Listed on my blog, The CRM Lady (www.crmlady.com) is a link list of many other Microsoft Dynamics CRM blogs that you might find interesting. (If you find a blog that is not listed, let me know.)

Here are a few links that might be of interest:

The CRM Lady Blog: http://www.crmlady.com (And there is a long list of other links on CRM Lady.)

Microsoft Resource Center: http://rc.crm.dynamics.com/rc/regcont/en_us/ onlinedefault.aspx

The Microsoft Dynamics CRM Development Team Blog: http://blogs.msdn.com/crm/

The Microsoft Dynamics CRM Video Gallery: http://www.democrmonline.com

The Microsoft Dynamics CRM Developer Center: http://msdn.microsoft.com/en-us/dynamics/crm/bb501031.aspx

Workshop

Robert has an active veterinarian practice. He offers a quarterly shots clinic for all existing and potential clients and yearly exams based on the first date that a client visited. Robert also specializes in cats; all his patients are cats. Robert uses Microsoft Dynamics CRM to track each patient and the relationship that his patients have with other patients. For instance, there is a golden tabby named Gifted whose mother is also a patient. The history that Robert collects on each patient allows him to more accurately predict, prevent, and treat common cat diseases, particularly hereditary diseases. Robert also works with the local town where his office is located. Robert offers a place for the local town to enter all the registered cats. In this way, Robert can also potentially have insight into the history of a particular cat whose parents are not patients.

Robert does not use all of Microsoft Dynamics CRM, but he would like to use more. One of his first tasks is to document some of the processes that happen in his office that are not part of his Microsoft Dynamics CRM system. He uses a billing system for medical billing and he has a packed filing cabinet.

Q&A

Q. *Our process is constantly changing. How can Microsoft Dynamics CRM keep up with all these changes?*

A. Microsoft Dynamics CRM offers users the power of workflow, which is a feature that power users can use to define, modify, and automate their own processes. A system administrator can also add or modify fields associated with specific entities, and a CRM architect can make changes to fine-tune the system as you use it.

Q. *What are some other places to find information on Microsoft Dynamics CRM?*

A. The Microsoft Dynamics CRM Development team has a great blog at http://blogs.msdn.com/crm/, which includes links to many other resources.

Q. *We are putting together a team to document some of the company processes and want to know who would be the best representatives for the team?*

A. Good representatives for the team include staff members who have a long historical perspective of the existing business processes as well as someone who is has fresh eyes and is learning about the business processes from a brand new perspective. You might also want to include a mix of information technology, finance, management, and staff representatives.

Q. *What is an example of a process that may be good to automate?*

A. An alert when an opportunity is created that is outside the bounds of normal for the company or a reminder to follow-up when a case is closed on an A-level client or a set of tasks that are created in association with completing a stage in a sales process.

Quiz

1. What process associated with Robert's quarterly shots clinic could Robert document and further automate?

2. Why process change occurs when Microsoft Dynamics CRM is installed and adopted?

3. What is a sample process that can be automated?

4. Name four different roles, such as a sales person, that could be users of Microsoft Dynamics CRM.

5. What is Microsoft Dynamics capable of doing when a piece of data is saved in the system?

Answers

1. Robert could document and automate how he alerts his customers and prospects to an upcoming shots clinic.

2. Many process changes can occur, but it is up to the Microsoft Dynamics CRM customer to decide what he wants to change through automation.

3. A sales process or the process of fixing a broken product.

4. Sales person, administrator, financial officer, marketing expert, business engineer, software developer, or network administrator.

5. Microsoft Dynamics CRM's workflow functionality can automatically create an email or activity when a piece of data is saved.

Exercise

Document a process from a big-picture "above the tree" perspective using either flow-chart boxes or detailed pictures. Now, pick a smaller piece of that process and drill down into the explicit details and document these details. If you give the details to someone unfamiliar with the process, could that person follow everything that you have written down? How does this process relate to what you know about Microsoft Dynamics CRM? How does this process relate to your business requirements as they relate to the use of Microsoft Dynamics CRM?

HOUR 4

Infrastructure Choices

What You'll Learn in This Hour:

▶ The Cloud, the Data, the Software

▶ How It All Works Together

▶ Asynchronous Services and Microsoft Workflow Foundation

▶ Diving into Development

▶ Integration Options

▶ Big Business Versus Small Business

In this hour, we dive into all the different options that surround the installation of the software. There are many choices within the world of Microsoft Dynamics CRM, and consideration and careful thought about these choices can make a big difference in the success and adoption of this powerful application for companies. This hour also offers insight into where any particular person might want to focus more of their training and which roles within a company might be best suited to mastery of which pieces of the Microsoft Dynamics CRM environment.

The Cloud, the Data, the Software

Microsoft Dynamics CRM is all about choice, and although choice is a wonderful thing, it also offers more opportunity for learning. When it comes to where Microsoft Dynamics CRM is "installed," it is important to understand what your options are and why.

Microsoft Dynamics CRM On-Premise

Companies have the choice to purchase the Microsoft Dynamics CRM software in an On-Premise model. Microsoft Dynamics CRM On-Premise is installed locally in a company's server environment, and it allows for full internal control of all application files and associated data. The actual program files, the database where all the data is stored, the connection to the company's Microsoft Exchange email environment, the web interface, plug-ins, and any customizations are all stored, managed, and installed locally.

In this situation, it is highly recommended that an experienced (and ideally, a Microsoft Dynamics CRM Infrastructure Certified) expert is available for the initial installation and the ongoing responsibility for the maintenance of the infrastructure environment. Mastery of the infrastructure of Microsoft Dynamics CRM is a unique set of skills and this mastery is required for long term error-free success. These new skills are best mastered by someone with a background as a network architect, network engineer, or network administration. Experience in the following areas is also extremely helpful:

▶ Hosting web environments and mastery of Internet Information Services (IIS)

▶ Managing the sharing and integration of data between different applications and systems

▶ Analyzing and interpreting system logs and error messages

▶ Microsoft Server 2005 and 2008

▶ Performance tuning and management of Microsoft SQL Server Databases

Microsoft Dynamics CRM On-Premise offers a corporation total control over the entire environment. Data is under the protection of the corporation; the software is under the change management and upgrade systems within corporate; and the ability to change, customize, add on to, and expand is not impacted by external partner companies.

A diagram of the Microsoft Dynamics CRM architecture is located within the Microsoft Dynamics CRM Developer Center at http://msdn.microsoft.com/en-us/library/bb928229.aspx.

Microsoft Dynamics CRM Online

Microsoft Dynamics CRM Online is basically the same software. The key difference is Microsoft Dynamics CRM Online is hosted by Microsoft Corporation. Microsoft Dynamics CRM Online also offers a few additional features and has a few limitations. Additional features include Internet lead capture and marketing campaign optimization, and a few limitations include the inability to upload custom Microsoft SQL Server Reporting Service reports and a set prebuilt report set.

Mastery of the infrastructure, having the right hardware, investing in a Microsoft Dynamics CRM infrastructure specialist, and other infrastructure specifics are not required. You also have access to a much larger environment with powerful hardware that can offer more scalability to small and midsize businesses that might be pushing their own hardware environment to the limits.

In addition, Microsoft takes on the responsibility of offering you long-term maintenance on the software and a level of uptime of 99.99 percent, with financial backing. An article on the announced service-level agreements for Microsoft Dynamics CRM Online can be found at http://crm.dynamics.com/deployment/ondemand.aspx and in a press release at www.microsoft.com/presspass/press/2009/mar09/03-10CRMConvergence09PR.mspx.

You can choose to install one piece of local software with Microsoft Dynamics CRM Online: the Microsoft Dynamics CRM Outlook Client. Yes, even with Microsoft Dynamics CRM Online, you can have integration to your local version of Microsoft Outlook email.

What you can't have in the world of Microsoft Dynamics CRM Online are hosted custom code sets and extensions that need to be installed on the same server as the Microsoft Dynamics CRM software and custom Microsoft SQL Server Report service reports. This server environment is owned, managed, and operated under the Microsoft umbrella, and, therefore, it has to be standardized for many different tenants of Microsoft Dynamics CRM.

Microsoft Dynamics CRM Hosted

Microsoft Dynamics CRM Hosted is similar to Microsoft Dynamics CRM Online, but it is hosted by an independent vendor. This external vendor can be a Microsoft Partner or one of the many hosting companies offering Microsoft Dynamics CRM. One of the benefits of working with a Microsoft Dynamics CRM Hosting partner is that you might have access to more third-party add-in products that are also hosted, such as integrated phone system software, Microsoft SharePoint environments, the Black-Berry server with Microsoft Dynamics CRM BlackBerry mobile support, and more. In addition, some third-party hosting partners have an offering for customers who want to host their own integrated custom code.

How It All Works Together

There are so many pieces. How do we put them all together?

A picture definitely expresses a thousand different words, and the relationship between the Microsoft Dynamics CRM infrastructure and the existing infrastructure and an almost unlimited choice of add-in options is no exception. In addition, how the hosting of Microsoft Dynamics CRM changes your understanding can be an eye-opener. For instance, the details that a hosting provider needs to know (or even a large enterprise who might host many xRM projects) differ significantly from the details that a small On-Premise-install network administrator needs to master.

xRM
xRM stands for relationship management software, where the x might mean something other than a customer (as in CRM). Microsoft Dynamics CRM is an xRM platform.
An example of an xRM solution includes configuring Microsoft Dynamics CRM to manage staffing and human resources.

Still, some items are core design, no matter where Microsoft Dynamics CRM lives. We will look at some of the pieces that make up the Microsoft Dynamics CRM infrastructure in the next sections.

Microsoft Dynamics CRM Infrastructure Components

When it comes to mastering the Infrastructure components in an On-Premise environment, one of the best pieces of documentation is the Microsoft Dynamics CRM Installation Guide and although, in this busy world, it is easy to skip much of the documentation that comes with applications, this guide is worth its weight in gold and is worth reading a few times. If you choose to ignore the Microsoft Dynamics CRM installation documentation, you do so at high risk.

Microsoft Dynamics CRM Application Software

The Microsoft Dynamics CRM program files, comprising the application, are generally installed to a designated CRM server. The install design and architecture of the application takes into consideration that independent software companies (ISVs), Microsoft Dynamics partners, and Microsoft Dynamics CRM customers, will extend, modify, customize, and configure the core application.

In addition, the architecture of the software platform takes into consideration that long term ongoing updates and upgrades will be part of the solution and will be released from the Microsoft Dynamics CRM development team on a regular basis. Further considerations in design provides for the need of the hosting providers and the Microsoft CRM Online team who have one set of shared CRM application software and yet many different instances of Microsoft Dynamics CRM databases (many tenants).

What Is a Tenant?

A tenant is generally related to one specific company's Microsoft Dynamics CRM data footprint; although in large enterprise clients, you might find different independent projects and non-CRM projects using their own set of databases (their own CRM tenant).

Microsoft Dynamics CRM SQL Server Databases

Microsoft Dynamics CRM stores all of its data in a set of Microsoft SQL Server databases. You can find out more about Microsoft Dynamics SQL Server 2008 or earlier versions at www.microsoft.com/sqlserver/2008/en/us/default.aspx.

For those familiar with Microsoft SQL Server, there is one key fact to keep in mind when working with Microsoft Dynamics CRM and Microsoft SQL Server: Data within the world of Microsoft Dynamics CRM is designed to be secure. It has specific rules related to it that are driven by the security rules defined in Microsoft Dynamics CRM, the business unit configuration defined in Microsoft Dynamics CRM, and by the user authentication setup through Windows Server. Given all these variables, it is a bad idea to directly add data into the Microsoft Dynamics CRM SQL Server databases or change any of the data within the databases through any method other than using the Microsoft Dynamics CRM software and software extensions designed with knowledge of Microsoft Dynamics CRM. Doing so is unsupported and can cause significant data corruption and application issues.

Microsoft Dynamics CRM actually uses a concept called filtered views. Data is served up by a filtered view to honor security roles. These filtered views can be added to or used to display data in a number of different formats.

In terms of database versions, Microsoft Dynamics CRM version 4.0 supports the use of either Microsoft SQL Server 2005 or Microsoft SQL Server 2008. Microsoft SQL Server 2008's upgrade path was focused on business intelligence, graphical displays of data, and analysis; so, if these items are important to you, consider upgrading the core database engine.

Multitenant

Microsoft Dynamics CRM v4.0 also supports multitenants. Multitenant support allows hosting companies to efficiently offer Microsoft Dynamics CRM within the world of the large, shared, and secured data center. When using a tenant of a multitenant environment, there are a few rules to consider, particularly if you are adding your own custom additions.

The first is that a few of the pieces of Microsoft Dynamics CRM v4.0 continue to be shared and have not yet been upgraded to multitenant. The first is Microsoft Dynamics CRM Help. The core Help files reside with the Microsoft Dynamics CRM application directory. You can customize Help, but the customizations will be seen by all users of the Microsoft Dynamics CRM software. Help is configured to allow you to add documentation to specific new custom entities, but on a wide search others might see this new documentation.

The second is that any changes to the core application files will impact everyone sharing these core application files. This is one reason why you are not allowed to upload your own custom software to extend the application if you are a Microsoft Dynamics CRM Online customer. The other significant reason is that allowing outside code on internal servers is at best risky.

Microsoft SQL Reporting Services

When you access the standard reports within Microsoft Dynamics CRM (from the Reports menu), you are accessing reports that were created in Microsoft SQL Reporting Services (SRS). If you are a Microsoft Dynamics CRM On-Premise customer, you can create your own Microsoft SRS reports and upload them into Microsoft Dynamics CRM. Figure 4.1 shows a list of some standard Microsoft SRS reports.

Other reporting choices include the Microsoft Dynamics CRM Ad Hoc Report Wizard that is built into the software, the Microsoft Dynamics CRM Analytic Accelerators found in Codeplex, and integration to Microsoft Office Excel through security-enabled dynamic Excel spreadsheets. More on reporting can be found in Hour 20, "Utilizing the Power of Microsoft Excel with CRM Data," and Hour 21, "Reporting and Query Basics."

Microsoft Windows Server and Microsoft Dynamics CRM

Microsoft Dynamics CRM On-Premise requires Microsoft Windows Server and other components that have been mentioned in this hour.

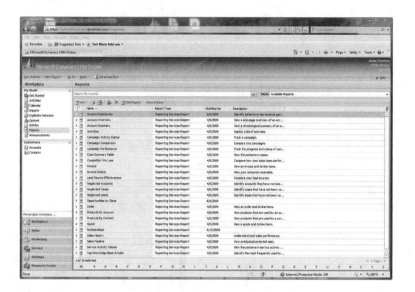

FIGURE 4.1
Reports from
Microsoft SQL
Server Reporting
Services.

If you are a CRM On-Premise customer, when you open Microsoft Dynamics CRM, the system does not ask you for a username and password. Why not? Microsoft Dynamics CRM already knows who you are based on the fact that you have already been authenticated to your company's environment when you logged in to your computer.

The CRM security model uses Windows-based authentication (Kerberos/NTLM) and internally driven authorization. It then offers further role-based layers of enhanced security based on additional configuration options. In Hour 5, "Security," you dive into the details of the application security.

Microsoft Dynamics CRM Email Router Software

Microsoft Dynamics CRM offers an independent and yet integrated solution to sharing email with Microsoft Exchange, and this option is available for both On-Premise and online environments. This component is called the Microsoft Dynamics CRM email router. The email router can live independently and yet definitely has an interest in all the mail coming into Microsoft Exchange. You also have the option of not using the Microsoft Dynamics CRM email router, choosing instead to configure Outlook to communicate directly. If you configure Outlook, you must configure each and every instance of Outlook to track email. Using the Microsoft Dynamics CRM email router is more efficient. For a conceptual peek, look at Figure 4.2.

FIGURE 4.2
The email router
in a multiple
Exchange envi-
ronment.

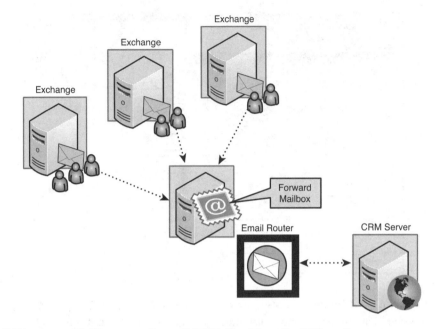

Microsoft Dynamics CRM Outlook Clients

There are two Microsoft Dynamics CRM Outlook clients. The first is the Microsoft
Dynamics CRM Outlook client, which supports the ability to go offline and is
designed for a laptop environment. This piece of software has continual drip synchronization between the Microsoft Dynamics CRM database and the local laptop
Microsoft SQL Express database. This design allows users to undock their laptop without specifically choosing to Go Offline. This creates more overhead, so you do not
want to install the Microsoft Dynamics CRM Outlook client for the laptop where it is
not needed (such as on a desktop machine).

The second version of the Microsoft Dynamics CRM Outlook client is designed for a
desktop machine or a Citrix or Terminal server environment. This version of the software allows multiple users using the same machine to work with the Microsoft
Dynamics CRM Outlook client, and it has less overhead because it does not need to
communicate with a local copy of a Microsoft SQL Express database.

Microsoft Dynamics CRM MobileExpress

Microsoft has recently released a new Microsoft Dynamics CRM mobile client called
MobileExpress v4.0 for Microsoft Dynamics CRM 4.0. The announcement can be read
on the Microsoft Dynamics CRM Team blog at http://blogs.msdn.com/crm/archive/

2009/07/09/product-release-mobile-express-for-microsoft-dynamics-crm-4-0.aspx. The mobile client is a free piece of software for clients who already own Microsoft Dynamics CRM. If the Microsoft-released mobile client doesn't meet your needs, you can find powerful and extremely well-proven solutions from third-party vendors, such as Ten Digits (www.tendigits.com) and CWR Mobility (www.cwrmobility.com).

Asynchronous Services and Microsoft Workflow Foundation

One of the key powers of Microsoft Dynamics CRM is the standard Microsoft Windows Workflow Foundation (WWF). Workflow allows for a number of different functionalities, from the automation of simple and complex business rules to the more advanced programming logic for parallel processing.

.NET

A major goal of the latest release of Microsoft .NET 4.0 is to make Workflow a standard part of the programming toolkit for all .NET developers, from small business to enterprise. You can read more about this at http://msdn.microsoft.com/en-us/library/dd851337.aspx.

Did you Know?

Microsoft Dynamics CRM takes Workflow one step further than just a tool for programmers. Microsoft Dynamics CRM makes Microsoft Workflow a user-enabled built-in function, empowering users who are not necessarily programmers to automate and organize.

When it comes to the infrastructure and the moving parts of Microsoft Workflow, we must mention asynchronous services. One of the key building blocks of Microsoft Dynamics CRM is the asynchronous services. The asynchronous service executes long-running operations independent of the main Microsoft Dynamics CRM system process. They are often associated with Microsoft Workflow and a component of things, such as queue processing. They can also be hosted on a different server, thus taking the load off the main CRM server in enterprise architecture. The Microsoft Dynamics CRM Software Developer's Kit (SDK) is a great place to learn more about the asynchronous services used by Microsoft Dynamics CRM. The SDK is available for download, or you can access the asynchronous services section directly from http://msdn.microsoft.com/en-us/library/cc151103.aspx.

Diving into Development

We can't leave this hour without commenting on the potential for experienced developers to become masters of Microsoft Dynamics CRM development. Developers diving into the world of Microsoft Dynamics CRM have a number of areas of expertise to master, and here are just a few of them:

▶ Extending the core Microsoft Dynamics CRM code

▶ Microsoft Windows Workflow Foundation (WWF)

▶ Form- and field-based scripting and scripts

▶ Icing on the cake: Silverlight integration

▶ Microsoft SharePoint (WSS/MOSS) for complementary unstructured data support

▶ Integrating to the world of finance and enterprise resource planning (ERP) with products such as DynamicsAX, GP, SL, and NAV

▶ Dashboards and business intelligence tools and techniques

▶ Mobility

▶ Changes to the Microsoft Dynamics CRM Outlook Client

Integration Options

What about connecting with all the other applications that we use? Hour 22, "Integration to the Other Applications," Hour 23, "Microsoft Dynamics CRM Utilities You Can Add" and Hour 24, "Microsoft Dynamics CRM as a Development Framework," take an in-depth look at the world of integration, so I make just a small comment here. Microsoft Dynamics CRM is built for and often expects long-term integration. Just as a salt goes with pepper, Microsoft Dynamics CRM goes with many other complementary applications, either from other Microsoft departments, outside vendors, or from Microsoft partners.

Big Business Versus Small Business

Despite, perhaps, assumptions otherwise, small businesses often use more functionality of Microsoft Dynamics CRM than big businesses. Small businesses often have the same needs and yet fewer people to get many of those core customer service, prospect management, and marketing tasks completed. People working within small businesses wear many different hats, leveraging and learning new skills as the job demands. It is not uncommon to find someone working in small business who has service, grassroots marketing, and a consultative sales technique (and experience to match all three). In addition, these power users have skills related to their chosen industry, and their tasks lists are long, detailed, and diverse. When it comes to Microsoft Dynamics CRM, any given person in a small business might use many, if not all, the features and functionality within the system. On the other hand, small business users might not have to keep track of all the details associated with working with their peers. The internal activity and appointment list might be a lot smaller.

When it comes to managing the hardware and infrastructure installation of Microsoft Dynamics CRM in small business, the balance is delicate. Microsoft Dynamics CRM integrates with many other applications, the operating system, and core functionality. If you layer this on top of a single server, the hardware needs to be beefy enough to handle the extra layer. There is good reason to outsource the hosting of Microsoft Dynamics CRM in the world of small business (not only because of hardware, but because of the labor required to maintain this new layer of integration).

In the world of big business, there are occasionally many more people and departments to juggle, and the interconnection between who is doing what and when is a key factor for getting things done. The functions of Microsoft Dynamics CRM within big business might be divided among different roles and departments, such as the marketing department using the marketing functions and features, the service department focused on service scheduling and cases, and the sales department using the sales features. This division of labor doesn't always mean the division of information. In big business, security layers become more important, as does the security offering. Needs for role-based, feature, and function and division security are not uncommon.

Now that you have a better understanding of many of the choices surrounding Microsoft Dynamics installation and use, let's dive into a workshop including a few questions for review.

Workshop

Chase Boats is a company that manages the funding and sponsorship of crews and tall ships entered into various worldwide races. Given that many of the races are held all over the world, Chase Boats needed a customer relationship management software package that could handle multiple currencies, localized dates and time, and the organization and management of potential sponsorship dollars. Chase Boats already had a good accounting system managed by its accounting firm, but it wanted a CRM product that could empower each staff member to be more organized, more collaborative, and more responsive to the sponsors and crews that they work with. Charlie Chase is the CEO of Chase Boats. He accesses his Microsoft Dynamics

CRM software from all over the world; his company uses Microsoft Dynamics CRM Online. In addition, because Charlie might spend a month or two in different countries, he sets Microsoft Dynamics CRM to the country he is in and gets immediate localized settings.

Chase Boats also has staff who resides in different locations. When a big race is happening, Charlie works closely with the staff in numerous different locations to coordinate logistics. Microsoft Dynamics CRM email and activity tracking allows Charlie to quickly see all the conversations from around the world that are happening with any given sponsor or crew member.

Q&A

Q. *Our Microsoft Dynamics CRM software keeps having difficulties. It seems like we keep having issues.*

A. Microsoft Dynamics CRM needs to be installed correctly and managed by an experienced network administrator. If the software is installed incorrectly from the beginning, it can give you continuous issues. Do it right, and you will not have any problems.

Q. *We are waffling between Microsoft Dynamics CRM Online and Microsoft Dynamics CRM On-Premise. Are there any other resources to help us decide?*

A. Talk with one or two Microsoft Dynamics CRM partners and the Microsoft Dynamics CRM Online team. This choice can be determined by key factors such as whether you need to create complex custom reports or the resources that are available for you to manage the infrastructure. You might also consider talking with one of the many existing Microsoft Dynamics CRM users.

Q. *What are some of the best resources for our people to get more training?*

A. Some of the Microsoft Dynamics CRM boot camps are excellent. IMG, Inc., also has a long history of running great classes (www.imginc.com/aboutimg/Pages/default.aspx), as does BizITPro (www.bizitpro.com).

Quiz

1. What is one reason why a large corporation might want to use Microsoft Dynamics CRM Online rather than Microsoft Dynamics CRM On-Premise?

2. What is one benefit that Charlie Chase gets out of using Microsoft Dynamics CRM?

3. Name three other applications that Microsoft Dynamics CRM might work well with.

4. What can't you do in the world of Microsoft Dynamics CRM Online?

5. What does multitenant mean?

6. What are two areas that a developer new to Microsoft Dynamics CRM can choose to master?

Answers

1. Microsoft Dynamics CRM Online offers the application without requiring the skilled infrastructure specialists and hardware requirements needed for a robust On-Premise application.

2. Charlie Chase depends on the localization of dates and time, as well as the management and handling of multiple currencies associated with his products and services.

3. Microsoft Excel, Microsoft Office SharePoint Services, and Microsoft Word.

4. Import custom Microsoft SQL Server Reporting Service reports.

5. Multitenant means that you have the ability to have many different instances of Microsoft Dynamics CRM databases sharing the same set of core application program files.

6. The core Microsoft Dynamics CRM .NET code, Silverlight, and form- and field-based scripts.

Exercise

If you are considering an On-Premise solution, you want to dive into this exercise. Download the Microsoft Dynamics CRM Installation Guide and the Microsoft Dynamics CRM SDK. Spend some time familiarizing yourself with key areas of these two documents. You might not be a software developer or the person or team who has or will install the software, but these two documents offer real insight in a number of different areas.

HOUR 5

Security

What You'll Learn in This Hour:

▶ Principles Behind the Microsoft Dynamics CRM Security Model

▶ How to Create and Manage Your Organization (Business Units and Users)

▶ How to Use and Maintain Security Roles

▶ Principles Behind "Sharing" Data

The security model within Microsoft Dynamics CRM is extremely comprehensive and has been designed to protect data integrity, provide an efficient mechanism for accessing data, and facilitate easy collaboration.

Microsoft's goals for the security model include the following:

▶ Provide users with access only to the information required to perform their job functions

▶ Categorize types of users to define roles and restrict access based on those roles

▶ Support data sharing for collaboration, so that users can be explicitly granted access to data they do not own

Successfully implementing security within Microsoft Dynamics CRM requires an understanding of the three core elements that make up the security model:

▶ Business units

▶ Users

▶ Security roles

Figure 5.1 shows that these three elements are located on the Administration interface, which is accessible from the Settings menu.

All persons (users) who access your Microsoft Dynamics CRM system must be uniquely identified, and the system must know where they sit in the organization structure (business unit) and what they are allowed to do (security role) once logged in.

FIGURE 5.1
Where to access business units, users, and security roles.

Watch
Out!

Can't Log In Without This

All three pieces of information must be defined for a person to log in to the system. If one of your users is unable to log in, check that she is enabled, has been assigned to a "business unit," and has a "security role."

Both users and security roles are stored within a business unit. Therefore, when we add a user to the system, we must define the business unit that user belongs to and the user's security role within that designated business unit. It is possible to have different/unique security roles within each business unit, but it is not a recommended practice. (We discuss this in more detail in the "Security Roles" section.)

Business units form the basis of your organization structure, and it is helpful to work from an organizational chart when setting these up. However, it is important to remember that a key reason you are building this hierarchical structure is to govern access to data. The structure you build in Microsoft Dynamics CRM might not directly match your physical organizational structure. You want to ensure that your users have access to all the right information they require to perform their job function, but at the same time you want to be able to limit access to any sensitive data.

Before we delve into the security model itself, we need to understand how data is referenced in Microsoft Dynamics CRM so that we can better understand how and where we might need to control access to it. There are two kinds of data records in Microsoft Dynamics CRM:

▶ **User owned:** User-owned records are typically records that relate to a customer (for example, a lead, account, contact, opportunity, order, invoice, case, contract, and activities). Typically, these types of records are managed by or actioned by users.

▶ **Organization owned:** Organization-owned records are typically those used for reference data and are associated with a business unit (for example, a product, services, queues, teams, and resources). In other words, they are not directly related to or associated with any user.

Exception to the Rule

By the Way

Three special items in CRM can be created, which by default are individually owned, but may be promoted to the organization:

▶ Reports

▶ Mail Merge Templates

▶ Email Templates

Individual security privileges govern if users can create these items, and a separate privilege also exits to determine if a user can promote them to be available to the organization.

Every record in Microsoft Dynamics CRM is automatically marked with its respective "owner." When you access Microsoft Dynamics CRM and select any of the key customer-related record types (lead, account, contact, opportunity, and so on), by default, you are provided with a list of "your" records. This is because the default view (My Active Contacts) filters and selects records owned only by you to help you focus on those you manage.

Figure 5.2 highlights by default, Microsoft Dynamics CRM filters "My" records wherever possible to simplify finding and accessing those records that relate to that user.

The owner of the record is displayed on the Administration tab of the record itself; although it is possible to change the owner of a record, the ability to do this is governed by a *security privilege* within the security role, which allows control over whom can perform this kind of function.

FIGURE 5.2
Records filtered
by owner.

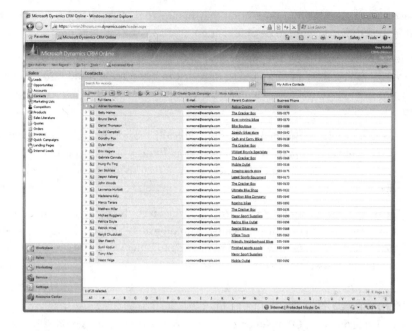

Figure 5.3 displays where the owner identification is located for each record.

FIGURE 5.3
Record owner
displayed on the
Administration
tab.

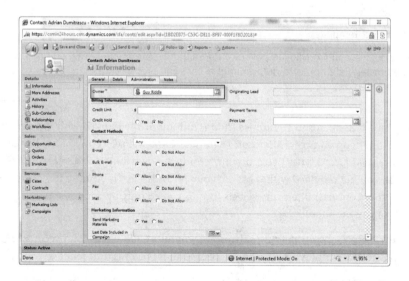

This concept of a security privilege is key to the Microsoft Dynamics CRM security
model.

A Privilege is an inherent component of the security role itself, which is made up of hundreds of these privileges, each one governing every action that can be performed within the system.

How It All Comes Together

When we bring together these three core elements of business unit, user, and security role, we can see how the security model works.

We might have one or many business units, and within these we add users. This gives us our organizational structure. At this point, however, we have not declared what users are permitted to do or what they can access, because this comes from the security role. Remember that security is primarily determined by the security role, not by which business unit a user is assigned to.

A security role is three dimensional, but we will first look at it in a two-dimensional way and build upon what we learn.

Table 5.1 illustrates how a two-dimensional security role, as a matrix of "actions" against specific record types (entities), might look.

TABLE 5.1 If Security Roles Were Two Dimensional

	Create	Read	Write	Delete	Etc.
Account	Yes	Yes	Yes	No	
Contact	Yes	Yes	Yes	No	
Opportunity	Yes	Yes	Yes	No	
Case	No	Yes	No	No	
Activity	Yes	Yes	Yes	Yes	
Etc.					

If the security role were just two dimensional, we would not be able to define on which set of records a user may perform this action (because there is no qualification). In Table 5.1, the action for Write Opportunity is Yes, which would give the ability to update any opportunity in the system. However, in reality, it is more likely that *only* the salesperson who is managing that opportunity would be allowed to update it. So, we might want to restrict the Write privilege to only those records that the user owns. This is where the third dimension or "qualifier" comes into play and completes the picture of the security role. The qualifier will allow you to grant privileges to specific sets of records (for example, opportunities that the user owns).

Table 5.2 shows how the two-dimensional Yes/No actions have been replaced with qualifiers to give the three-dimensional aspect, exactly as they appear in Microsoft Dynamics CRM.

TABLE 5.2   Sample Microsoft Dynamics CRM Security Role Structure

	Create	Read	Write	Delete	Etc.
Account	■	■	■	○	
Contact	■	■	■	○	
Opportunity	■	■	◕	○	
Case	○	■	○	○	
Activity	■	■	◕	■	
Etc.					

Key:

Organization (System wide) – (■)

User (own data only) – (◕)

None – (○)

In the preceding example, we have explicitly declared the appropriate action on a particular set of data records. For example, users can

▶ Read any account, contact, opportunity, case, or activity in the entire Microsoft Dynamics CRM system

Terminology

The action Write refers to the ability to update (change) a record.

▶ Write any account or contact in the entire Microsoft Dynamics CRM, but not a case, and can only update opportunities and activities they own

Table 5.2 is for example purposes only and does not cover all the possible privileges. We cover the full extent of the security role later. However, these principles form the basis of the security role concepts.

Tailoring Security Roles to Match Job Roles

It is important to understand that certain actions can apply to some users who perform a specific job function, but not to others within your organization. This is why Microsoft Dynamics CRM provides the capability to define many security roles, so that you can tailor each role to apply to a particular job function/role within your organization.

Business Units

The top-level business unit is automatically created when your Microsoft Dynamics CRM system is provisioned and has the name of your organization. (This is the only one that does not have a parent.)

A business unit can be defined as a subsidiary, division, operating unit, branch office, and so forth, depending on how your specific organization is structured.

There is nothing wrong with having a single (the default) business unit and every user in your organization sitting in that one business unit. Although not a rule, it is often the case that, for smaller organizations, it makes sense to have everyone in the same business unit because the lines of demarcation between job roles and responsibilities are often blurred and overlap (because people tend to wear many hats in smaller companies). Therefore, we need to make sure that people have access to all the information they need to fulfill the role that they perform. If you initially place every user in the same business unit, you can at any time in the future add business units and move users as required.

Creating a business unit is a straightforward process. As shown in Figure 5.4, we can see a list of existing business units, and from here, we can click the New button in the toolbar to create a new business unit (see Figure 5.5).

Reorganizing Your Business Unit Hierarchy

It is possible to reorganize your business unit hierarchy. (Any business unit, except the top-level parent, can be repointed to another parent business unit.)

There are two methods:

▶ From the list of all business units, highlight the one that needs to change. Click the More Actions button in the toolbar, select Change Parent Business, and select the new parent from the dialog box.

▶ From the list of all business units, double-click the required business unit to open the record. Click the Actions button in the toolbar, select Change Parent Business, and select the new parent from the dialog box.

You Can't Rename or Delete a Business Unit

Once created, a business unit name cannot be changed or deleted. After creating a business unit, you can simply "disable" it so it can no longer be referenced.

FIGURE 5.4
List of existing
business units.

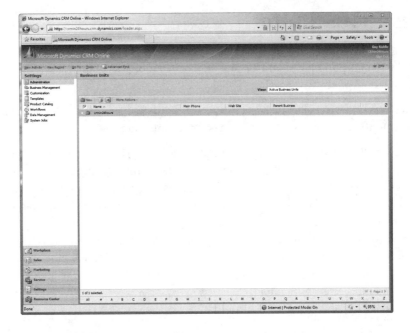

FIGURE 5.5
Create a new
business unit.

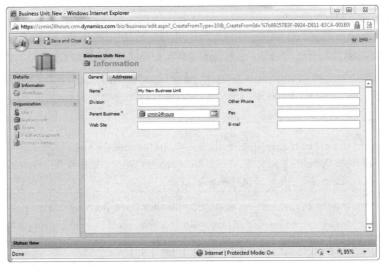

Users

Users represent each and every person who will access the Microsoft Dynamics CRM system. Each user is uniquely identified by a network logon identifier Microsoft Dynamics CRM On-Premise and, in the case of Microsoft Dynamics CRM Online, by their Windows Live ID.

Users represent each and every person that will access the Microsoft Dynamics CRM system and each User must be uniquely identified.

For an on-premise deployment, each user will have their CRM User record associated with their Windows network logon identifier; and in the case of Microsoft Dynamics CRM Online, the association will be with their Windows Live ID.

Microsoft Dynamics CRM caters to three different scenarios for a user license, and this information is stored within the user record itself. The type of client access license (CAL) determines what users can do with Microsoft Dynamics CRM. Organizations usually have a limited number of each type of CAL. A CAL is licensable, and it is the responsibility of each organization to ensure that it has licensed sufficient numbers of CALs for its users. A CAL is required for each user, except those with administrative access. When a user is created in Microsoft Dynamics CRM, we need to specific which type of CAL that user will be assigned:

▶ **Full:** User will have full access to any part of Microsoft Dynamics CRM that he or she has the security roles and privileges to access.

▶ **Administrative:** User will have read-only access to the Sales, Marketing, and Service areas and full access to the Settings area. This type does not consume a CAL.

▶ **Read-Only:** User will have read-only access to the Sales, Marketing, and Service areas that he or she has the security roles and privileges to access.

CALs Can Either Be User or Device

For On-Premise deployments, Microsoft allows CALs to be assigned to a device rather than a named user. This is useful for organizations that have a lot of part-time workers or shift workers (for example, call centers).

By the Way

Depending on whether you are using Microsoft Dynamics CRM On-Premise or Microsoft Dynamics CRM Online, there are two slightly different procedures for creating users. In both cases, you need some minimum pieces of information before you can create the users:

▶ Network login and email address (for CRM On-Premise) or Windows Live ID (for CRM Online)

▶ First and last name of user

▶ Business unit

Each user must be assigned to a business unit (this defaults to the top-level unit), and this is automatically set for CRM Online users. This can be changed at a later date if required (as discussed later in this hour).

Creating CRM On-Premise Users

From the Microsoft Dynamics CRM Administration page, we can access users. Figure 5.6 shows a list of existing users.

FIGURE 5.6
List of existing users.

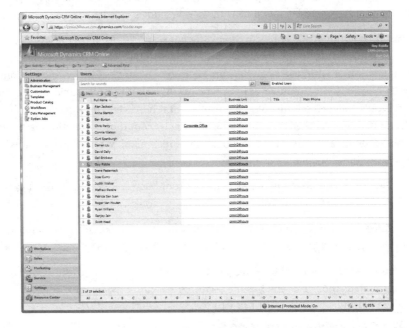

When we click the New button in the toolbar to create a new user, we are presented with two options (see Figure 5.7). We can either add a single user or multiple users.

FIGURE 5.7
Options presented to create users.

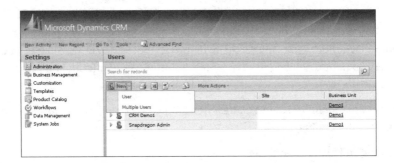

OPTION 1

Select User to add a single user to the system, and you will be presented with a user interface (see Figure 5.8).

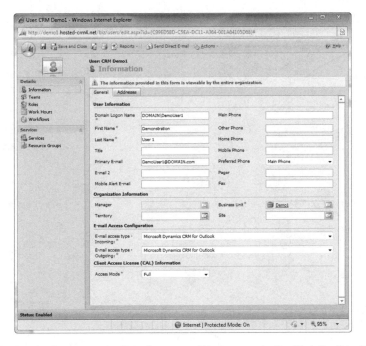

FIGURE 5.8
Options presented to create users.

Using this method, you must select the correct business unit; it will default to the top-level business unit in your hierarchy.

You must also append to the user a security role after the user has been created; otherwise, the user will not be able to access the system. To add a security role to the user, click the Roles button in the side navigation pane. The User's Roles interface will appear, as shown in Figure 5.9.

To add a security role, click Manage Roles in the toolbar. A dialog will appear in which you can select an appropriate security role for that user from the list of security roles available within the business unit to which the user has been assigned (see Figure 5.10).

After a security role has been assigned to a user, the user is can then log in to the system.

OPTION 2

Select Multiple Users to create one or several users at one time. Note that when you choose this option to create new users, they will all be created with same following values:

- ▶ Same business unit
- ▶ Same security roles
- ▶ Same license type

FIGURE 5.9
User's security
roles.

FIGURE 5.10
Available secu-
rity roles.

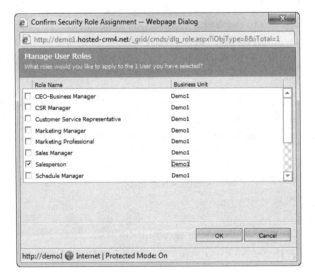

If you choose this method, you are taken through a wizard to define the new users, as shown in Figures 5.11 through 5.15.

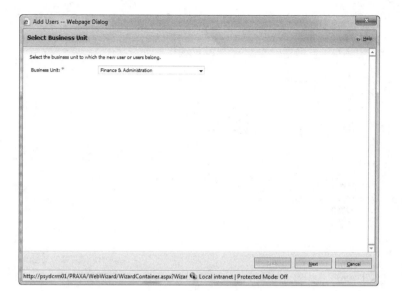

FIGURE 5.11
Wizard step 1: Choose Business Unit.

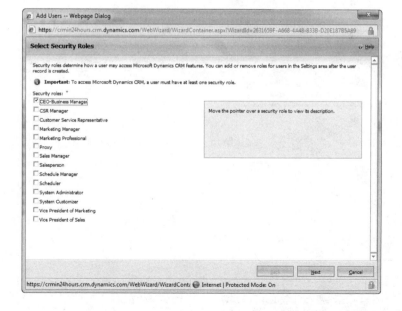

FIGURE 5.12
Wizard step 2: Choose Security Role(s).

FIGURE 5.13
FIGURE 5.13
Wizard step 3:
Select License
Type.

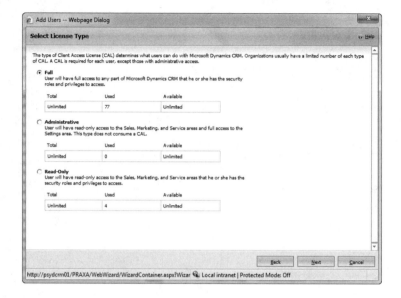

FIGURE 5.14
Wizard step 4:
Select Users
from Your
Domains/Groups.

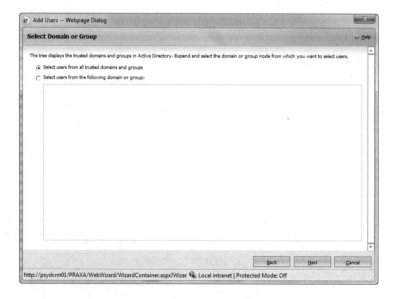

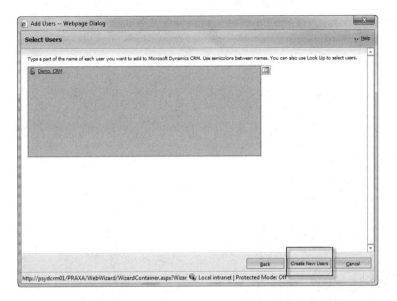

FIGURE 5.15
Wizard step 5:
Select Users
from your
Domains/Groups.

After all of your users have been selected from your Domains/Groups, click the Create
Users button to have them all created as Microsoft Dynamics CRM users.

Crting Microsoft Dynamics CRM Online Users

From the Microsoft Dynamics CRM Administration page, we can access users.
Figure 5.16 shows a list of existing users.

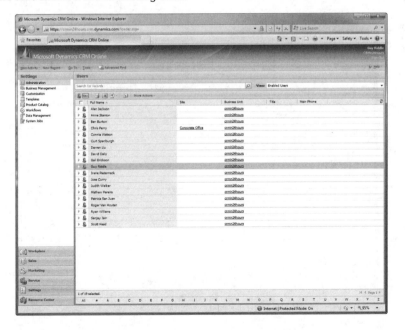

FIGURE 5.16
List of existing
users.

When we click the New button in the toolbar to create a new user, we are taken through a wizard to define the new users, as shown in Figures 5.17 through 5.19.

FIGURE 5.17
Wizard step 1:
Choose Security
Role(s).

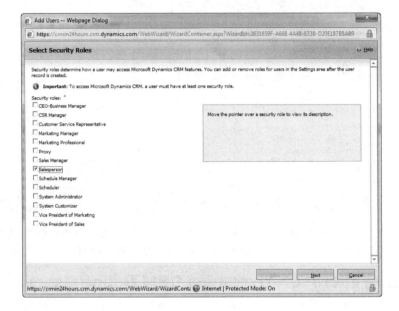

FIGURE 5.18
Wizard step 2:
Add Users.

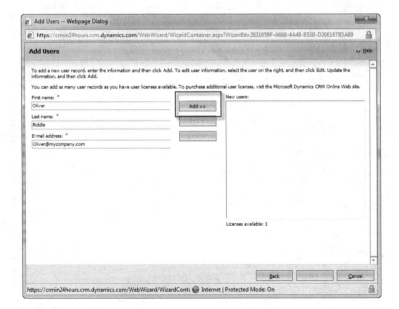

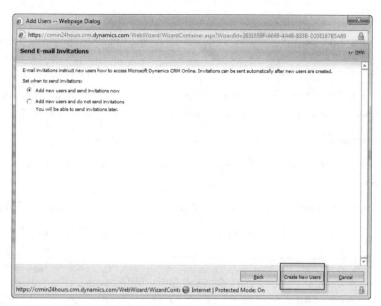

FIGURE 5.19
Wizard step 3:
Send E-Mail Invitations.

On this page of the wizard, you can enter the details of one or many users you want to add to the system. At the bottom of the screen, you will see the available number of licenses decrease as you add more users.

You can choose not to send invitations, but it is recommended to do so in order that the user receives an email with the correct URL to access your Microsoft Dynamics CRM system. If you choose not to send invitations now, you can send them later. This is done from the users list view (refer to Figure 5.16). You just select the users you want to send the invitation to, click the More Actions button in the toolbar, and then choose the Send Invitation option.

After you decide on your preferred option for sending email invitations, click the Create Users button to have them all created as Microsoft Dynamics CRM users.

How to Change the Business Unit of a User

From the list of all users, highlight the one that needs to change. Click the More Actions button in the toolbar, select Change Business Unit, and then select the new parent from the dialog box.

From the list of all users, highlight the one that needs to change. Click the More Actions button in the toolbar, select Change Business Unit, and then select the new parent from the dialog box.

From the list of all users, double-click the required user to open the record. Click the Actions button in the toolbar, select Change Business Unit, and then select the new parent from the dialog box.

N.B. The same procedure applies if you have assigned the user a "manager" and want to change it at a later date.

User Administration

When users leave the organization, a few housekeeping functions should be carried out:

- ▶ Reassign their records to another user.

- ▶ Disable their Microsoft Dynamics CRM user record. Doing so automatically frees up their CRM licenses so that they can be used for other users.

To reassign all a user's records to someone else, follow these steps:

1. On the Actions menu, click Reassign Records and then click Assign to Another User.

2. Click the Lookup icon, type a part of the other user's name, and click Find.

3. In the results list, double-click the employee's name and then click OK.

To deactivate a user record, follow these steps:

1. In the navigation pane, click Settings. In the Settings area, click Business Unit Settings and then click Users.

2. Find and open the user record for the departing salesperson.

3. On the Actions menu, click Disable and then click OK.

By the Way

> ### You Can Change the Information You Capture About Your Users
>
> The Microsoft Dynamics CRM record type "User" is customizable. Therefore, you can extend the information that is captured about a user using standard Microsoft Dynamics CRM customization techniques.
>
> However, remember that any user record is visible to any user within the system.

Security Roles

Security roles govern what a user can do after access to the system is granted. Microsoft Dynamics CRM ships with 13 predefined security roles, each comprising almost 350 individual security privileges (see Table 5.3).

TABLE 5.3   Shipped Security Roles

Shipped Security Role
CEO-Business Manager
CSR Manager
Customer Service Representative
Marketing Manager
Marketing Professional

TABLE 5.3   *Continued*

Shipped Security Role
Sales Manager
Salesperson
Schedule Manager
Scheduler
System Administrator
System Customizer
Vice President of Marketing
Vice President of Sales

Generally, the components of a security role fall into two categories:

▶ **Entity:** Relates to a record type of data/information captured and entered into the system (for example, account, contact, product, quote, case, activity) and typically maintained by our users

▶ **System features:** Specific functions that we can perform within the system (print, export to Excel, import data, mail merge, override quote pricing, and so on)

When it comes to understanding the security role, we have to understand how the privileges for them are defined. System features are simple: You can or you can't perform the privilege; whereas with entity privileges, we have to qualify where the privilege may be performed. An Entity Privilege has three elements:

▶ Entity (record type)

▶ Action

▶ Access level (qualifier)

Actions

For any given entity (record type), we can perform eight actions on it. The security role must know all of these for every entity.

Table 5.4 shows the actions that a user may perform against any given entity.

TABLE 5.4   List of Actions

Action	Description
Create	Creates a new record.
Read	Views or open an existing record.
Write	Saves changes to an existing record.
Delete	Deletes an existing record.
Append	Appends (attaches) this record to another record.

TABLE 5.4 *Continued*

Action	Description
Append To	Appends (attaches) other records to this record.
	The Append and Append To privileges typically work in conjunction with each other.
	For example, if you want to add a note to an account, you must have the Append privilege on the note and the Attend To privilege on the account.
Assign	Assigns this record to another user.
Share	Shares this record with another user (or team).

Access Levels

Five access levels (qualifiers) define what set of records a user can perform the respective action.

Table 5.5 shows the list of access levels to determine where a user could perform an action against any given entity.

TABLE 5.5 List of Access Levels

Access Level	Symbol	Description
Organization	■	Can perform this privilege on any record in the system
Parent/Child	◉	Can perform this privilege on any records in the same business unit as the user and any records in any child business units sitting under the user's business unit
Business Unit	◖	Can perform this privilege on any records in the same business unit as the user
User	◔	Can only perform this privilege on records owned by the user
None	○	No access to perform this privilege at all

Table 5.6 shows a list of example privileges to highlight how the three elements come together to define a privilege.

TABLE 5.6 Privileges

Entity	Action	Access Level	Result
Account	Write	Organization	Can update any account record in the entire system
Contact	Write	User	Can only update contacts that are owned by the user
Opportunity	Read	Business unit	Can only read opportunities that are owned by the user and any that are in the same business unit
Activity	Delete	User	Can delete any activities that are owned by the user
Contract	Read	None	Has no access to view any contracts at all (and therefore this option will disappear from any screen where it would normally appear for that user)*

*As a user navigates through Microsoft Dynamics CRM, each user interface is dynamically rendered, based on the security privileges within their security role. This means that if a user does not have the privilege to perform a system function or access certain types of data records, those corresponding buttons on the user interfaces will disappear.

In the case of system features, it is based on the ability to perform the function; in the case of entities, it is based on the Read privilege. For example, if I set the Export to Excel privilege to None, the button will disappear from every user interface to which in normally applies. If I set the Invoice entity Read privilege to None, the user will not see the Invoice button on any user interface in the system.

This process is the recommended method for removing unwanted items from the user interface for each of your security roles as required.

By the Way

> **Users Can Have More Than One Security Role**
>
> It is permissible for a user to be granted more than one Security Role. In this case, you might find that a conflict arises. If this happens, Microsoft Dynamics CRM always applies the least restrictive principle. For example, if we give a user Role A that denies a specific permission, but we also give him a second Role B that grants the permission, using the least restrictive principle, he will be granted permission.

Maintaining Security Roles

Although Microsoft Dynamics CRM provides 13 "out of the box" security roles, we do not have to use them. In fact, we can define our own security roles from scratch, or we could modify any of the shipped roles. Both of these capabilities are possible, but it is not a recommended practice. Preserving the original roles (even if you don't use them) allows you to go back and reference them if ever you need to in the future. The best practice is to copy an existing role and then modify it to meet your exact requirements. That way you only have to make changes by exception.

By the Way

> **Review the Shipped Security Roles Before You Use Them**
>
> By default, every shipped security role (except System Customizer) permits the user to
>
> ▶ Read almost every record in the entire system
>
> ▶ Delete any record that the users owns
>
> Therefore, review each security role to ensure that they meet your requirements before using them.
>
> You can edit any of the default security roles, except the System Administrator role.

From the Microsoft Dynamics CRM Administration page, we can access security roles. Figure 5.20 shows a list of existing security roles.

From the list of existing security roles, we can highlight which role we want to copy, click More Actions in the toolbar, and select the Copy Role option.

We can also provide a name for the new security role we are creating (see Figure 5.21).

If we leave the check box selected, the new role will automatically open for us after it is created (see Figure 5.22).

Because almost 350 privileges make up a security role, there are too many to display on one screen. Therefore, the privileges have been grouped logically onto eight individual tabs. Figures 5.23 through 5.30 show the privileges for the default Salesperson security role.

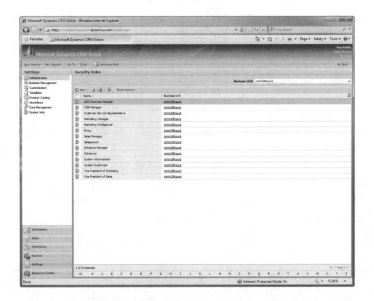

FIGURE 5.20
List of existing security roles.

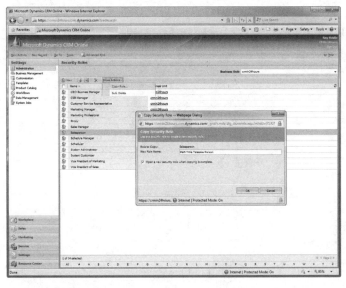

FIGURE 5.21
Name new Security role.

Don't Forget Permissions for New Entities

If you add a custom entity to Microsoft Dynamics CRM, it will automatically be enrolled into every security role, and there will be a set of security privileges relating to it. However, by default, every privilege will be set to None (no access). The exception is with the System Administrator role, which has the Organization privilege for every action. This allows you to then explicitly define what privileges you require for each of your security roles.

Watch Out!

FIGURE 5.22
Security role.

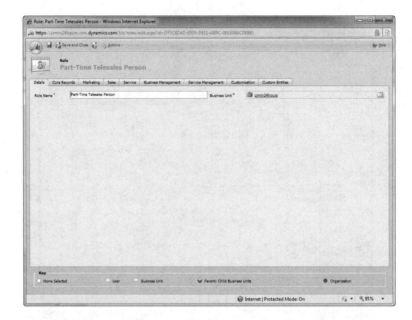

FIGURE 5.23
Salesperson:
Core Records.

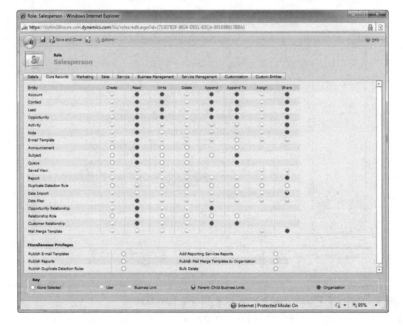

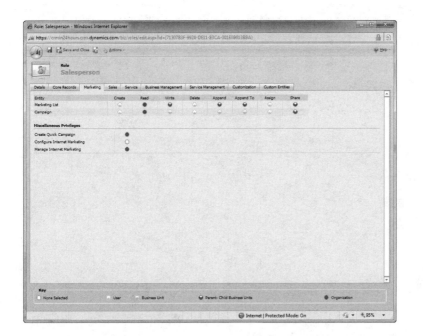

FIGURE 5.24
Salesperson:
Marketing.

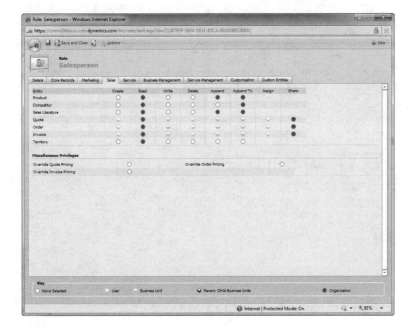

FIGURE 5.25
Salesperson:
Sales.

FIGURE 5.26
Salesperson:
Service.

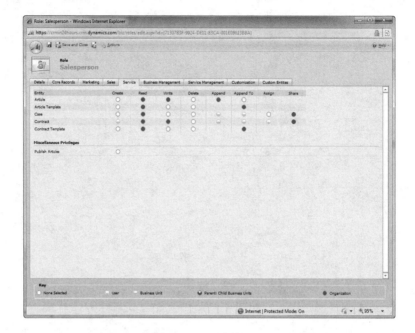

FIGURE 5.27
Salesperson:
Business Man-
agement.

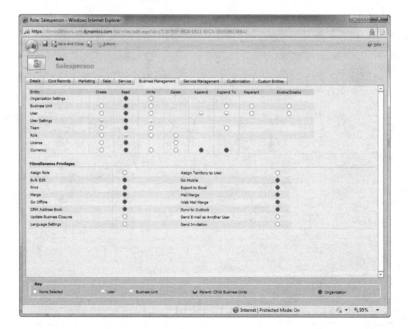

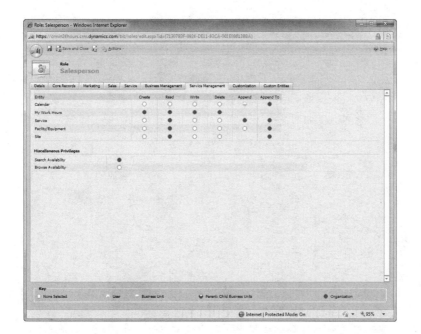

FIGURE 5.28
Salesperson:
Service Manage-
ment.

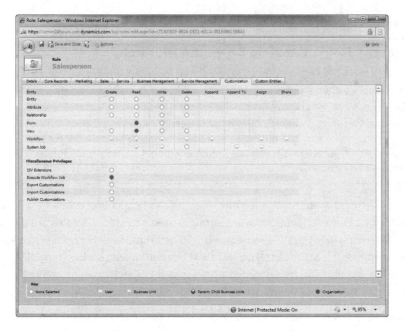

FIGURE 5.29
Salesperson:
Customization.

FIGURE 5.30
Salesperson:
Custom Entities.

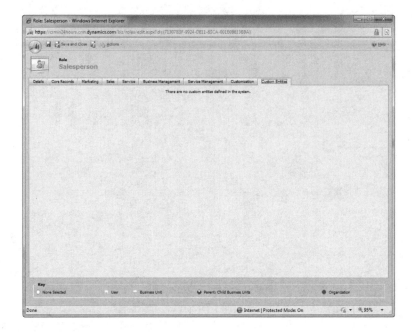

FIGURE 5.30
Salesperson:
Custom Entities.

Sharing Records

Security Roles Cascade Down the Hierarchy

Security roles are created and associated with business units.

Each time we create a new business unit within our hierarchy, it inherits all the security roles associated with the parent business units.

Because Microsoft Dynamics CRM inherits security roles to children business units, you cannot vary the privileges of a security role to be different for each business unit. Alternatively, you can create additional security roles for each business unit as required.

We have learned that, through security roles, we can restrict user access to specific data records. However, sometimes a user might need access to a data record that isn't included (access-wise) in their security roles. To accommodate this need, we can collaborate through a Microsoft Dynamics CRM concept called sharing. Typically, any record in CRM that can be associated with a customer (lead, account, contact, opportunity, case, quote, and so on) can be shared.

Security roles govern what we can do in Microsoft Dynamics CRM, and because sharing is an action, there is also a privilege associated with it. Therefore, to share a record with another user, we must have the ability to share that record type. This is so that we can control who can share records (and which types) in the system.

You might not need to be concerned about sharing in your organization. Because, by default, every shipped security role permits every user to "read" every record, you might find that the need for sharing (and explaining this feature to your users) is not necessary.

Sharing is an explicit process, initiated by users. You can share a record in Microsoft Dynamics CRM in two different ways. In both instances, a Sharing User interface will display. In that, the user must define whom the record is to be shared with and what privileges are assigned to the user.

At first glance, it might appear that when you share a record with another user that you could grant security privileges that change the user's security role. This is not actually the case. The user's underlying security privileges will prevail. What you are granting are privileges to that specific record itself, but only if the user already has the privilege to perform the similar action to his or her own records.

For example, if I share a Contact record with another user and grant her the Delete privilege, the user will not be able to delete the record if her base security role has the Delete Contact privilege set to None.

Removing the share of a parent record removes the sharing properties of the records that it inherited from the parent. Therefore, all users who previously had visibility of this record will no longer have visibility of the child records either.

It is possible that some child records might still be shared to a user if they were shared individually.

After a sharing request is initiated, a user interface opens (see Figure 5.31). Through this interface, users can nominate whether they want to share records with a single user, several users, or a team.

Either single or multiple records can be shared at a time.

As shown in Figure 5.32, with an individual record open, the user can click Action in the toolbar and select the Sharing option.

Figure 5.33 shows that with a list view open, the user can select several records in the list, click More Actions in the toolbar, and select the Sharing option.

By the Way

Hidden Option

Share reassigned records with original user?

A system setting determines whether records are shared back to the original owner when they are assigned.

If your CRM environment is locked down so that users can only see their records, this might be a useful feature; otherwise, the user who created the record (or previously owned it) might lose access to it.

FIGURE 5.31
Setting the sharing options.

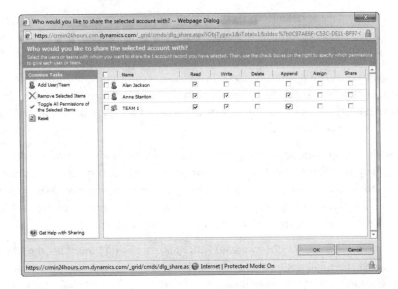

FIGURE 5.32
Share a single record.

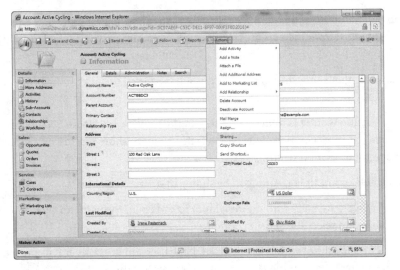

Owner Sees Everything

The "owner" of a parent record will always see every child-related record.

If our security model is set up such that salespeople cannot see others opportunities, we need to be mindful of sharing. For example, John is the owner of an account, and he shares the account with Mary. Usually, if Mary adds an opportunity, John would not normally see it. However, if she adds the opportunity to the account that John owns, John will see that opportunity.

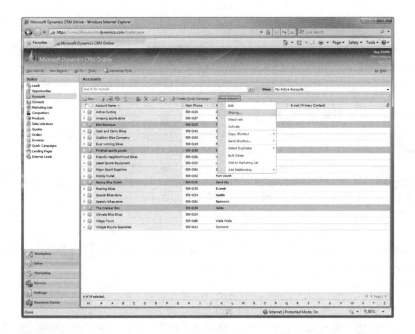

FIGURE 5.33
Share multiple records.

Teams

Teams only have relevance if you are planning to implement sharing. A team is a group of users. A team does not actually own any data and does not have a security role assigned to it.

When a user shares a record, it is an explicit action associated with a specified user. (For example, a user shares a record with a named coworker.) In some situations, users might have to share a record with several users, and this can be laborious for the user. A feature of sharing is that instead of sharing a record with a named user, we can elect to share the record with a team.

The key benefit of this approach is that if a new employee joins the organization, as soon as we add the new employee to the team, he or she is automatically shared with all the records that the team has been granted access to. Similarly, if a user is taken out of a team, that user's right to access those shared records is removed.

A user can be a member of several teams.

Defining and maintaining teams is a straightforward process. Team definitions are accessed via the Administration interface from the Settings menu.

Teams Are There to Stay

An annoying "gotcha" exists with Teams—once created, they are there to stay. Unfortunately, no facility exists to delete or disable a Team after it is created.

Where this becomes further annoying is that a Team is associated with a business unit—if you accidently create the Team within the wrong business unit, you cannot move it to a different one.

Figure 5.34 shows a list of existing teams. From here, we can click the New button in the toolbar to create a new team (see Figure 5.35).

FIGURE 5.34
List of existing teams.

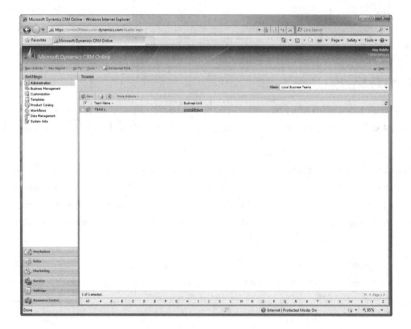

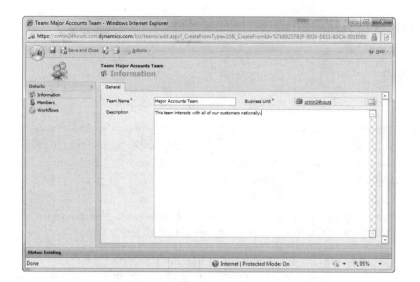

FIGURE 5.35
Create a new team.

Team members can be managed from the team record. Users can be added or removed (as shown in Figure 5.36).

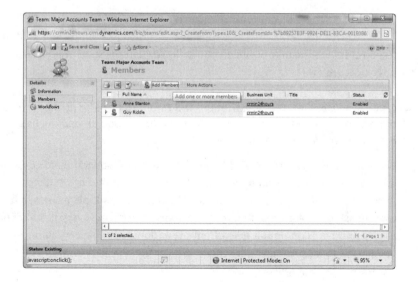

FIGURE 5.36
Manage team members.

Workshop

Q&A

Q. *I created a business unit by mistake. How do I get rid of it?*

A. Business units cannot be deleted. If you no longer require a business unit, simply make it inactive via the option on the Actions menu. Be sure to move any users first before you disable the business unit, because deactivating a business unit will also deactivate any users within it.

Q. *One of my users has been promoted, and I now need give him more access through his security role. What do I need to do?*

A. Open the user's record, and in the left navigation pane, click Roles. In the toolbar, click Manage Roles and choose the appropriate security role for the user. Remember that a user might have more than one security role if required.

Q. *I moved a user to a different business unit, and now she can't log in to the system. What did I do wrong?*

A. When a user moves business units, their security roles are automatically removed. This is so that you can explicitly select the appropriate role to fit her responsibility in the new business unit. To log in to the system, a user must have a security role.

Q. *One of my users left the organization, and I want to transfer all his records to the new person taking over his role. Can I do this in one procedure, or do I have to manually reassign each record?*

A. Records can be "assigned" individually or in bulk. On individual records, you can simply take the Assign option or just change the Owner attribute on the record itself. Bulk records can be changed by selecting multiple records in a list and choosing the Assign option in the toolbar. Transferring every record of one user to another is an option taken from the Actions menu when you have opened the user's record; you just have to enter the new user to whom all the records will be reassigned.

Q. *I need to add a new user, but I have run out of Microsoft Dynamics CRM licenses. I have a user in the system who recently left. How can I reuse her license?*

A. Navigate the list of users in the Administration section from the Settings menu. Select the users who have left the organization and, from the Actions menu, choose Disable. Doing so disables the users so that they will no longer be permitted to access the system, and it also frees up their licenses for reuse.

Q. *We have a new employee, and she is going to be doing both sales and marketing. Which security role do I give her: Salesperson or Marketing Professional?*

A. You can give her both roles. A user can be assigned multiple security roles where it makes sense to do so. If there are conflicts in security privileges between the assigned roles, a "least restrictive" rule applies. For example, if one role stipulates a user cannot do something, and the other says he can, he will be permitted to perform the action.

Q. *I sometimes use temporary staff to do telesales. I have given them the Salesperson security role so that they can access the sales-related information. Because they are temporary staff, however, I don't want them to be able to export to Excel. Is there a way to achieve this?*

A. This is a great example of where a new security role could be created to achieve this business requirement. Navigate to the list of security roles from the Administration section from the Settings menu. Highlight the Salesperson security role, click the More Actions button in the toolbar, and select the Copy Role option. Enter the desired name for the new role (perhaps Telesales Temp Staff, in this instance). When the new role opens, click the Business Management tab. Locate the Export to Excel privilege on the right side of the lower half of the screen; click the green dot and it will change to a red circle (signifying None). Save and close the new security role. Any users who now have this security role assigned to them will not see the Excel button on any screen.

Q. *I have created a "personal view" of all the opportunities in my pipeline and now a colleague also wants to use it. Can this be done automatically, or does my colleague have to set it up himself?*

A. From the Advanced Find screen (where personal views are created), click the Saved Views tab. Highlight the view required to be shared, click the More Actions button in the toolbar, and then select the Sharing option. The view can now be shared with other users/teams.

Q. *I created a team some time ago, but the need for that team no longer exists. Can I remove the team?*

A. Unfortunately, teams cannot be deleted or disabled. You can rename a team to something more appropriate if you want to continue using it, or you can give it a revised name that highlights that it should not be used.

Quiz

1. Which of the shipped security roles permit users to see almost every record in the system and delete any records for which they are marked as the "owner?"

2. How do you gain the license back from a user that leaves your organization to make it available to use for another user?

3. How do you display a list of which users have been assigned which security roles?

Answers

1. All of them except the "System Customizer" (who has reduced access to core customer related records). While seeing everything in the system is less of an issue it is worthwhile reviewing what you will allow users to delete. Consider the scenario where a disgruntled employee decides to leave your organization–you probably don't want them going through the system deleting all their records. It is a better practice to get users to use the native feature of deactivating a record if it is no longer current/active rather than deleting records.

2. A user cannot be deleted from the system–this is so that any 'history' is maintained for your business–however, you can via the Actions menu on the user record disable a user. By 'disabling' a user, their license count is released back into the available pool of licenses.

3. Unfortunately, no predefined feature provides this information. However, using the Report Wizard, you can build the report easily. When you run the report wizard, make sure you select Roles as the Primary record type and Users as the Related record type.

Exercise

Let's look at a scenario of how we might need to control access to data and how we could implement that through the Microsoft Dynamics CRM security model.

Scenario

We are a company based in San Francisco with sales offices in Seattle, New York, and Atlanta. We have an eastern sales manager based in New York and a western sales manager based in San Francisco. Both can see all the opportunities of their respective regions but not nationally. We also have a marketing manager who is based in Atlanta and needs access to everything. The sales teams in each office are permitted to see the sales opportunities within their own office (so that they are not stepping on each other's toes) but not allowed to see those in the other offices.

Possible Solution

To segregate the data between what the sales managers can see and what each sales-person can see, we need to establish a business unit hierarchy to achieve this. Therefore, we have opted to create four additional business units under the default one, as shown in Figure 5.37. Hierarchically, we have also placed Seattle and Atlanta under San Francisco and New York, respectively; this is because we need the sales managers to be able to cascade down their respective branches of the hierarchy.

FIGURE 5.37
Possible solution for business unit hierarchy.

In this model, the sales staff will be assigned to each business unit related to where they work. Each will be given an appropriate security role; but in particular, their roles must stipulate that they have Business Unit privilege for opportunities (so that they can only see any opportunities in their own business units).

The eastern and western sales managers will be assigned to the New York and San Francisco business units, respectively. They will also be assigned appropriate security roles; but in their cases, we must make sure that they have Parent Child Business Unit privilege for opportunities (to ensure they can see all the opportunities in the business unit to which they belong as well as the opportunities in the business units below them).

The marketing manager could be placed in the Atlanta business unit (where he physically resides) or he could be placed in the top-level business unit (perhaps representing his position within the organization). The key here is that we must give him the appropriate privilege depending on where we place him. If he is placed in the Atlanta business unit, he must have Organization privilege for opportunities, which allows global access to all opportunities in the system (because he will need to look up the organizational hierarchy as well as across it). If he is placed in the top-level business unit, he could be assigned Organization or Parent Child Business Unit privilege for opportunities (because here, he really only needs to look down the hierarchy).

HOUR 6

Managing Leads

What You'll Learn in This Hour:

- ▶ A Little History

- ▶ Importing New Leads

- ▶ What Data to Capture and the Import Process

- ▶ Distributing Leads

- ▶ A Deeper Look at a Lead

- ▶ From Lead to Prospect

Managing leads is the beginning of a sales process and one core reason for using a CRM application. In this hour, we dive into the world of leads and the meaning of leads in the world of Microsoft Dynamics CRM. A lead is an unqualified person that has the potential to become a new customer.

A Little History

A lead is an unqualified contact that is associated with a company. This unqualified contact can come from a number of places, including a collected business card, a purchased list, a referral, a trade show, a seminar, or a random phone call. In Microsoft Dynamics CRM, there is a special place in the system for these unqualified contacts (Leads). There are two core reasons for this separation. The first is that many companies purchase large lists of contacts, and it is generally good practice not to dump a huge list of unqualified contacts in with your nice clean qualified data. There is definitely something to be said for not having to sort through 50,000 extra Lead entities (record types) when trying to run a sales funnel report.

The second reason is that Microsoft Dynamics CRM takes a multilayered approach to the tracking of everything that happens around relationships, and yet when data is collected from many other places and systems, it tends to be rather flat (or normalized for you developer gurus). The Leads feature of Microsoft Dynamics CRM allows for a flat company contact record to be converted to a more robust structure, including Account, Contact, Opportunity, and all the associated activities, history, and notes.

The most common way to create Lead entities (record types) is to import them from a purchased or acquired list. The functionality to import leads into Microsoft Dynamics CRM is robust and an area of confusion to many, and yet given how often it is used, we take a good piece of hour six to talk about importing new data into the leads area of Microsoft Dynamics CRM.

Importing New Leads

Microsoft Dynamics CRM has a nice tool that imports data from any file that is formatted as a comma-separated value file. You will see people refer to this type of file as a "CSV" file, but the general gist is that every value in the file is separated by a comma, and the set of data ends with a carriage return. The system and wizards can then understand where one piece of data ends and the next begins, as well as when one record of information ends and another begins. This file is also an industry standard, so if you purchase data from another company or if you get a list of leads from a trade show, you will most likely be getting that list in either Microsoft Excel or Comma Separated Value (CSV) file format. If you are familiar with Microsoft Excel, you can save any Excel file as a CSV file. If you use a field separator in your data, such as the comma in Smith, Smith and Jones LLP, you must also enclose the field in a data delimiter, such as double quotes. An example of what a few lines of a CSV file might look like is as follows:

Name, Topic, Phone Number
John Doe, Interested in large purchase, 425-111-1111
"Smith, Smith and Jones LLP", Dropped by booth, 425-333-2222

CSV files separate each value with a comma or each value with a comma *and* double quotes. The double quotes are nice when you have company names with commas in them, such as the company name Smith, Smith and Jones LLP.

In Figure 6.1, you will see that the Microsoft Dynamics CRM Data Import Wizard lets you choose what separators are used in your CSV file.

The other key item that you want to be careful of when preparing or reviewing your data for import is that special characters are not always digestible by the system. For instance, an @, #, &, or * often have other meanings to computer software, and if they are embedded in your data, they can cause the system to literally choke. International characters can also have the same effect. Microsoft Dynamics CRM will check for characters that are not agreeable and will prevent data from being uploaded that does not fit.

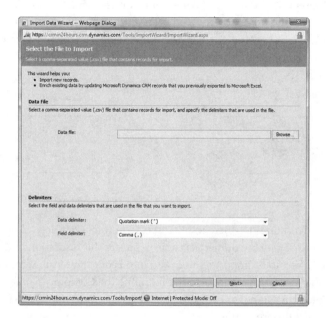

FIGURE 6.1
Data separators.

What Data to Capture and the Import Process

There are a number of different needs and interests when it comes to putting data into Microsoft Dynamics CRM. These needs and interests are driven by the timing of the Microsoft Dynamics CRM project, the department and people with the interest, and the business processes. In general, no matter what the interest, most data tends to lend itself to being imported as a Lead so that you can use the system convert functionality to create relationship depth and the interconnection between records. An Account has a primary Contact, and a Contact has a relationship to an Account. Although you can import directly into Contacts, the Lead convert feature creates interdependence that you would otherwise have to manually enter.

There is an interest in importing data after a trade show or when a list of potential leads has been purchased and the interest list can go on. There is often a need to import data when a new staff person is hired or when a merger or acquisition occurs. With each need and interest, it is important to consider which tool to use to import data because each tool offers different advantages.

Data Import Wizard: Data Format

The Data Import Wizard enables end users to map Microsoft Dynamics CRM data fields to fields represented in the CSV file. For instance, if you know that the first field in your CSV file is the Company Name (because the first column in your Excel spreadsheet is Company Name), your map would associate the first field in the CSV file to the Account name in Microsoft Dynamics CRM. Figure 6.2 illustrates this.

FIGURE 6.2
Data mapping.

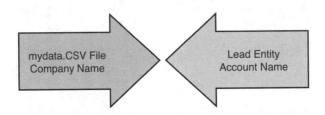

Another consideration is to where in Microsoft Dynamics CRM do you want to import this data? There are numerous choices, but for this discussion and in general, you are more likely to be importing this data into Leads than into Accounts or Contacts. To further expand, you are actually mapping the Company Name in your CSV file to the Company Name in the Leads pool (also known as the Leads entity [record type]). Figure 6.3 illustrates this.

FIGURE 6.3
Company Name
mapping to
Account Name.

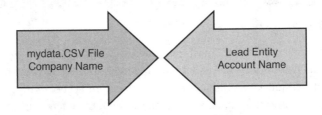

The following is a look at a data mapping from the Data Import Wizard as we follow a process of importing a CSV file that contains two leads into the Leads pool in Microsoft Dynamics CRM:

1. Select Imports from the My Work section of the left navigation pane.

2. Choose New.

Once a new import is chosen, you will see the first import screen, as shown in Figure 6.4.

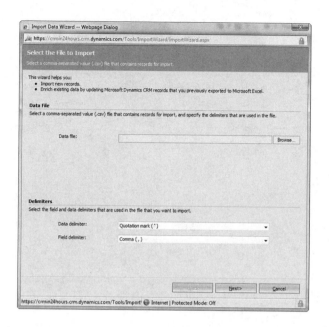

FIGURE 6.4
Starting a data
import.

On this initial screen, you need to tell the system what the name of your CSV file is, where it is located, and how the data is delimited. Is the data separated by only commas or by commas and quotes? Are the quotes single quotes or double quotes?

You then proceed to the next screen (see Figure 6.5). This screen requests that you tell the system where in Microsoft Dynamics CRM you want to import your data and what data map to use to map the data in your file to the data in Microsoft Dynamics CRM. In our example, we import data into the Leads entity in Microsoft Dynamics CRM. We do not have an old data map to use, so we will create one in the following figures.

Because a data map does not exist that defines the data within the data file I am using in this example, I choose to create a new data map by clicking the lookup icon next to the data map field in Figure 6.5. Once this is selected, Figure 6.6 appears.

Create a new data map and continue to the creation of the details associated with the data map. The details include general details so that the map can be used again and the specific attribute mapping of the data fields in your data file (referred to as columns if you import sample data). It also shows how they relate to data fields in Microsoft Dynamics CRM (CRM refers to these as attributes), and if mapping to a list. Lastly which items from your data file will map to which items in the predefined list. Figure 6.7 shows the general details, which include the name of the data map so that it can be used again, who created it, and when it was created.

FIGURE 6.5
Select Record
Type and Data
Map.

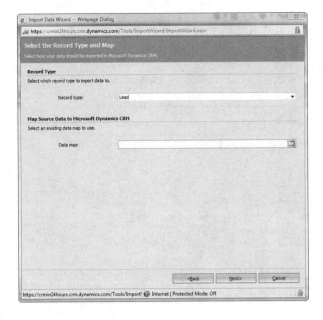

FIGURE 6.5
Select Record
Type and Data
Map.

FIGURE 6.6
Creating a new
data map.

In Figure 6.8, we actually map columns from your data file to attributes (fields) in
Microsoft Dynamics CRM. Microsoft Dynamics CRM understands your data file because
Microsoft Dynamics CRM offers the ability to upload a sample. The system uploads the

first record from the data file, which is often the header row from a Microsoft Excel file. In my example, I included the names of the columns in the first row. Notice the section labeled Column Headers in Figure 6.8. The Target section of Figure 6.8 shows all the attributes (fields) in the Microsoft Dynamics CRM Lead entity (record type), and these can be selected and mapped to the column headings from your data file.

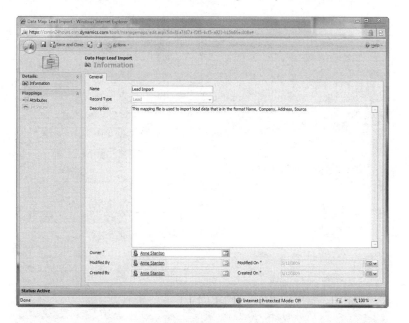

FIGURE 6.7
Name the data map.

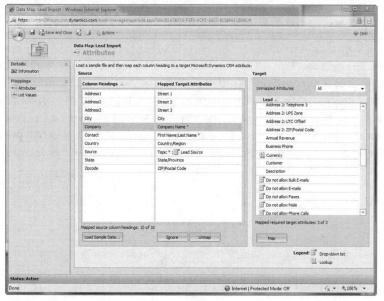

FIGURE 6.8
Mapping attributes.

In Figure 6.9, we take it one step further. We actually map a piece of data called source in our data file to the Lead attribute (field) source, which is a drop-down list. If the data does not exactly match items in the list, we must tell the system how the data in our source field maps to items in the source drop-down list attribute in Microsoft Dynamics CRM.

FIGURE 6.9
Matching drop-
down list items.

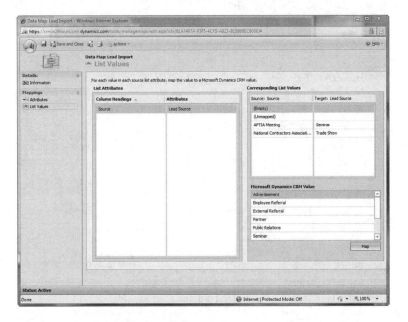

After the data map is created, configured, and saved, we return to the data import process. The next step is to tell the system who will be assigned as the owner of the lead after data is imported and whether duplicate records should be included. We show how the system asks these questions in Figure 6.10. Note that most all core records within Microsoft Dynamics CRM have an owner. This owner could possibly be a specific user or the system, depending on what type of entity (record type) we are talking about. With regard to Leads, the owner is a specific Microsoft Dynamics CRM user.

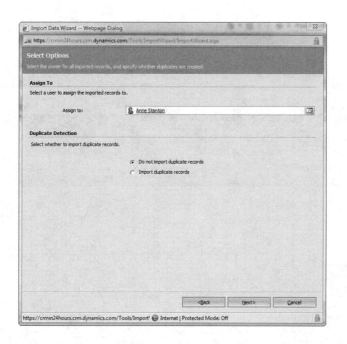

FIGURE 6.10
Assign and dupli-
cates.

Figure 6.11 shows that you can apply a name to the total import, offering easy reference when looking at the system messages regarding how many leads were imported
and how many were errors.

FIGURE 6.11
Name the
import.

Figure 6.12 and Figure 6.13 show how the import process appears when first started and how it reports when the data is completed.

FIGURE 6.12
System mes-
sages: Import
Started.

FIGURE 6.12
System mes-
sages: Import
Started.

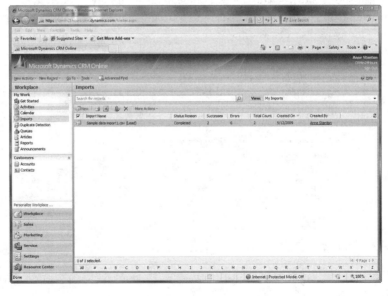

FIGURE 6.13
System mes-
sages: Import
Completed.

We then moved to displaying the new records as a list of new Leads as you can see in Figure 6.15. Figure 6.14 shows the data that was entered into Microsoft Excel and how it looks in Leads view.

FIGURE 6.14
Original data in
Excel 2007:
Leads to Import.

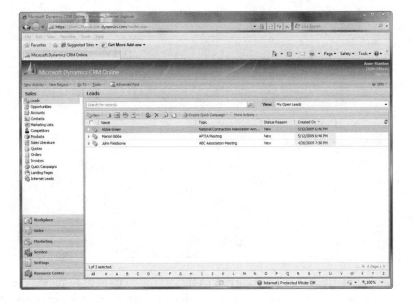

FIGURE 6.15
Leads: Import
Completed.

We can also select a specific Lead and drill down into the details, change the details, or add to the details that were uploaded. After Leads are imported, the sales process usually goes through a qualification process. After a Lead is qualified, the Lead is converted to an Account.

Microsoft Dynamics CRM can also automate the process using the features and functionality of the Microsoft Windows Workflow Foundation (WWF). Hour 16, "Workflow: Creating Simple Workflow," focuses on creating simple workflows, but it is worth mentioning here that the system can be designed to automatically kick off an automated sales process when a Lead is converted or when an Opportunity is created.

Distributing Leads

When a Lead is entered into the system, core information can be used to distribute this Lead to the appropriate salesperson. Microsoft Dynamics CRM can be configured with business rules using workflow functionality that kicks in on the creation of a Lead. For instance, if a Lead has a zip code that begins with a specific set of numbers, a workflow rule can run that automatically changes the sales territory or owner of that new Lead record to the appropriate sales territory or salesperson.

Figure 6.16 shows an example of a simple workflow set up to associate all leads with a zip code starting with 05 to a specific salesperson.

FIGURE 6.16
Distribution of
leads workflow.

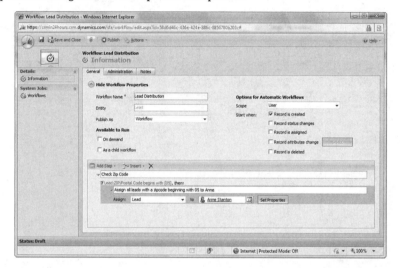

When you get to Hour 16, remember this example. The concept of changing the owner and sales territory of Leads when they are created is a great beginner workflow to start practicing with.

A Deeper Look at a Lead

After a Lead is imported, the details can be fine-tuned and changed. Figure 6.17 shows the General tab of the Lead. Before any configuration, the Lead form is made up of four tabs: General, Detail, Administration, and Notes. Configuration also allows you to add more tabs, remove tabs, or add more data fields to existing or new tabs.

Let's discuss four fields on the Lead General tab. The first is Topic. If you are looking at a long list of many, many Leads, the Topic field helps distinguish two Leads with exactly the same information. For instance, you might have two Leads with different

Contacts, but perhaps they work in the same company. The Topic field can be renamed through system customization; however, it cannot be removed. Given that the Topic field is a required system field, some consideration is needed to decide how your company wants to use Topic. Some examples for Topic include where the Lead came from, how the Lead is categorized, and to what division the Lead is assigned.

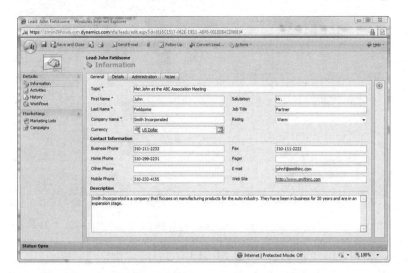

FIGURE 6.17
General tab of the lead.

The next field worthy of discussion is the Currency field. In Microsoft Dynamics CRM, you can assign different currency to different Leads. This enables a global corporation to track local Leads in the currency of the country where the Lead is being worked. Currency also impacts other entities (record types) in the system that has associated money, such as Opportunity, Quotes, Orders, and Invoices. When setting up system configuration within Microsoft Dynamics CRM, you can also enter a currency-conversion rate table. The currency rate table does not automatically update, but it can be manually changed as needed.

We also see a Rating field on the Lead General tab with a drop-down list of Hot, Warm, and Cold. The value on this field maps to the Opportunity during the convert process. This rating helps a salesperson prioritize the Leads when making decisions regarding which Lead to call first to qualify and flows through as an indicator on the Opportunity to offset the core sales funnel analysis fields, such as estimated close date, sales stage, and percent probability. If a Lead or Opportunity is cold and the estimated close date is within a couple of weeks or days, the sales manager might want to have an offline discussion with his salesperson.

Finally, there's the Description field. It is tempting to use the Description field for Notes; however, the field is limited in size. The best use of the Description field is for a brief profile of the company with which the Lead is associated. This profile might be a cut and paste from the company's website or it might just be local knowledge. Figure 6.18 offers an example of the Detail tab of a Lead.

FIGURE 6.18
Details tab of
the Lead.

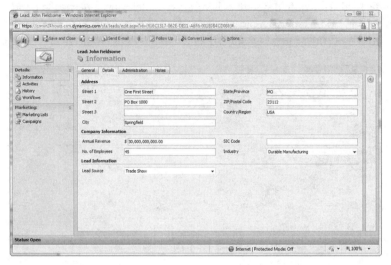

Notice that, on the Details tab, the last field displayed is the Source field. This is one of the most critical fields within the Lead, and if you have not already considered it, you might want to change this to a required field and perhaps move it to the General tab. The next tab we are going to look at is the Administration Tab as seen in Figure 6.19.

FIGURE 6.19
Administration
tab of the Lead.

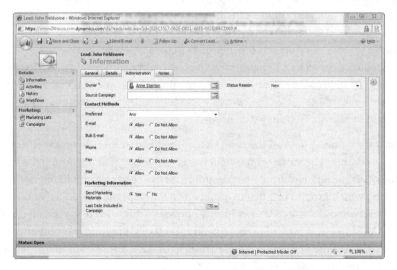

The fields on the Lead Administrative tab control some of your business process compliance when in the To Qualify stage (items such as whether the Lead has requested that you do not call them, but you are allowed to send them information via email). Should the Lead be flagged for a certain marketing campaign to heat them up a bit, or perhaps marketing materials have been sent to them and you want to flag and show the last campaign this Lead was included in. In addition, if this Lead was acquired through a new marketing campaign, the Lead Administration tab displays what source campaign generated the Lead.

Mapped Data

Activities and details on the Lead do not necessarily get copied to the Account or Opportunity during convert. If you are going to be working on the Lead past the qualification phase, convert it so that your detailed activities, notes, and work is organized around the Account or Opportunity.

From Lead to Account: Convert

Figure 6.20 shows the change from Lead to the more complex Account and related entities.

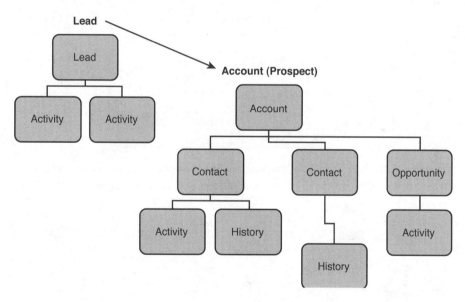

FIGURE 6.20
From lead to prospect.

Microsoft Dynamics CRM has a convert process that takes a flat "Lead" and expands it to the dimensions needed to track a complex company and sales process. The three things that a Lead can be converted into are Account, Contact, and Opportunity. You have the choice of converting a Lead to all three or any combination of the three. Depending on the company, you might find that all three entities are used or only one. Even within the blog world, you will see different debates on this subject.

Once a Lead is converted, a sales process can kick off, a salesperson can add more Contacts, and any other numerous Activities can be associated. With regard to the Opportunity, you are kicking off a "thing" that is called an Opportunity that tracks the dollar value of the potential sale and other key sales information; this thing lives in the sales funnel until it is closed and relegated to history (won or lost).

Figure 6.21 shows the choices you have when converting a Lead.

FIGURE 6.21
Convert Lead.

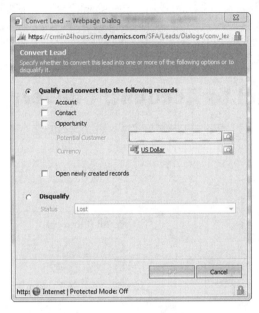

In Figures 6.22, 6.23, and 6.24, you can see the Account, Contact, and Opportunity record that was created from the convert process of the Lead in Figures 6.20 and 6.21.

FIGURE 6.22
The created
Opportunity.

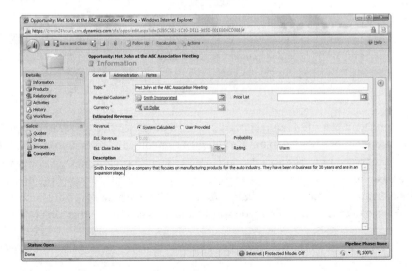

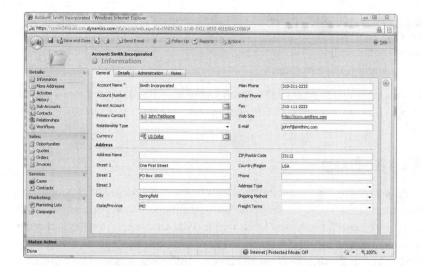

FIGURE 6.23
The created account.

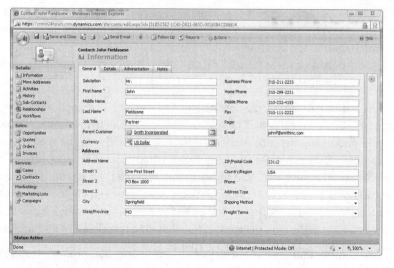

FIGURE 6.24
The created contact.

Notice that the Topic field and the Description field in the Opportunity are populated with data from the Lead.

Although Microsoft Dynamics CRM enables users to import Leads and then convert Leads to Account, Contact, and Opportunity, the feature does not have to be used as part of your sales process. You can enter an Account, select Contact from the left navigation pane, and enter the Contact (which can autopopulate with Account details). Later, when you are ready, you can create an Opportunity to track the promised deal.

The Lead feature offers a few key benefits. The first is the ability to keep the long, long list of unqualified Leads separate from your shorter list of qualified Accounts of type prospect. The second is that it offers some efficiency around creating new Accounts, Contacts, and Opportunities. It also offers a flat normalized table for data import that is similar to a user's experience with Excel and allows for field matching with a common-sense approach.

Like many Microsoft products, Microsoft Dynamics CRM gives you many choices when it comes to the eventual business processes you decide to use.

Workshop

Smith Incorporated is a company that sells manufacturing products to auto body shops around the world. On a regular basis, the marketing department at Smith Incorporated purchases lists of Leads that include all the new auto body shops in the United States. The lists that it purchases are downloaded and are in the format of a text file. The marketing department takes the list, opens it in Microsoft Excel, and adds a column labeled Source. It populates the Source column with the name of the list it purchased. The department also deletes one or two columns of the spreadsheet that contain data that it can immediately see is not of interest. When it finishes the review, the department saves the file as a CSV file and imports it into the Leads entity (record type) pool of Microsoft Dynamics CRM.

After the Leads are imported, they are assigned to specific salespeople within Smith Incorporated based on zip code. The salespeople schedule activities and start making their calls, prioritizing the calls based on the rate associated with the Lead. When a call is completed, they complete the phone call Activity and either schedule another call or convert the Lead based on a conversation. When a Lead is qualified through a phone call and a positive conversation with a Contact, the Lead is converted to an Account, Contact, and Opportunity. If the Lead is disqualified through a conversation, the Lead is run through the convert function, and it is closed as disqualified.

New Opportunities that are created kick off an automatic sales process, starting at sales stage one. Sales stage one has five associated Activities with it, including update estimated close date, probability percentage and rating, follow up with prospect by sending requested initial sales material, and confirm that the Lead received and reviewed the information and is ready for an appointment. The goal of sales stage one is to start the sales process and further qualify the Lead. Sales stage two includes activities associated with meeting the prospect face to face.

Q&A

Q. *Is it necessary to use Leads? Or can we bypass that feature?*

A. You can bypass the Leads feature, but you might want to add a source field to either the account or contact to capture where your new accounts or contacts came from. Traditionally, source is part of the Lead entity (record type).

Q. *I uploaded a spreadsheet into Leads incorrectly, and I now want to delete everything I uploaded. Is there an easy way to do this?*

A. Yes, in Microsoft Dynamics CRM, you can select the first lead and the last lead you want to delete and then press the black X.

Q. *I did a data import, but all the data in my Excel spreadsheet is not in Leads. What happened?*

A. Microsoft Dynamics CRM keeps track of which leads were uploaded and what were failures because of various issues. Under Imports from the Left Navigation Pane, change your view to Completed Imports. Double-click your import to choose it and show more details, including documented failures.

Q. *We want our leads to be associated to a specific salesperson depending on the state. Can this be supported?*

A. Yes, Microsoft Dynamics CRM supports this scenario by offering users the option to define workflow rules.

Quiz

1. What are the four fields on the General tab of a lead that are worthy of more consideration?
2. How will you use the Lead Topic field? What are some examples?
3. How does Lead rating relate to Opportunity rating?
4. Can data be imported into other record types?
5. Why does the system support a lead and a prospect, and why are they different?
6. What are possible data separators?

Answers

1. Topic, Currency, Rating and Description are the four fields.

2. The Lead Topic will be used to help classify different leads. An example includes two leads from different contacts at the same company.

3. The lead rating can map to the opportunity rating and can indicate how active, hot or cold the lead and potential sale is.

4. Yes, data can be imported into a variety of record types including Accounts, Contacts, and Leads.

5. A Lead is an unqualified prospect. A prospect is a classification of a type of Account and associated contacts. A Lead it an entity (record type).

6. A possible data separator is a comma or a comma and quotation marks.

Exercise

Create a data file using Microsoft Excel. Include company name, contact name, contact address, telephone number, email, web page, and source. Save this file as a CSV file and import it into Microsoft Dynamics CRM. During the import, you are asked to create a data map. Map each of your fields from your Excel file to fields within the Lead entity in Microsoft Dynamics CRM. Notice that you have to upload a sample data file and, if you have not added a header row to your Excel spreadsheet, the sample data file might be a bit tougher to map to the Lead entity. You might also notice that it is beneficial to have a first-name column and a last-name column in your data file because the Lead entity has the name split into three fields. For the Topic field, map the company name and the source. Notice that you can map two fields, creating a merge effect.

After the leads are imported, check the system messages. Did all the leads get imported, or were there errors?

Now, open one of your new leads and populate a few more fields. Now, try converting it to an account, contact, and opportunity. What data gets moved during convert?

HOUR 7

The Account in More Detail

What You'll Learn in This Hour:

- ▶ Account Form
- ▶ How the Account Relates to Other Entities (Record Types)
- ▶ What the Account Can Impact
- ▶ How the Account Can Be Redefined

In this hour, you will master the consistent structure throughout the application for data capture through the use of the data entry form. Additionally, you learn the pieces of the form that offer options for more usability and the areas of a form that connect to related data.

Account Form

Figure 7.1 shows the initial Account form. This is what you will see when you create a new Account.

Capturing or displaying all the details on an Account includes the common assumed information, such as address and telephone numbers, but also the very specific industry or audience niche information. Figure 7.1 shows an example, but let's dive into more detail.

First, the Account Form is built with a number of different building blocks, all of which offer the user different options. "Forms," such as the Account form, appear in their own window, although it note that you can open many forms at once. This ability to open many forms at once is the first significant difference between Microsoft Dynamics CRM and other CRM systems. In Microsoft Dynamics CRM, you can multitask working on many of the same entities (record types) or a combination of entities (record types) at the same time. If you want to enter three new Accounts, for instance, you can have three Account forms open. Microsoft Dynamics CRM gives the user the option of the multiple-window experience when working with forms. You will grow to love this if you are a multitasker or if you have leveraged the power of instant messaging and carrying on two, three, or four conversations at once. Additionally, newer hardware technologies, such as the use of multiple monitors or the use of one of the new much large monitors, really emphasizes the power of this feature.

FIGURE 7.1
The Account form.

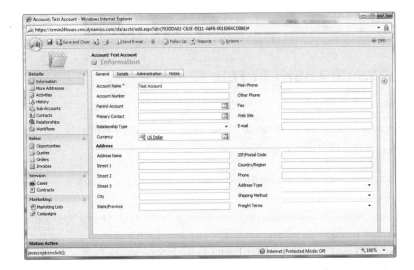

This feature could confuse and frustrate you if you are not a multitasker and if you are only comfortable with having one window open at a time. You can avoid this confusion by understanding this feature and just choosing not to use it.

First Building Block

The first building block of a form is the leftmost menu, which is called the left navigation pane. Figure 7.2 shows this section.

The left navigation pane contains a list of all other related entities (record types). (Remember, we discussed those entities (record types) in Hour 1, "What Is Microsoft Dynamics CRM?"). These entities (record types) have a close and direct relationship to the displayed entity (record type) (Account), and these related entities (record types) are served up with a filter. When one of the left navigation pane entities (record types) is selected, the information that is available is specifically for the displayed Account. If you select Contact, the Contacts displayed will be only those Contacts associated with that Account. In addition, if you select one of these entities (record types) and create a new entity (record type), such as a new Contact, all information from the selected Account is available to the system, and the system pre-populates the related fields in the new entity (record type). For instance, if you open an Account and then select Contact, New, you will see that the Contact's address is pre-populated with the Account's address, and the parent Account is pre-populated with the Account name. This saves on data entry effort. An example of other related entities (record types) to an Account are an Activity, a Contact, an Opportunity, a Subaccount, More addresses, or a Case. Figure 7.3 shows the main entry screen or form of the Account entity (record type).

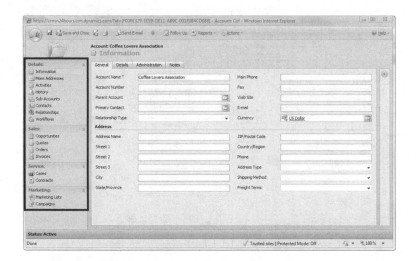

FIGURE 7.2
The left naviga-
tion pane.

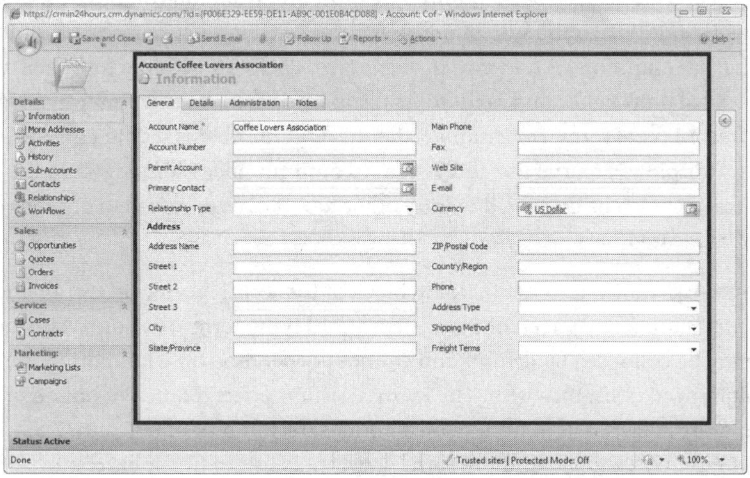

FIGURE 7.3
The Account's
main entry
screen.

The second building block is the main entry screen. This is your work area and where data is entered. The main entry screen displays a list of different fields for data entry. These fields are specific to the Account entity (record type) and include default fields that come with the system, such as Name, Address, Phone Number, and Parent Account, but can also include fields that were defined during the setup and configuration of your Microsoft Dynamics CRM system. Most default system fields can be turned off, and some default systems fields are available that are not displayed before you configure the system. Figure 7.4 shows the Account Form; notice the Tabs across the top just under the word Account.

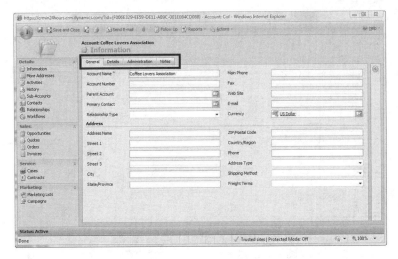

FIGURE 7.4
The Account form tabs.

The main entry screen is also organized by tabs, and each tab can have different data fields on it. When the system administrator configures Microsoft Dynamics CRM, he can eliminate or add tabs to each form. Each tab within a form has a unique set of data fields, and no data field can be offered twice within any given entity (record type) form. For instance, the Account number is a data entry field that is usually displayed on the first tab. If the Account number is displayed on the first tab, it can not also be displayed on any other tab. It can be moved to another tab, but not replicated.

The Form Assistant is another building block of the form. It is located on the right side of the main entry screen of the entity (record type) form. The Form Assistant pane may be collapsed by default and changes depending on what part of the form you might need assistance with. The Form Assistant offers a different option of adding and retrieving data from related entities (record types). In Figure 7.5, we selected Primary Contact, and the Form Assistant is listing available contacts. In the Account form, the available Form Assistants include Parent Account, Primary Contact, Currency, Territory, Price list, Preferred Service, Preferred Facility/equipment, Preferred user, and follow-up. Most all of these items refer to retrieving data, except for follow-up. The Follow-Up Form Assistant enables users to quickly add an Activity (phone call, task, email, and so on) to the Account, all from within the first displayed entry screen.

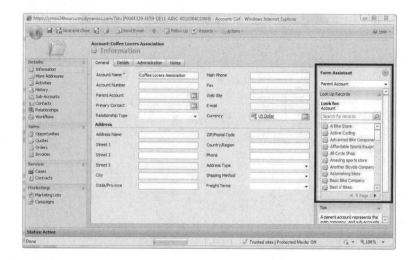

FIGURE 7.5
The Account
Form Assistant.

Account Data

The Account data is divided up amount a number of different tabs. Let's take a look at each tab as it defaults when Microsoft Dynamics CRM is first installed.

General Tab of the Account

The General tab of the Account Form is shown in Figure 7.6. On this form are specific fields that are worth a closer look. These include the Parent Account, the Primary Contact, Relationship, and the Address Phone number.

As mentioned, when it comes to data fields on the Account form and on the first tab, a few require a good explanation. We will talk about fields on other tabs in later paragraphs. The first is the field displayed on the Account form called Parent Account. For any given Account, there can be an assigned Parent Account. The Parent Account is not required, but if entered offers a tree of related connections. Parent Accounts are no different from Accounts, so a listed Parent Account can also have a parent of its own. In this way, you can capture a hierarchy within a corporation or other hierarchies depending on the situation. A Parent Account could be corporate headquarters, and the Account could be a divisional office. A local store could have a Parent Account of regional headquarters, and a regional headquarters Account could have a Parent Account of U.S. operations. The list is almost endless. As a paradigm shift, if you were capturing cows and farms within the system, the Parent Account could be the farm where the cow was purchased, and the current Account could be the farm where the cow is residing.

FIGURE 7.6
Data fields of particular interest.

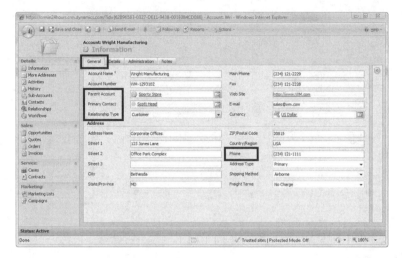

The next field that is worthy of mention and discussion, from the General tab, is the Primary Contact. Within Microsoft Dynamics CRM, you can have an unlimited number of Contacts associated with an Account; however, for each Account, you have the option of selecting only one Primary Contact. This Primary Contact displays on Account-specific views and in other locations such as an Account centric report. The Primary Contact can mean different things to different companies and can even be renamed. An alternative name to Primary Contact might be Key Decision Maker, Primary Buyer, or Company Champion. The Primary Contact could be any number of different people, such as the mentioned main decision maker, or the chief financial officer, or your key target. The decision as to who to associate with the Primary Contact in smaller clients is usually relatively simple; however, in larger prospects or clients, choosing just one Primary Contact for an Account can be much more difficult. Not to worry: Microsoft Dynamics CRM offers a huge variety of options when it comes to configuration, customization, and capturing and creating associations and relationships.

Our next focus is on the Relationship Type field. This drop-down list of options is customizable, but from a pre-configuration standpoint, it contains the following default items: Competitor, Consultant, Customer Investor, Partner, Influencer, Press, Prospect, Reseller, Supplier, Vendor, and Other. The relationship type is a way to describe what this account is with regard to how it relates to your company. The most common relationship types that are in use are prospect and customer.

Lastly, on the General tab, there is a Phone field listed under Address. This is the address phone number and is placed and captured here as references to the phone number a company, such as Federal Express or United Parcel Service (UPS), would use when trying to deliver a package. The delivery fields on the General tab can be turned off and are often not needed (depending on the model of the business using Microsoft Dynamics CRM).

Details Tab of the Account

Figure 7.7 shows a picture of the Details tab of the Account form. Within this Details tab, there are some key fields worth further discussion, including Territory, Industry, Description, and Ownership.

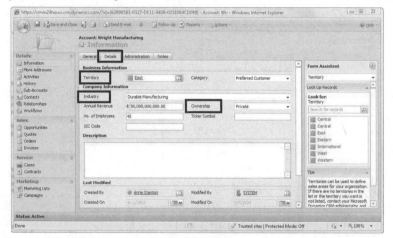

FIGURE 7.7
Data fields of particular interest.

The Detailed tab also has a number of fields that are worth a more detailed discussion. The first is Territory. Territories in Microsoft Dynamics CRM are defined by the company using Microsoft Dynamics CRM and are set up on the System Configuration, Administration menu when the system is configured after installation. Territories can be adjusted, added to, and changed. Territories are not just a defined acronym and association, but they also each have functionality and association to other information within the system.

More Details on Territories

Figure 7.8 offers a look at how Territories are setup in the system.

I want to take a slight side step and give you just a little more insight into territories. If you look at Figure 7.8, you will see that a territory also has associated with it a territory manager and an association to an unlimited number of members. Members are users in the Microsoft Dynamics CRM system, such as salespeople, who are associated to a specific territory. So, a territory could be associated to a specific account and a specific set of members (or salespeople). This association greatly expands what you can do with reporting or views, which we discuss in later hours. You can also define specific processes and associate them with specific changes to territories. You will see the word workflow in the left navigation pane in Figure 7.8. Workflow is the automation of a business process and many companies have territory-specific work flow processes.

FIGURE 7.8
Sales territory setup.

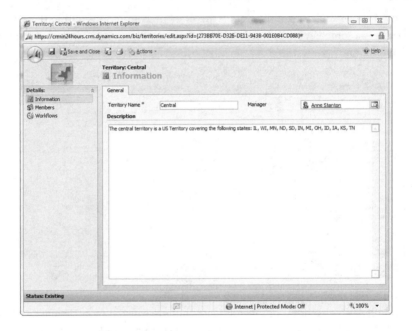

Microsoft Dynamics CRM comes with a long list of industries for the drop-down list associated with the Industry Data field. Some examples include eating and drinking places, public relations, durable manufacturing, financial, wholesale, and social services. The Industry Data field is similar to SIC or NACIS, but is more focused on the description that you might classify the Account as opposed to a recognized standard. SIC is also a default and available data field associated with the Account. If industry is important to your classification and firm, one option is that you set up the industry drop-down list to correspond with the descriptions associated with the SIC code. Another option is to let Industry indicate what your sales team would classify the Account as and then complement this with a SIC or NAICS classification. Industry, SIC, NAICS and other similar fields tend to be used or not used depending on the company using Microsoft Dynamics CRM. When setting up Microsoft Dynamics CRM, it is important to ask the right questions to get input on this specific area.

The Description field is a little deceiving because it is a text field, but it is limited in size. If you were thinking of using the Description field on an ongoing basis to add notes, for instance, be aware that you will run out of space. The Description field is much more appropriate as a corporate profile or a place to put a brief summary of the account. Notes, on the other hand, are unlimited. We talk more about notes in a bit.

Administration Tab of the Account

Figure 7.9 shows the administration tab of the Account form. Fields worthy of further discussion on this tab include Owner, Originating Lead, Price List, and Last Date Included in a Campaign.

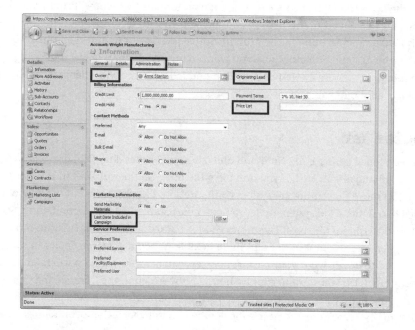

FIGURE 7.9
Data fields of particular interest on the Administration tab.

On the Administration tab, the first data field that jumps out is the Owner field, notice that next to the owner there is a small red asterisk (*). This red star indicates that this is a required field. The owner must be a Microsoft Dynamics CRM user or a staff member at the organization using Microsoft Dynamics CRM. The Owner field is one of the security controls that can be used with regard to who has access to which Accounts. The Owner field also drives a number of reports and views. You can rename the Owner field, but you cannot eliminate this field from being required and displayed. Some examples of an Owner could include the Account Manager, the primary salesperson, or the assigned customer service representative.

In earlier chapters, we talked briefly about a Lead versus an Account of type prospect. When a Lead is entered into the system, it can be converted to an Account, Contact, and/or an Opportunity. The Originating Lead data field is a system field that displays where this Account came from if it came from a Lead. A system field is a data field that the software keeps updated automatically. As a reminder, the best way to think of a Lead is as an unqualified contact.

A Price List can be associated to an Account. If you are using Microsoft Dynamics CRM for Orders, Quotes, and Invoicing, you would set up Price Lists, Products, and Discounts. When you assign a default Price List to the Account, you don't have to add a default Price List to the associated Orders, Quotes, and Invoices.

The associated Last Date Included in a Campaign is another system field. When you use the Microsoft Dynamics CRM campaign features, the system will capture and track the last date that this account was associated with a campaign. It then displays this field on the Account on the Administrative tab. This is useful when thinking about the Account either because you want to include them in a new marketing campaign or you are interested in calling and following up with them regarding the last material that was sent.

Notes Tab

As mentioned earlier i, the Notes tab and associated Notes data field are definitely worth talking about. First, if you don't like the notes all the way over in this fourth tab, just move the feature via system configuration. I have found that users who are used to a flatter CRM system prefer to have notes on the first tab. Second, in true Microsoft fashion, Microsoft Dynamics CRM is packed with choice. This can make the system more complex, but also more flexible. When it comes to choice in notes, you need to decide what your business process will be with regard to where notes will be captured. Do you want to capture notes on the Account, the Contact, the Opportunity, the Activity, or all of the above? Perhaps you want to only add profile type notes to the Account and very specific detailed notes to each Contact it relates to. You also have to decide between what goes into Description (or if description is even turned on) and notes. At the Account level, Description is a great place to put the Account profile (often from their website), for instance, but at the Contact and Activity level it gets a bit more difficult.

Figure 7.10 shows an example of the Notes tap with two different notes entered.

I can hear the question now: Is there an executive summary on the Account that pulls all the associated notes from associated Contacts, Activities, Opportunities, and more onto one display? The answer is yes and no. Microsoft Dynamics CRM does not currently come with an executive summary of all notes; however, numerous third-party solutions offer this, and it is something that can be built with development resources if you want to build it yourself. In addition, with the right business process, it does not become an obvious need.

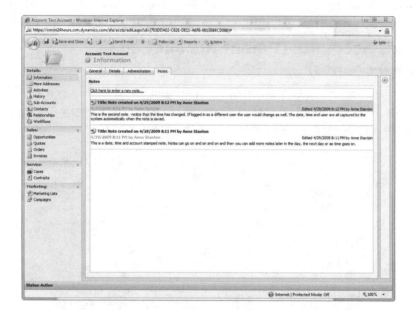

FIGURE 7.10
Notes.

How the Account Relates to a Few Other Entities (Record Types)

Account is a core entity (record type) in Microsoft Dynamics CRM. It has numerous other associations to other entities. Let's look at a few of these other entities and the relationship they have to Account.

Contacts

Account relates to a number of other entities (record types), and each relationship is slightly different. The first, and possibly the most obvious, relationship is the relationship between an Account and its various Contacts. An Account can have an unlimited number of associated Contacts. In addition, within the Account, there is an optional Primary Contact. The Primary Contact would appear on Account-specific views and reports, whereas all the other Contacts might not. This keeps the Account reports and views cleaner and easier to read. Another feature within the relationship between Account and Contact is the ability for the Account to share information with a new Contact when a new Contact is created from the Account form. This reduces user data entry and maintains data integrity. For instance, when a Contact is created after choosing the Account, the Account address details and Account name would be duplicated to the new Contact record. If the Contact was created without the Account open, data will not populate.

Other Accounts (Parent Account and Subaccounts)

Subaccounts can be used when setting up an Account that is a subset of a larger Account structure such as an umbrella company or a very large corporation that has different accounting practices. Figure 7.11 shows an example of using Subaccounts.

FIGURE 7.11
Subaccount example.

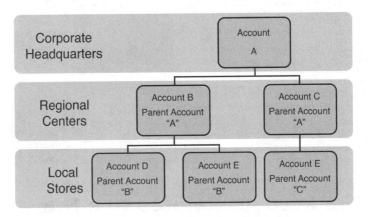

You also don't have to use Subaccounts, because you can set up an Account as a parent, and each Parent Account can have a parent, and so on. Figure 7.12 shows an example of a Parent Account structure.

FIGURE 7.12
Parent account example.

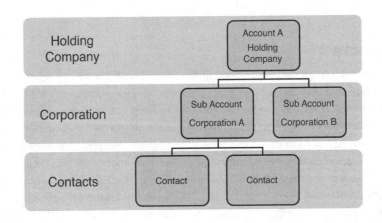

What the Account Can Impact

The Account is one of the core entities (record types) within Microsoft Dynamics CRM, and it is related to many other entities (record types). The Account has an impact on many other functions and features within Microsoft Dynamics CRM. Therefore, if you are thinking of renaming the Account, consider a few things.

First, you want to consider that features that you might not want to use today might be features you want to use tomorrow. If you decide to rename Account to Prospect and set up some other database structure for Client, for example, your entire service module prebuilt within Microsoft Dynamics CRM is semi-useless because it would be tied to Prospect rather than Client.

Other features and functions are also built on the core building block Account, including the relationship function, the Contract features, the Service Calendar, and even such functions as duplicate checking and inactivation. The Account is a key building block in the greater scheme of Microsoft Dynamics CRM.

The Account globally unique identifier (GUID) can also be used to connect many different systems. It can be used to tie to an Account specific document folder created and maintained in Microsoft SharePoint to the Account in Microsoft Dynamics CRM. It is also used by third-party independent software vendors (ISVs) who offer Microsoft Dynamics CRM plug-ins and add-on applications.

When working with Microsoft Dynamics CRM, it is easy to get lured into the ability to change and add everything; however, without good vision into the long-term impact, it is always good to talk with an experienced Microsoft Dynamics CRM architect first. At the very least, post your ideas to the Microsoft Dynamics CRM forums and see what type of feedback you get from the field.

How the Account Can Be Redefined

Software Architecture Insight Could Be Helpful

The following shows major changes to the Microsoft Dynamics CRM system that do not require the experienced skills of a software developer or software architect. Reproduce at your own risk.

Watch Out!

In the first two hours of this book, there were a few hints as to how the Account could be redefined, but let's take a deeper dive now that you understand that changing the Account has wide-ranging impacts.

A company purchases buildings and then hires a rental management company to handle the leasing of the offices within the buildings. In this particular case, the company wants to track all the buildings as the core building block of their system. After careful consideration by the Microsoft Dynamics CRM architect and review of the implications with the client, the Account entity (record type) is renamed toBuilding.

In Figure 7.13, you see that by renaming the Account entity (record type), the top of the screen displays the word Building as opposed to Account. On the other hand, there are specific data fields, which still have the name account, associated with them. In this particular example, the Microsoft Dynamics CRM system customizer would also have to rename each data field (attribute) that has the word Account as part of the data field (attribute) name. There are only a few, but as you can see in Figure 7.13, they definitely need to be changed. In addition to changing the entity (record type) title, you need to consider the text associated with error messages, the names of any Account-specific system views, and any reports that have Account as part of any of the descriptive information. Although this seems like a lot of information, the name of the Account and all associated data fields can be changed fairly efficiently using available tools and a dash of Microsoft Dynamics CRM experience.

FIGURE 7.13
Renamed
Account to Building in system
customization
(nothing else
changed).

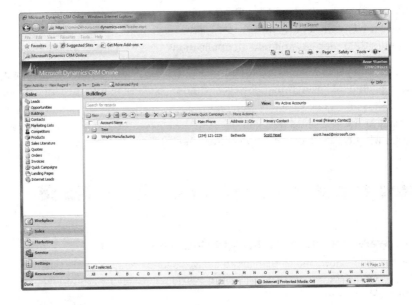

Workshop

A financial investment company, Wood Finance, has a staff of ten financial planners. Each planner has many relationships, specifically with consumers who work with individuals from Wood Finance to manage their long-term and short-term investment portfolios. In addition, Wood Finance offers corporate discounts and corporate "lunch and learn" seminars to those corporations who offer the services of Wood Finance to their staff members interested in more detailed financial planning.

Wood Finance uses Microsoft Dynamics CRM to manage its relationships. The Account captures corporation details, but it also captures a family surname so that families of individuals can be grouped and potentially viewed or reported on together. Wood Finance uses the subaccount, and it uses it rather creatively. The company uses the subaccount to capture the details of other surnames within a family tree. For instance, the Smith family has a master surname of Smith, which is an Account within Microsoft Dynamics CRM; however, Mr. and Mrs. Smith have two daughters who are both married. Wood Finance would like to track all that happens within the world of the married children, too, and they want to track that the married children have a relationship to the Smiths. A Subaccount has been created for the James family in Microsoft Dynamics CRM for the James family as Mrs. James is Mr. and Mrs. Smith's married daughter.

Figure 7.14 shows an example of "The Family" Account building blocks.

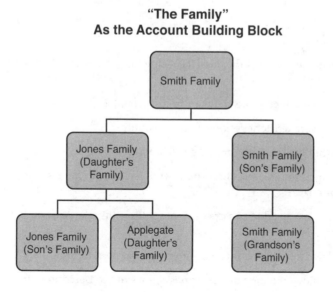

**"The Family"
As the Account Building Block**

FIGURE 7.14
If the Account is a family surname, the subaccounts contain related family surnames.

Q&A

Q. *We track NAICS and SIC, but sometimes, we just want to associate a general less standard industry. Is this possible?*

A. Yes, you have two choices. You can use a drop-down list of industries that are common to your company or you can create a text field to capture any combination of typed in text that describes industry.

Q. *Many of our accounts have a complex hierarchy of relationship to other accounts. How is this handled?*

A. An account can have a parent account, a parent account can have a parent account, and so on up the ladder. You also have the option of associating subaccounts.

Q. *We email around a ton of attachments, but we do not necessarily want to capture those attachments within Dynamics CRM associated with email tracking or notes. Can we turn off attachments?*

A. Yes, you can block attachments.

Quiz

1. What are some of the impacts of changing the name of an Account to something else?

2. Are parent accounts different from Accounts?

3. How are territories related to an Account?

4. What are the four components of a form?

5. Why is the Address Phone number different from the main business phone number?

6. How many addresses are attribute fields within the Account Entity (record type)?

7. How many tabs can you create on the Account form?

8. Would you enter your descriptive notes in the Description field or the Notes field?

Answers

1. "If you decide to rename Account to prospect and set up some other database structure for client, for example, your entire service module prebuilt within Microsoft Dynamics CRM would be semi-useless because it would be tied to Prospect rather than Client."

2. No.

3. Every Account is associated to a Territory and every owner of an Account is associated to a Territory.

4. Left Navigation Pane, Form Assistant, Main Entry Screen, and the Tabs.

5. The Phone Number field associated with the address is provided for companies, such as Federal Express or UPS.

6. Two.

7. Eight.

8. No, because the Descriptive field is limited in size. The Notes field is not limited in size and is designed for an unlimited amount of notes.

Exercise

Using Microsoft Visio, paper, or a large white board, diagram the following scenario: The Wild Adventure Corporation (WAC) organizes tours of local nature preserves as a team-building exercise for large local corporations. The WAC needs to keep track of the nature preserves that it visits and the corporations who purchase its nature preserves tour team-building services. How would you use the Account in this scenario?

HOUR 8

The Sales Funnel

What You'll Learn in This Hour:

▶ Some of the Sales Styles and Choices

▶ Tracking Opportunities

▶ Working with Sales Percentages and Sales Stages

▶ Creating a Sales Process Workflow

In this hour, we look into the world of sales and how sales, sales processes, sales funnels, and overall sales styles are tied to Microsoft Dynamics CRM. We dive into different industry sales methodologies, and we look closely at what the sales funnel is all about, such as what it is used for and why it is important.

Sales Styles and Choices

It is hard to talk, think, and learn about Microsoft Dynamics CRM without some discussion about personal styles. It is even more difficult to talk about the application, as true sales force automation or customer relationship management software, without discussing the impact of sales styles.

Sales Cultures

Relationship-oriented salespersons, approaching a sale from a prospect-oriented and personal touch, place an incredibly high level of value on the relationship that they have with individual contacts. They might be more hesitant to enter data into the system, but they need to keep all the details of all their various contacts organized and available for them so that they can work on the maximum number of accounts. They are also interested in buzz and information about their prospect and customer accounts within the system that might come from the Internet or other sources. This arena of sales audience can gain benefit from integration of Microsoft Dynamics CRM with external sources, such as a data cleansing services or repositories of additional information on specific businesses, such as Hoovers (www.hoovers.com), Dun & Bradstreet (www.dnb.com), and others. They often also have an interest in integration with some of the social media and Web 2.0 toolsets, including websites such as LinkedIn (www.linkedin.com) and Twitter (www.twitter.com).

Product-oriented salespeople might be more interested in capturing all the details of their specific product, engineering and sales techniques for selling the product, their market, and the competition selling the same type of commodity product. Product-oriented salespersons need to keep track of their prospects or incoming sales calls, but they might also need Microsoft Dynamics CRM to keep all the product and competitor details organized and accessible. They might use the system to track weaknesses in comparable products on the market, competition specials, product defects and recalls, available inventory, and perhaps key knowledge on use and configuration (and additional details).

Neither of these primary focus cultures is exclusive; in fact, they overlap. A person selling a set of commodity products might have a well-established network of clients that he upsells to in addition to incoming calls for orders, and a salesperson focused on selling services through relationships might also have a wide range of product offerings. Each of these sales styles can overlap. Microsoft Dynamics CRM handles this overlap by offering support for both services and product cultures. The software offers a product catalog and quote, invoice, and order functionality, and it offers a robust company hierarchy to support complex relationships. The goal for you is to dive in and master the pieces of the software that best apply to your selling culture and methodology.

Corporate Selling Methodologies

For any given company, there are many different sales methodologies. These range from industry standard methodologies, such as Sandler Sales (www.sandler.com), Miller Heiman (www.millerheiman.com), and Richardson (www.richardson.com), to custom (perhaps more industry-specific) sales process methodologies designed and matured within a specific company. One of the keys to success with Microsoft Dynamics CRM is to understand the selling methodology that you want to use with the product.

If your company does not currently have a formal selling methodology, it most likely has business processes in use that can give additional insight into how using Microsoft Dynamics CRM might work best within the environment.

The Existing Sales Method Built Into Another Application

If your company is currently using a different CRM application, you might have a methodology built into the software that was or is in use today. This methodology could be something that everyone loves or hates, and it could also be limited or crafted to fit the software in use. One of the key shifts when moving to Microsoft Dynamics CRM is to not only move existing sales processes, but to also consider these sales processes as they might mature and change based on new functionalities. Take, for instance, a company that uses the XYZ CRM application (name changed to protect the vendor). In this software, you cannot define a sales process, but it captures notes, contact details, appointments, and scheduled calls. It is robust enough, but it is not everything that the company needs. When this company moves away from the XYZ CRM application to Microsoft Dynamics CRM, it has the option to define a standard sales process because Microsoft Dynamics CRM offers it a place to define the process and the functionality to make the sales process more efficient.

The Ad Hoc Sales Method

What about a company that is not using an industry-level CRM application? For instance, a company heavily vested in using Microsoft Outlook for much of its day-to-day sales work. It might not have an existing CRM application, but through the use of Microsoft Outlook, it categorizes information, captures communication, organizes contact details, creates reminders, sets appointments, tracks tasks, and perhaps follows a routine that works for it. The company might also be supplementing Outlook with a variety of Microsoft Excel spreadsheets to forecast, set budgets, analyze open opportunities, and compare goals to actuals. It does not have a true collaborative environment, but it does have processes. Letters, mailings, and other efforts might be part of the process, perhaps supported by Microsoft Word. The reality is that technology is being used. It might not be the best technology for the job, but it is being used.

If you add in its collaborative need for a service department that captures details on what is going on with current clients and that this service department has ideas and efforts about selling additional product and services, this company really needs that one place to organize and collaborate.

Microsoft Dynamics CRM pulls all of this into a total solution, organizing and pairing technology with methodologies and business process and bringing a new dimension to the table, which offers different complementary layers of collaboration and organization. Microsoft Dynamics CRM takes all the pieces and applies the right piece to the right job, Outlook for email, Word for letters, and Microsoft Dynamics CRM to collaborate on what needs to get done to close an opportunity.

Opportunity Tracking

Earlier hours talked about what makes up an opportunity. This section reviews what opportunities are used for. The opportunity is the core building block of most sales processes. It is the "object" or "the potential sale" that moves through the sales funnel and that is classified, won or lost, closed, analyzed, compared to goals, reviewed, and tracked. An opportunity has a life all its own, with a beginning, a middle, and an end. It is also associated with a prospect. The opportunity starts with the awareness that a potential sale is within reach or worth going after and ends with the winning, losing, or postponement of that sales opportunity.

When courting a potential prospect, the loss of an opportunity does not necessarily mean that you will not try to sell that same prospect again in a year or so. The loss of an opportunity also does not mean that the prospect is not a prospect. The loss of an opportunity signals the end of a sales process, which was supposed to result in success or perhaps the closing of an open door because of a locked-down budget or problems in the economy.

The other advantage of an opportunity is that for any given prospect you could potentially have multiple opportunities depending on your business model. For instance, you might have two departments that sell different products to the same company, or you might have a product division and a service division. The product division might have an opportunity to sell a specific set of products, and the service department might have a different opportunity to sell complementary services. Each opportunity can be unique and have its own close date and its own set of processes, and the success of each is independent.

Sales Percentages

The sales percentage or the probability of a win is related to the opportunity. Microsoft Dynamics CRM supports defining a probability of a win in any number of different formats. Many companies like to have a common definition of their probabilities and so will relate the percent probability to a stage within the sales process. Still other companies tolerate the free-will choices of their sales team and can interrupt the probability based on individual salesperson's style. Others offer three to six options, such as 0%, 10%, 25%, 50%, 75%, and 99% (or a similar series).

One of the key concepts with probability percentages is that the probability is generally used to offset the predicted and anticipated revenue in the pipeline. If there is a potential deal for $10,000 with a probability of 25 percent, the analysis determines this potential sale is worth $2,500 dollars (10,000 * .25).

When the anticipated revenue is offset based on the salesperson's or sales team's predictions, a CEO, board of directors, or even venture capitalists can better understand what might be closed.

Sales Stages

A sales process is made up of a set of sales stages. For each stage, there might be a set probability percentage, a set temperature or rating, and a defined set of actions. As actions are completed, the idea is that you move closer and closer to the goal of moving a prospect to a new client. For each set of actions completed, a sales stage is completed, and the sales process moves forward. The following is an example of a sales process:

▶ Stage One: Establish a dialog and an initial relationship with the prospect.

Potential activity items

Phone call: Follow-up to initial conversation

Send letter with more details and further introduction

Phone call: Follow-up to letter

After connecting with the prospect, thank you email or email with promised info

Update sales stage and probability percentage

▶ Stage two: Understand and document the needs as defined by the prospect.

Potential activity items

Prepare custom PowerPoint presentation (focused on prospect needs)

Outline your understanding of what they are looking for

Research prospect history for supporting information

Make appointment to meet

Meet face to face to reiterate what you have learned

Update sales stage and probability percentage

▶ Stage three: Validate to the prospect that you have heard their needs by communicating back your understanding of what they are looking for.

Potential activity items

Meet face to face to reiterate what you have learned

Update sales stage and probability percentage

▶ Stage four: Share your company's culture, vision, and history with your prospect.

Potential activity items

Follow-up to meeting

Update sales stage and probability percentage

▶ Stage five: Answer any questions your prospect might have about the company.

Potential activity items

Phone call

Continue to build and mature your relationship with the prospect.

Update sales stage and probability percentage

▶ Stage six: Share with the prospect how your offering can meet their needs

Potential activity items

Demonstrate product

Update sales stage and probability percentage

▶ Stage seven: Present proposal.

Potential activity items

Prepare proposal

Negotiate details

Update sales stage and probability percentage

▶ Stage eight: Close deal.

Close opportunity as won!

Each stage can have any number of activities, which can include any variety of different tasks, phone calls, letters, emails, and even specific goals. Stages can also call workflow or have automatic functions that occur, such as the automatic generation of an email. In addition, Microsoft Dynamics CRM supports your ability to standardize and automate a sales process using the Microsoft Dynamics CRM Workflow engine. There is more about workflow later in the day; however, in the next section, we look at a simplified example that was configured in Microsoft Dynamics CRM Workflow.

Automating the Sales Process with Workflow

In this section, we walk through setting up a piece of a full sales process and the end result. We start by creating a new workflow and then add the sales stages to this new workflow. Figure 8.1 kicks off the process.

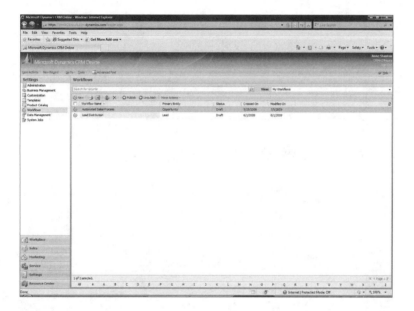

FIGURE 8.1
Automated sales process (workflow).

Creating a New Workflow for the Sales Process

Figure 8.1 shows a new workflow that was created and saved. This is how your new workflow will appear in the list of available workflows. Now let's set up the sales stages and the associated steps for this new workflow. We start by creating a new workflow, and because we are focusing on a sales process, we associate this new workflow with the opportunity record. In Figure 8.2, a name has been assigned and the entity opportunity has been selected from the entity list.

The scope of the new automated sales process will be organization. Figure 8.3 shows the scope in the upper-right corner.

FIGURE 8.2
Creating the new automated sales process workflow.

FIGURE 8.3
Scope.

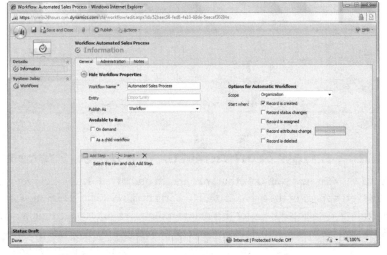

Adding Sales Stages

Did you Know?

Individual Sales Processes

You can also create individual sales processes for specific subsets of salespeople for a less-standardized and more custom offering. Depending on your organization, this option might be embraced or strongly rejected.

In Figure 8.4, we take our first step toward creating a sales process in the workflow. We add a stage. Stages categorize a set of steps and often a set of activities and a section of the sales process. They can also indicate or help classify what needs to be done within a level or section of the sales funnel.

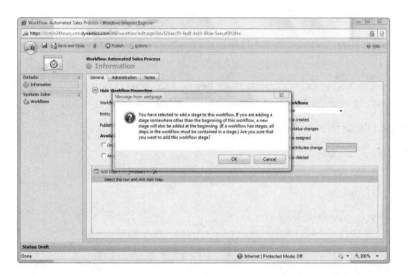

FIGURE 8.4
Adding a stage to the workflow.

In Figure 8.5, two steps have been added to the first stage of the sales process. We have added "stage one: establish initial relationship" and the two steps, which are phone call and letter activities. The concept is that when an opportunity is created, a phone call activity and a letter activity are automatically created and added to the owner of the opportunity's to-do list.

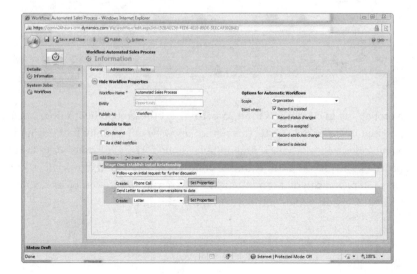

FIGURE 8.5
Stage one: Establish initial relationship.

Adding Steps

To add a new stage, do the following:

1. Select Add Step.

2. Select Stage.

3. Select Stage Description and enter a description for stage two.

Figure 8.6 shows an example with stage two added. Stage two moves the prospect further along in the sales process.

Now, add the details for the first step under sales stage two:

1. Select Add Step.

2. Select Check Condition.

FIGURE 8.6
Stage two:
Understand and
document the
needs as
defined by the
prospect.

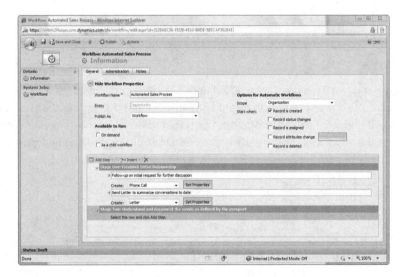

If the probability to close is less than 25 percent, set the probability to close to 25 percent, as seen in Figure 8.7. We do this so that any new opportunity that has had stage one completed will have a probability assigned. There are other ways to skin this beast, but this serves as an example of the condition option of workflow. Within any given step, you can add conditions that when true or false can be associated with activities or can update attributes in the opportunity.

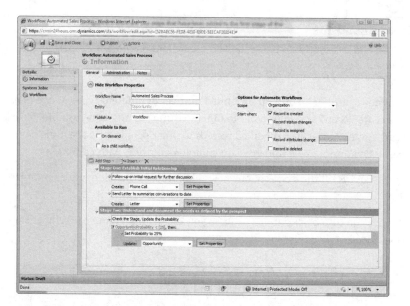

FIGURE 8.7
Step 1: Conditionally setting the probability on the opportunity to 25 percent.

Using a Conditional Statement in a Step

In Figure 8.8, we add a new task to prepare the PowerPoint presentation. We go a bit further by showing that the task can also be customized to include details that might be important to remember and dynamic variables that pull data from the opportunity entity (record type) when the stage is activated.

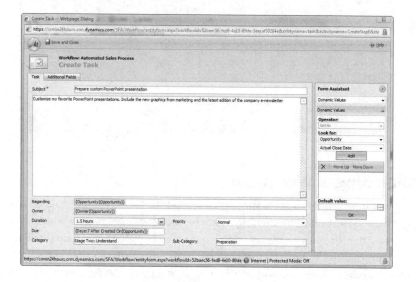

FIGURE 8.8
The task for preparing the PowerPoint.

> **Form Assistant**
>
> You can add dynamic data using the Form Assistant on the Set Properties page of the task.

We can now continue to add an unlimited number of different types of activities using Create Record or add updates to other existing records using Modify Record. You can also assign new or modified records to other people who are users of Microsoft Dynamics CRM, and you can complement these with conditions.

Figure 8.9 shows all the stages of our new sales process. The stages are minimized for clarity.

Each stage can also be expanded to show you the details. Figure 8.10 shows stage one expanded.

FIGURE 8.9
The defined sales process within a workflow.

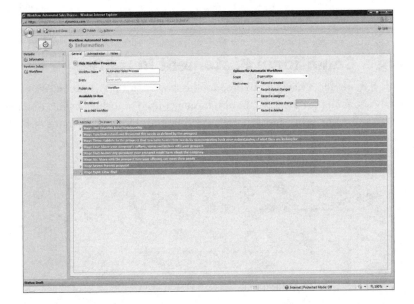

Publishing a Workflow

The sales process can be a set of simple tasks to get started or it can be multilayered and complex. Start small by creating a two- to three-step sales process with one or two activities. After the sales process is created, you need to publish it to access and use it, or if it is automated, to have it start processing. You can make a sales process automatic *or* manual. Manual allows you to control when the sales process starts, because you choose the Run Workflow option when you are ready to run the workflow.

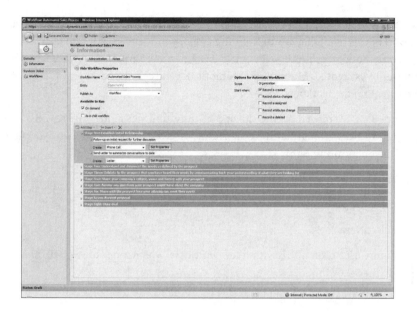

FIGURE 8.10
Stage one expanded.

Figure 8.11 shows the Publish option.

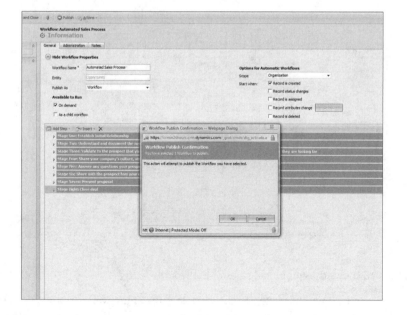

FIGURE 8.11
Publishing the workflow.

To publish, select Publish from the top of the Create Workflow form.

After the workflow is published, it is available to run. In our example, our new manual workflow is available to run from the Opportunity screen. If it had been created as an automatic sales process, the process would run automatically when a new opportunity is created. Manual or automatic depends on the configuration choice when creating the workflow.

In Figure 8.12, we moved over to the opportunity, and we created and saved a new opportunity. Notice that after the opportunity is saved, we have the Run Workflow on top of the opportunity form:

1. Select Sales.

2. Select Opportunity.

3. Select New.

   Figure 8.12 prompts us with a few warnings, which, once answered, allow us to do the following:

4. Choose Workflow.

5. Choose your new workflow.

FIGURE 8.12
The opportunity
workflow.

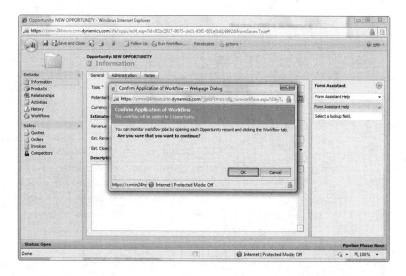

Figure 8.13 shows the completed steps of the workflow.

In our example, if we choose to run the workflow, the entire workflow runs from start to finish, and we can see the final process. In our sales process workflow, we did not add in any conditions (such as an activity has to be completed to move to the next step) or wait states (such as a condition has to be met to do the next action). The system does what it was told and displays back to us what was accomplished and what is still pending in the sales process. We now want to add in some timing logic and progress based on timing, dates, and the completion of activities. So, we need to build in to our sales process workflow some wait conditions.

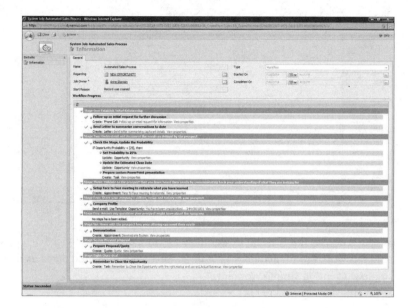

FIGURE 8.13
Completed steps
of the workflow.

Editing an Existing Workflow

If you want to change a workflow that has already been published, you need to do two things: Check the workflow and see whether it is actively running or waiting, and then unpublish the workflow so that it can be edited. To unpublish, do the following:

1. Select Workflows.

2. Select the workflow of interest (in our example, the sales process workflow).

3. Select the Unpublish option.

The status of the workflow will be set back to Draft, as shown in Figure 8.14.

FIGURE 8.14
Workflow status.

We leave you with just this little bit of workflow for now, and we will pick back up on expanding this workflow to include wait states, more conditions, and dates in Hour 16, "Workflow: Creating Simple Workflow."

Workshop

Wild Landscaping is a landscaping company that specializes in native species. It focuses on bringing hardy and local plants to each area that it services, and it offers services and has offices all over the world. Each office has a variety of teams, including long-term maintenance, administration, planning and architecture, consumer sales, business sales, and the weekend dream makeover speed team.

The company sells its services to both businesses and consumers. Businesses often purchase the long-term maintenance plan, whereas consumers are more partial to the weekend dream makeover offering.

Wild Landscaping has a successful sales process that it has used around the world. It uses its sales process in two different ways with two different sets of associated activities depending on the audience. It uses its sales process as it applies to the business prospects and the business sales team, and it uses its sales process when approaching consumers.

The business sales team must ultimately find out who the key decision makers are within the company it wants to approach. It does this by starting with a warm referral to someone within the company, and then it leverages the relationship to learn more about the company.

Q&A

Q. *We use five different sales processes. Can we create these and then associate different sales processes to different accounts?*

A. You can create each of the sales processes as manual processes and then associate them as you need them. You can also automatically associate them if you have a clear business rule, such as the owner of the opportunity that helps the system to act on a specific set of conditions.

Q. *We use the Miller Heiman sales methodology. Is there a plug-in that automatically configures Microsoft Dynamics CRM with the Miller Heiman templates, worksheets, and configurations?*

A. Third-party options offer the Miller Heiman sales methodology plug-in.

Q. *We recently created a workflow, but it is not running. What did we forget?*

A. Most likely, you forgot to publish the workflow. A workflow stays in draft mode until it is published.

Quiz

1. What is the probability to close used for as it applies to opportunity? Why would this variable be of value to a group of venture capitalists?

2. Name two sales methodologies that can be incorporated into Microsoft Dynamics CRM.

3. Can the system handle a sales process that is oriented around selling a specific set of services as opposed to a set of products?

4. How many opportunities can you have on any one given prospect?

Answers

1. The probability percentage on an opportunity is used for analysis to offset the estimated revenue based on a salesperson's interpretation or a step in the sales process. This offers a more realistic expectation of expected revenue.

2. Richardson, Sandler Sales, or Miller Heiman.

3. Yes. Microsoft Dynamics CRM can automate, document, and follow a services-oriented sales process.

4. You can have an unlimited number of opportunities on any given prospect.

Exercise

Create a simple sales process that includes the following items: Automatically create a new activity of type task to remind a specific salesperson to update the close date, estimated revenue, and probability to close on the opportunity. Plan for and schedule a demonstration of a product and follow up on the demonstration.

Outline the sales process that Wild Landscaping might be using. Start with a warm referral to a person within a company in your area. What happens after that introduction? Can any of these steps be automated? Which steps? What are some of the other things you might have to do if you start with this warm lead?

HOUR 9

Marketing Campaigns

What You'll Learn in This Hour:

- ▶ Basic Campaign
- ▶ Creating and Tracking the Marketing Budget
- ▶ Capturing the Results
- ▶ Tracking the Steps, Activities, Tasks

Now that you have learned the different sales styles and how to track Opportunities in Hour 8, "The Sales Funnel," it is time to learn about the component that helps drive sales: Marketing Campaigns. Marketing Campaigns are one of the modules in Microsoft Dynamics CRM that enable you to build, manage, track, and report on the efforts that your team has put into promoting a marketing event.

The Campaign

A Campaign contains all the information related to a specific marketing effort over a period of time. One way to look at a Campaign is as an umbrella over a set of information. Take, for example, all the details that are involved with putting a trade show together. These details include tasks that need to be done, budgets that need to be put together and tracked, mailings and announcements and the responses to these, and more. A Full Marketing Campaign keeps track of all the planning Tasks, the Campaign Activities, and the Campaign Responses. It also lets you add target products and Sales Literature to the Campaign, which allows you to see all related information in one place in Microsoft Dynamics CRM. By having all the information in one place, you can see and understand the effectiveness of your Marketing Campaign.

Think of a Campaign as a container that holds all the information related to a marketing activity. The full Marketing Campaigns manage more complex marketing efforts where you want to create multiple activities, maintain several Marketing Lists, and keep track of planning tasks and responses.

To create a new Campaign, follow these steps:

1. Navigate to the Marketing area.

2. Select Campaign from the left navigation menu.

3. Click New.

For this example, you will create a full Marketing Campaign to manage your company's annual summer picnic.

On the Campaign entry form, as shown in Figure 9.1, do the following:

1. Select New.

2. Enter a name for your Campaign.

3. Select the Status Reason.

   Because you are creating a new Campaign, you can leave it to its default value, Proposed.

4. For the Campaign Type field, select the type of the Campaign you are managing. In this case, select Event from the drop-down list because you are creating a Campaign for an event.

5. For the Campaign Code field, you can enter your own code or leave it blank to have the system automatically generate a Campaign code.

FIGURE 9.1
New Campaign.

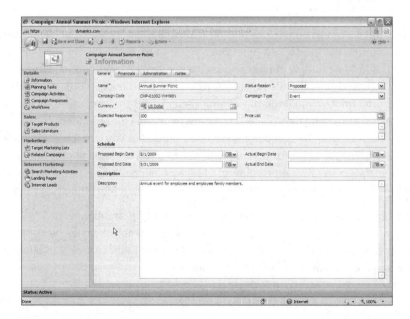

6. Save the Campaign.

   After you save your Campaign, you cannot change your Campaign Code.

7. By default, the Currency field is set to your system base Currency. In this case, it is set to U.S. Dollars.

8. The Expected Response holds the number of expected responses from managing this Campaign; you can leave the default value of 100.

9. Set the Proposed Begin Date and Proposed End Date for your Campaign under the Schedule section.

10. Enter the Description for your Campaign (optional).

After you populate the information on the General tab, click Save on the menu bar to save the Campaign. After the Campaign is saved, you can add Planning Tasks, Campaign Activities, and Campaign Responses.

Quick Campaign Versus Campaign

Quick Campaigns differ from full-blown Campaigns in Microsoft Dynamics CRM. A Quick Campaign is a light version of a Campaign. It contains only a single type of activity and works with a single marketing list. However, Quick Campaigns and Campaigns can share the same Marketing List and receive Campaign Reponses. We look at Quick Campaigns later in this hour.

Did you Know?

Marketing Lists

One of the important tasks to do for your Campaign is define the Marketing Lists. Marketing Lists contain the list of members which are either Accounts, Contacts, or Leads that will receive the marketing material.

If you have already created Marketing Lists in the Microsoft Dynamics CRM system, you can use your existing target Marketing Lists for your Marketing Campaign or you can create a new Marketing List. Because you are doing a new Campaign, let's create a new Marketing List.

Marketing List Members

Each Marketing List can only contain members from a single type of record. If your Campaign needs to be sent to all types of records, you need to create multiple Marketing Lists.

Watch Out!

To create a new Marketing List, follow these steps:

1. Navigate to the Marketing area.

2. Select Marketing Lists from the left navigation menu.

3. Click New.

4. On the Marketing List entry form, enter the Name for your new Marketing List.

5. Select the type of record (Account, Contact, or Lead) from the Member Type drop-down list.

6. Populate the Purpose, Cost, and the Description field (if desired).

7. Click the Save button on the menu bar to save the Marketing List.

8. After the Marketing List is saved, as shown in Figure 9.2, you can add Marketing List Members.

FIGURE 9.2
New Marketing
List for existing
Contacts.

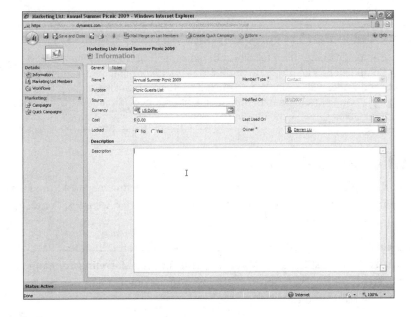

Marketing List members are existing contacts or accounts or leads from within your Dynamics CRM system. If you want to add someone to your Marketing List who is not currently a contact, you will need to first add the person as a contact or lead before associating him to a Marketing List.

Locking Marketing List

If you lock your marketing list by selecting Yes for the Locked field, as shown in Figure 9.2, you cannot add or remove members for the marketing list. To add or remove members, change the value to No and save the Marketing List. After you finalize your members, you can lock your marketing list by changing the Locked value back to Yes.

The Marketing List Members navigation is now enabled on the navigation menu. To add new members, follow these steps:

1. Click Marketing List Member.

2. Click Manage Members on the grid view menu. A Manage Members window will appear (see Figure 9.3).

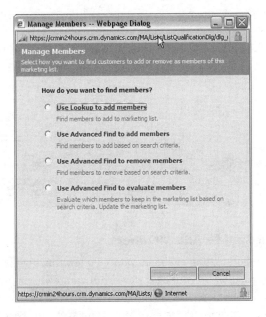

FIGURE 9.3
Manager member options.

3. Choose an option to manage members. You have four different options: Use Lookup to add members, Use Advanced Find to add members, Use Advanced Find to remove members, and Use Advanced Find to evaluate members. As long as the Marketing List is not locked, you can use the four options to change your members.

Use Lookup to Add Members

If you select the option to Use Lookup to add members, a Lookup dialog box will appear that enables you to search for the records that you have identified in the Member Type field of your Marketing List. Because the Contact type was selected, the system will perform the search against Contacts, and the active Contacts will be returned back to you.

1. Select the Contacts and add them to the right pane, as shown in Figure 9.4.

2. Click OK after you add members.

FIGURE 9.4
Look Up Records
dialog box to add
members.

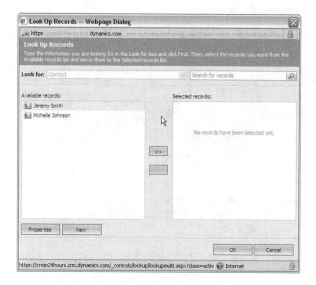

Use Advanced Find to Add Members

Advanced Find is a feature that will be introduced a few times within this 24-hour period. It is used for setting up your own views with your own queries (see Hour 11, "Configuring Your Interaction with Microsoft Dynamics CRM") and working with Excel (see Hour 20, "Utilizing the Power of Microsoft Excel with CRM Data"). If you select the option to use Advanced Find to add members, a common Advanced Find dialog box will appear, as shown is Figure 9.5. You can add your own filter criteria to identify the list of members as follows:

1. Choose your criteria (an attribute [field] and a value or range of values).

2. Choose View.

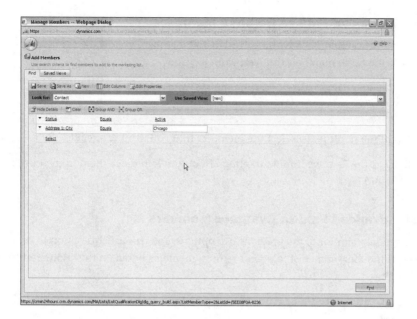

FIGURE 9.5
Advanced Find
dialog box to add
members.

3. On the result page, select the members that you want to include.

4. Click the Add to Marketing List button to add the found people or accounts to your Marketing List, as shown in Figure 9.6.

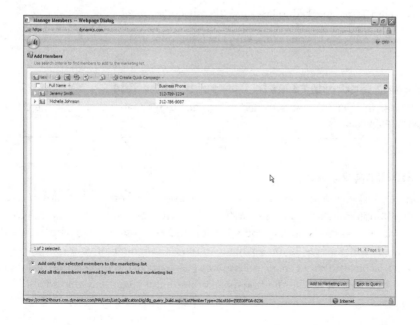

FIGURE 9.6
Advanced Find
dialog box to add
members search
result.

Use Advanced Find to Remove Members

This option is similar to Advanced Find to add members. Follow the same steps to identify the list of members that you want to remove:

1. Choose your criteria (an attribute [field] and a value or range of values).

2. Choose View.

3. On the result page, select the members that you want to exclude.

4. Click the Remove from Marketing List button to remove them from your Marketing List.

Use Advanced Find to Evaluate Members

This option is similar to the previous two options. You can use this option to evaluate the existing Marketing List to add or remove members based on the additional filtering criteria.

Add Marketing List to Campaign

After the Marketing List is created, you can use it in your Marketing Campaign. To tie your Marketing List to your Campaign, follow these steps:

1. Navigate to your Campaign.

2. Select Target Marketing List from the navigation menu.

3. Click Add to add your Marketing List (see Figure 9.7).

Watch Out!

> **Adding Marketing List to Campaign Activities**
>
> The Marketing Lists must be added to the campaign before you use it in the Campaign Activities.

Planning Tasks

Planning Tasks are Activities of type Task. It helps you organize your to-dos in a Marketing Campaign. Think of it as your "to do" list. After the Planning Tasks are created, you can assign the task to yourself or to others on your team to help launch the Campaign. For example, if you are going to run a Campaign for your company's summer picnic, you could create a Planning Task for booking the location, a Task for ordering the food, a Task for putting together the email invitations, and so on.

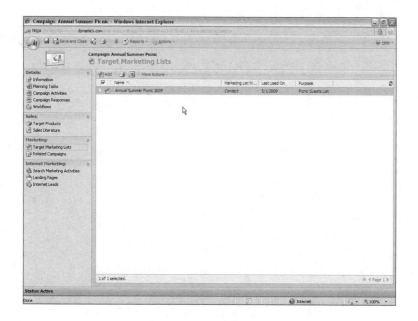

FIGURE 9.7
New Campaign,
Target Marketing
List quick view.

To create a Planning Task, follow these steps:

1. Open the Campaign.

2. Select Planning Tasks on the navigation.

3. Click New on the grid menu.

4. Enter the information for the planning task, including Subject, Detail, Owner, Duration, Due Date, and Priority, as shown in Figure 9.8.

5. Click the Notes tab to add additional information or attachments related to this planning task.

6. When you finish, click Save and Close to save your planning task.

Create Planning Task

You can create a Planning Task by selecting a new activity of type Task; just set the regarding field to a specific campaign.

Did you Know?

FIGURE 9.8
New Campaign,
Planning Task.

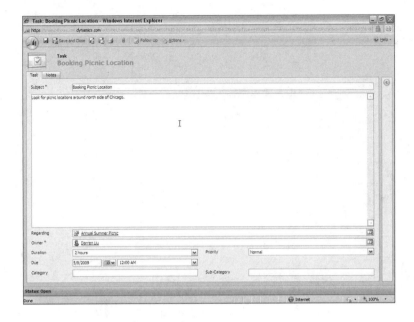

Campaign Activities

Campaign Activities are the core component of a Campaign. They are not the same as regular Microsoft Dynamics CRM activities. They are the actions that make up the Campaign, such as phone calls, appointments, letters, faxes, and emails. Campaign Activities contain information, such as scheduled start date, scheduled end date, priority, budgeted cost, and actual cost of the activity.

A Campaign can contain multiple Campaign Activities. For example, you can set up a Campaign Activity to send out an email Campaign and then follow up with phone calls. Campaign Activities have two categories: channel activities and nonchannel activities. Channel activities are communications such as a phone call, a letter, or an email that reaches the customer when the Campaign Activity is distributed. Nochannel activities are just to-dos for you and your team during the Campaign; a task will be created and added to the user's activity list. Campaign Activities can share a single Marketing List or use a different Marketing List within a Campaign.

To create a Campaign Activity, follow these steps:

1. Open the Campaign.

2. Select Campaign Activities from the navigation pane.

3. Click New from the grid menu.

4. On the Campaign Activity form, select the channel from the Channel dropdown list, as shown in Figure 9.9.

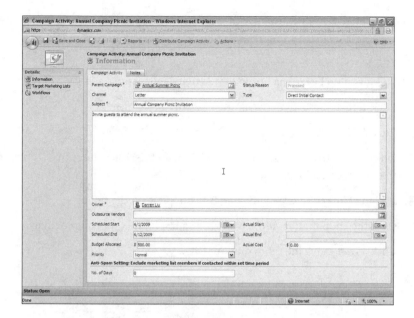

FIGURE 9.9
New Campaign,
New Campaign
Activity.

5. Enter a Subject for your Campaign Activity.

6. For the Type field, select the best option that describes the Campaign Activity that you are creating.

7. Verify the Owner. The Owner field, by default, is you because you are creating the Campaign Activity. You can assign it to another user if that user will be responsible for it.

Nonchannel Activity

If you want to create a nonchannel activity, select Other or just leave the Channel field blank.

Did you Know?

---

8. Assign an Outsource Vendor if your Campaign Activity involves an outside vendor. Enter the Scheduled Start, Scheduled End, Budget Allocated, and Priority information.

9. Under the Anti-Spam setting, exclude Marketing List members if contacted within a set time period, and enter the number of days you want to pass before a member in your Marketing List can be contacted again.

10. Click Save to save the Campaign Activity.

Every Campaign Activity must have at least one Marketing List. Because you added the Marketing Lists to the Campaign earlier, you can add that to your Campaign Activity.

To add a Marketing List to the Campaign Activity, follow these steps:

1. Click Target Marketing Lists on the navigation.

2. Click Add on the grid menu.

3. On the Lookup dialog box, as shown in Figure 9.10, click the search icon to get the lists of available Marketing Lists.

4. Add the Marketing List by moving it to the pane on the right.

5. Click the OK button to add the Marketing List to the Campaign Activity.

6. Click Save to save the Campaign Activity.

FIGURE 9.10
New Campaign, Add Marketing List Lookup dialog box.

Distributing Campaign Activities

After the Campaign Activity is created, your next step is to distribute the Campaign Activities. Distribution of the Campaign Activity kicks off and assigns the Campaign Activity to the specific people who need to accomplish them and associates the activities to the associated Accounts, Contacts, or Leads.

To distribute the Campaign Activities, click Distribute Campaign Activity on the menu bar.

A form opens based on the channel type that you specified. For example, if you select Email, a New Email form will show up. If you select Phone Call, a New Phone Call form will show up. In this example, a Letter was selected in this Campaign Activity, so a New Letter form appears, as shown in Figure 9.11. You can see some of the fields on the form are disabled because the system automatically populated those values.

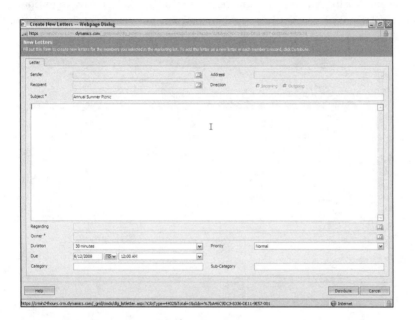

FIGURE 9.11
Distribute Campaign Activity.

After a Campaign Activity is distributed, the Activity owners can view the open Activities under Activities in their Workplace. They will have to complete the Activity, such as making phone calls or sending the email.

Campaign Activity Status

After the Campaign Activity is successfully distributed, the Status Reason from the Campaign Activity changes from Proposed to Completed.

Campaign Templates

Over time, you will invariably conduct similar Campaigns. Instead of recreating the Campaign every time, Microsoft Dynamics CRM offers you the option to create a Campaign and save it as a template. Then, the next time that you run a similar Campaign, you don't have to recreate the same task and activities. This saves you time in planning your Marketing Campaign.

There are two approaches for creating a Campaign template. The first approach is to create a new Campaign template by going to Campaigns and clicking the New Template button on the grid menu. When the new Campaign form appears, fill in the necessary information, and then click Save and Close to save the template. The second approach is to create a template from an existing Campaign. Just open your existing Campaign, click the Action menu, and select Copy as Template, as shown in Figure 9.12. The second approach is usually the most popular way to create a Campaign Template.

FIGURE 9.12
Creating a Campaign Template from and Existing Campaign.

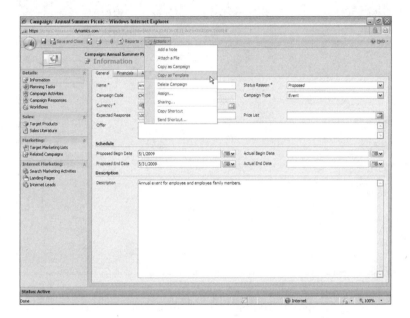

Watch Out!

Campaign Template

To identify the Campaign Template, it's a good idea to include the word Template in the name.

Quick Campaign

A Quick Campaign is a light version of a full-blown Campaign. It can only contain a single type of activity and works with a single Marketing List. The Marketing List can be a group of Accounts, Contacts, or Leads. After you decide what type of Activity that you are going to create and the owner of the Activity, creating the Quick Campaign is easy.

First, identify a list of recipients through the Advanced Find tool, as shown in Figure 9.13, or through one of the Account, Contact, or Lead views. In this example, you will launch a Quick Campaign from the search result of Contacts through Advanced Find, as shown in Figure 9.14.

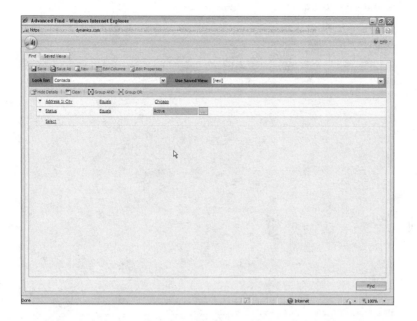

FIGURE 9.13
Advanced Find for Contacts in Chicago.

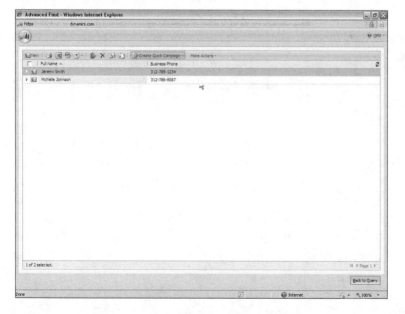

FIGURE 9.14
Advance Find result.

On the results screen, click the Create Quick Campaign button on the grid menu, and then select one of the three available options: For Selected Records, For All Records on the Current Page, and For All Records on All Pages. In this case, you are going to select all records. On the next page, enter the Name of the Campaign, and then click the Next button to continue, as shown in Figure 9.15.

FIGURE 9.15
Create Quick
Campaign Wiz-
ard—Enter Quick
Campaign Name
screen.

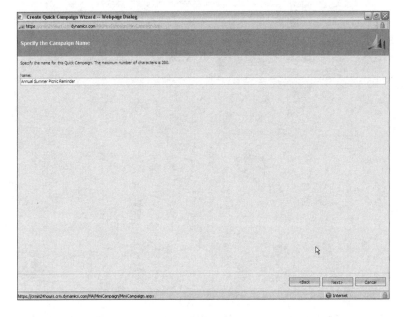

On the Select the Activity Type and Owners page, as shown in Figure 9.16, pick the type of Activity that you want to create and select the owner of the Activity. The

FIGURE 9.16
Create Quick
Campaign Wiz-
ard—Select the
Activity Type and
Owners screen.

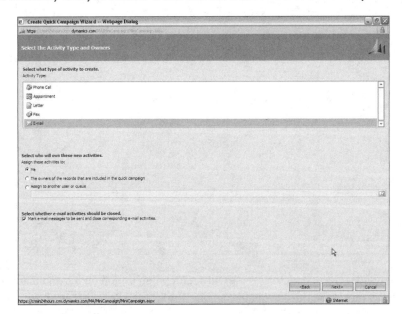

available Activity types are Phone Call, Appointment, Letter, Fax, and E-mail. If you select E-mail, you have the option to have Microsoft Dynamics CRM send out the email message and automatically close the email Activities.

Based on the activity type you select, the corresponding activity form opens. Populate the necessary information for the activity, and then click the Next button to continue. After confirming the details, click Create to create the Quick Campaign; the activities will be distributed immediately.

Creating and Tracking a Marketing Budget

The budget and the actual cost of a Campaign are located on the Financials tab, as shown in Figure 9.17. You can enter the Budget Allocated amount, Miscellaneous Costs amount, and the Estimated Revenue amount for a given Campaign. The Budget Allocated field indicates the dollar amounts that you have dedicated to this Campaign. The Miscellaneous Costs field contains the dollar amounts that are not incurred by the Campaign Activities, such as the cost of the Marketing Lists. The Estimated Revenue field contains the dollar amounts that you expect to generate from this Marketing Campaign.

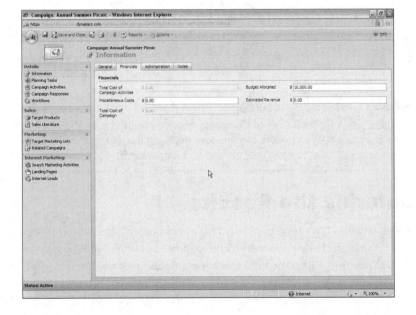

FIGURE 9.17
Campaign—
Financials tab.

The Total Cost of Campaign Activities and the Total Cost of Campaign have been disabled on the Campaign by default, because Microsoft Dynamics CRM will automatically calculate the values based on the financials from the Campaign Activities that are tied to the Campaign, as shown in Figure 9.18. The calculation of the total cost of the Campaign Activities amount is based on the actual costs of all the Campaign Activities. The calculation of the total cost of the Campaign amount is based on the total cost of Campaign Activities plus the miscellaneous costs recorded for the Campaign.

FIGURE 9.18
Campaign Activity; notice the Budget Allocated and Actual Cost fields.

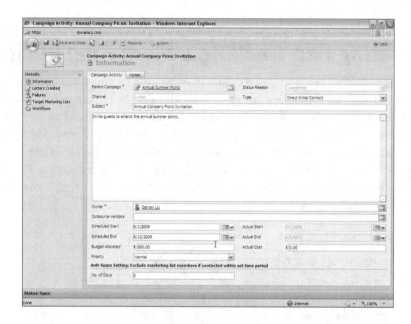

Watch Out!

Refresh Campaign Activity

If you don't see the Total Cost of Campaign Activities and Total Cost of Campaign values change after you update the financial fields on the associated Campaign Activities, refresh the campaign by closing and reopening it.

Capturing the Results

After the Activities have been distributed to your customers, they will start responding to your Campaign. Their responses will be captured as Campaign Responses in Microsoft Dynamics CRM. The total number of responses for the Campaign will be one of the ways to measure the effectiveness of the Campaign. After the Campaign Response is generated in the system, you can convert the responses into Leads, Quotes, Orders, or Opportunities.

There are multiple ways to capture the results in Microsoft Dynamics CRM. You can manually create the Campaign Responses from within the Campaign or create an Activity and convert it to a Campaign Response. If you are not connected to Microsoft Dynamics CRM, you can still record the responses of your Campaign in a text file and then import the records when you have access to your Microsoft Dynamics CRM system again. In addition, if email tracking is enabled in your Microsoft Dynamics CRM settings, incoming emails in response to your Campaign can be created as a Campaign Response in Microsoft Dynamics CRM automatically.

Manually Create a Campaign Response

To manually create a Campaign Response, follow these steps:

1. Open your Campaign.

2. Click the Campaign Responses on the navigation menu.

3. Click New on the grid menu. A new Campaign Response form displays for you to enter information, as shown in Figure 9.19.

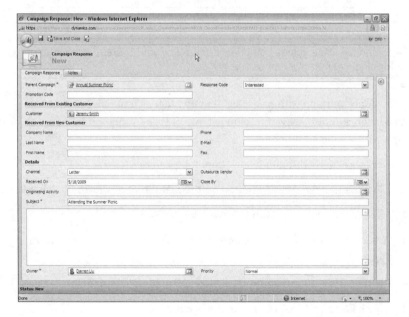

FIGURE 9.19
Campaign Response form.

4. Indicate the customer's response by populating the Response Code field on the Campaign Response form.

5. Associate this response to your existing Account, Contact, or Lead in Microsoft Dynamics CRM by clicking the lookup icon next to the Customer field.

6. After you finish, click Save to save your Campaign Response.

More Options to Convert an Activity to a Campaig Response

Watch Out!

Create New Customer

You might have to create a new customer by populating the Company, Last Name, First Name, Phone, E-mail, and Fax fields under the Received from New Customer section. Optionally, you can also populate the Details section here.

Did you Know?

Create Campaign Response

Another way to create a campaign response is to create a new activity and chose Campaign Response as the activity type. This can be done anywhere within the system that you can create a new activity.

Did you Know?

Response Code

The Response Code values can be customized by your system administrator to use the terminology that fits your business.

When you are working with a specific Activity, such as a phone call that you received, you can also convert it to an activity of type Campaign Response by associating it with a source Campaign.

To convert an activity through association, follow these steps:

1. Click the Convert Activity button on the menu bar, as shown in Figure 9.20.

2. Select To Opportunity from the available options.

3. A "Convert Phone Call to Opportunity" dialog box appears, as shown in Figure 9.21.

4. Populate the Customer and the Source Campaign lookup field.

5. Check Record a Closed Campaign Response.

6. Click OK.

7. A new Campaign Response will be created for the Source Campaign that you specified.

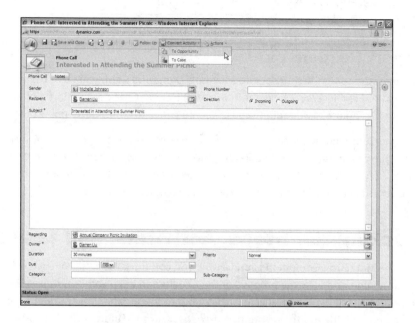

FIGURE 9.20
Phone Call Activity form; notice the Convert Activity button on the menu bar.

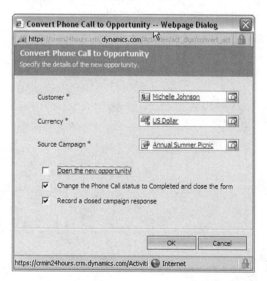

FIGURE 9.21
Convert Phone Call to Opportunity dialog box.

Did you Know?

Create Campaign Response
You can convert the following Activities into a Campaign Response: Appointments, Letters, E-mails, and Faxes.

Import Responses

To import Campaign Responses into Microsoft Dynamics CRM, you have many options. You can leverage the default Microsoft Default CRM data import tool, as described in Hour 6, "Managing Leads," or you can use a third-party import tool.

After the Campaign Responses are created, you can perform several tasks. You can assign the Campaign Response to another user on your sales team or assign it to a Queue. You can convert the Response into a Lead, Quote, Order, or Opportunity. Also, you can close the Campaign Response as completed or canceled.

Tracking the Steps, Activities, and Tasks

After the Marketing Campaign is underway, you can track the status of each step in the Campaign and view the progress of the Activities in Microsoft Dynamics CRM. To view the status of the Campaign Activities, go into the specific Campaign and select Campaign Activities on the navigation area, as shown in Figure 9.22. You will see a list of the Activities and the status for each of them.

FIGURE 9.22
Campaign, Campaign Activities view.

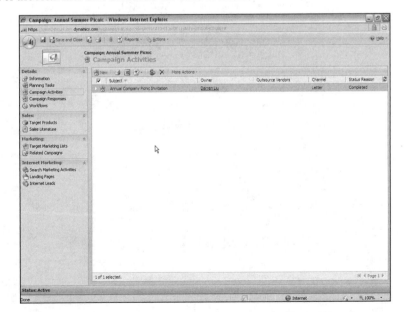

In addition, Microsoft Dynamics CRM provides three reports to track the progress and effectiveness of your Campaigns. Based on the information provided in these reports, your company can decide which Campaign should continue to run, which should stop, or which should be modified.

The reports available in the Reports section are Campaign Activity Status, Campaign Comparison, and Campaign Performance.

If the default reports don't contain the information you are looking for, you can always create an Advanced Find query or a Report Wizard report to get the data you need. For more information on finding, analyzing, and reporting, see Hours 20 and 21.

Summary

In this hour, you learned the essentials of Marketing Campaign in Microsoft Dynamics CRM. You should able to create a Marketing Campaign, a Marketing List, manage cost, capture Responses, and track Activities in a Marketing Campaign. Now, you can see that the Microsoft Dynamics CRM marketing module is a great tool for your company.

Workshop

Dragon Financials is a brokerage house that sells financial products and services to customers across the country. To get investors interested in its financial products and services, it participates in several national financial events every year. In addition to the national financial events, Dragon Financials hosts monthly online seminars to educate investors about the different financial products and trading platforms that it offers. The marketing department at Dragon Financials has leveraged the Marketing Campaign feature in Microsoft Dynamic CRM to help it to plan, keep track of activities and cost, and measure the effectiveness of its marketing activities.

Dragon Financials mainly focuses on the yearly national financial events. There are many things to prepare before attending the show. The marketing team creates a full Marketing Campaign to manage those events. The team uses Planning Tasks to lay out the action items that it needs to do for the event, such as reserving the booth space, preparing the booth, printing the brochures, making travel reservations, and inviting its top-rated customers to the financial events. Because its top-rated customers consist of private investors and institutions, the team creates two Marketing Lists in Microsoft Dynamics CRM for its Campaign. After the Marketing Lists are created, the marketing team creates and then snail mails the invitations to investors. Next, it follows up with them on a phone call after two weeks to make sure that they have received the invitation and to confirm their attendance. So, it has created two Campaign Activities: one for the invitations and one for the follow-up phone call. After marketing receives the confirmation of attendance, it creates a Campaign Response and associates it to the Campaign. The marketing team also uses the financial functions in the Campaign to keep track of its Campaign costs and report them to upper management when the Campaign ends.

In addition to the yearly national financial events, Dragon Financials hosts online seminars to educate investors. It needs to notify its potential investors and current customers about these seminars and to keep track of the registrations. It leverages the Quick Campaign feature in Microsoft Dynamics CRM to create an email Campaign to notify its investors. Because Dragon Financials have the Microsoft Dynamics CRM tracking setting turned on, all the email replies are automatically converted to a Campaign Response. After the Campaign Response gets into the system, Dragon Financials then assigns it to a salesperson to follow up with the investor.

As you can see, Microsoft Dynamics CRM provides the marketing features that Dragon Financials needs. It helps them organize many marketing events and streamline the process for maintaining constant communication with its investors.

Q&A

Q. *Does the financial data in the Full Campaign synchronize with my Accounting Software?*

A. No. Currently, the Marketing Campaign financial features do not integrate with any Microsoft ERP packages. A Microsoft Dynamics Partner is a good resource for you to get more information on available third-party solutions to integrate your two systems.

Q. *Does a contact have to exist in the system for me to add it to a Marketing List?*

A. Yes. If a contact does not exist, you need to first create the contact as a Contact, Account, or Lead, and then associate it with your Marketing List.

Q. *Why must I distribute Campaign Activities?*

A. Campaign Activities have an extra feature built into their functionality to allow a marketing department the flexibility to fully organize all the necessary activities associated with a full Campaign prior to actually assigning those to specific people to get accomplished.

Q. *Can I create a new Campaign from an existing campaign?*

A. Yes. You can use an existing Campaign as a Campaign template to create a new Campaign.

Quiz

1. What is the difference between a Full Campaign and a Quick Campaign?

2. What record types can be used in a Marketing List?

3. What is a channel in a Campaign Activity? What is a nonchannel Campaign Activity?

4. True or False: A Campaign Response can be converted to a Lead.

5. True or False: The total cost of a Campaign is calculated automatically.

6. What default reports in Microsoft Dynamics CRM help a marketing manager to track the progress of a Campaign?

Answers

1. A Quick Campaign is a light version of a Campaign. It only contains a single type of activity and works with a single Marketing List. It is more geared toward use by a salesperson at the end of the month or a sales department doing a quick announcement, special, or alert. A Full Campaign is geared toward use by the marketing department who have more coordination needs around complex events.

2. Account, Contact, Lead, and Opportunity.

3. A channel activity is an external activity, such as an e-mail, a letter, or a phone call, that initiates contact with the customer when the campaign is distributed. A nonchannel activity is an internal activity act, such as to-dos to track actions that must be performed during the campaign.

4. True.

5. True.

6. Campaign Activity Status, Campaign Comparison, and Campaign Performance.

Exercise

Imagine that you are the marketing manager for a real-estate company, and your company is going to host a presales event for a new residential building. You have to ensure the location of the event is booked, identify the list of guests that you want to invite, send email invitations, and call the guests to confirm the registration after they respond that they will attend the event. You have been given $10,000 for this sales event. Upper management wants to know the actual cost and effectiveness of this marketing event after it's over.

To do: Use this information to create a campaign in CRM to manage this marketing campaign.

HOUR 10

Entering Data as a Salesperson

What You'll Learn in This Hour:

▶ A Month in the Life of a Salesperson

▶ Capturing a Lead, Entering a Lead

▶ Converting a Lead to an Account and Contact

▶ Entering Notes

▶ Final Planning

In this hour, we will look at how a sales person might use Microsoft Dynamics CRM during a typical day and the following weeks. We will follow a scenario from day to day as a lead moves from lead to a new customer.

A Month in the Life of a Salesperson

David Daily works at a small company that locally roasts specialty organic coffees and dried organic tea leaves. The company, Semi-Roasted, Inc., not only sells specialty coffees that they locally roast and organic tea leaves that they dry, but it also sells associated hot drink items, such as coffeemakers, coffee cups, teapots, and other tea accessories. David's role is a consultative sales representative and coffee *afficionaire*, and his position requires that he find new prospects. He also manages his existing customers while continuing to sell them more value-added product.

To find new prospects, David participates in a national coffee roasters event where representatives from all the global coffee distributors present on the latest in the coffee farming industry in their respective countries. Attendees at the conference tend to be restaurant owners, wine and cheese shop buyers, consumers, and other food and beverage industry associated people. David's goal at the conference is to meet people who have a high-end audience of consumers and an appreciation for both organic and locally roasted product.

Different Ways to Create a Lead

There are many ways to create a lead or a new contact in Microsoft Dynamics CRM. These include entering directly into a mobile phone using a Microsoft Dynamics CRM Mobile client; scanning the information into a third-party scanning plug-in to Microsoft Dynamics CRM; typing the information into the mobile device contacts and synchronizing to Outlook Contacts, which then can synchronize to CRM contacts; or accessing Microsoft Dynamics CRM from any web-enabled machine and typing in the new Lead details directly.

Semi-Roasted, Inc. also regularly sends out mailings to their current customers and the people in their prospect list to promote their subscription service for the coffee bean of the month and for their local coffee tastings.

Lastly, Semi-Roasted, Inc. places a high value on its existing relationships with its customers. It manages a pre-release new product club and often has private tastings for local VIPs.

In the next few sections, we sit on David's shoulder and walk through a day and a week in his life at Semi-Roasted, Inc.

Capturing a Lead, Entering a Lead

David attends the national coffee roasters event and, at lunch, he meets Janice, a woman from a neighboring town to where Semi-Roasted, Inc. is located. After further discussion, David learns that Janice is the owner of a local restaurant called The Coffee House, which serves recipes cooked from seasonal locally grown fruits and vegetables for breakfast and lunch.

David and Janice exchange business cards because Janice is interested in adding locally dried tea leaf teas and locally roasted organic coffees to her menu. Janice then has to rush to another session.

David has a few minutes and he has his laptop, so he enters Janice's contact information directly into his Microsoft Dynamics CRM system. In Figure 10.1, David starts Microsoft Dynamics CRM and chooses Sales and then Leads.

In Figure 10.2, David creates a new Lead, and in Figure 10.3, he enters the details from Janice's business card. He first enters contact details into the Leads General tab.

David is a fast typist, so he does not mind typing in the information. He also enjoys the chance to further think about and memorize some of Janice's information. He uses a few memory tricks, including noting the color of her hair and associating to her company name. She has blonde hair with a small green braid, and he associates green braid with local produce, green and organic.

FIGURE 10.1
Creating a new lead.

FIGURE 10.2
Creating a new lead.

David continues to enter information (see Figure 10.4 and Figure 10.5).

Finally, David wants to capture a few notes given that the conversation is still fresh in his mind. He will meet a number of new people throughout the day, and if he does not take notes, he might forget some details. In Figure 10.6, David has entered some notes on the Lead.

FIGURE 10.3
Entering the general details.

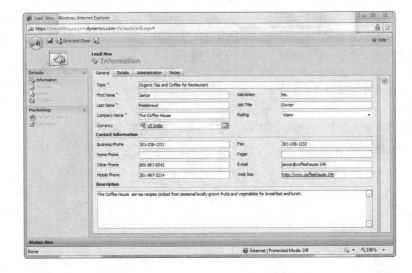

FIGURE 10.4
Entering the address details.

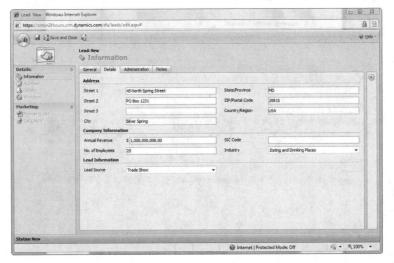

Now that Janice Fiddlehead has been added to David's Microsoft Dynamics CRM system, he can continue with the show. He runs to his next session.

Later that night, David decides to further qualify and follow up on his conversation with Janice. He jumps back into his Microsoft Dynamics CRM system to send Janice an email.

David uses the Microsoft Dynamics CRM search features to quickly find Janice in his long list of Leads. He types Janice into the search box at the top of the Leads view, as shown in Figure 10.7.

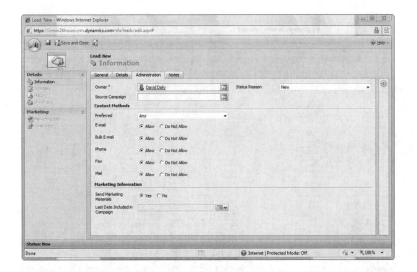

FIGURE 10.5
Entering the administrative and marketing information.

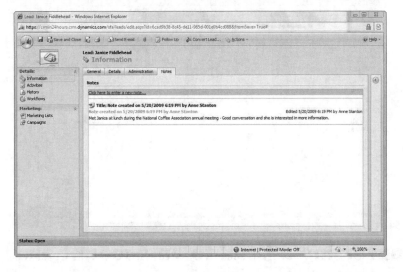

FIGURE 10.6
Entering notes.

Once he opens Janice's record, he chooses Activities from the left menu bar and creates a new Activity as type Email, as shown in Figure 10.8.

Another Option

He could also send an email to Janice from his Microsoft Outlook email and associate it to Microsoft Dynamics CRM if he is currently connected to his internal network or the next time he is connected to the network.

FIGURE 10.7
Search for Janice.

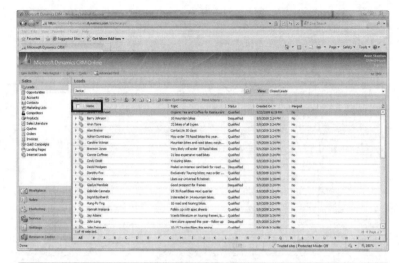

FIGURE 10.8
Create an email
from Dynamics
CRM.

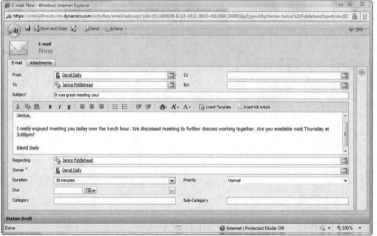

Converting a Lead to an Account and Contact

David finishes up his week at the conference and is back in the office on the next Monday morning. On return, he enters many other leads that he met at the conference and schedules and makes decisions regarding what he needs to do to qualify each of them.

Did you Know?

Another Option

David could also upload a list of Leads from Excel or he could use a third-party tool that supports scanning business cards into electronic Microsoft Dynamics CRM format to scan the business cards he collected.

Later in the day, he receives a response to his email from Janice. She is available on Thursday at 3:00 p.m. David converts Janice's Lead record to an Account and a Contact, now that a solid base of conversation has continued and Janice has agreed to meet.

Open Janice's Lead record.

▶ Select Convert Lead from the menu bar at the top of the form.

▶ Choose Account and Contact.

David is not ready to create an Opportunity for The Coffee House yet because he is not comfortable defining an estimated close date and probability of close until after his first meeting.

Once the Lead is converted, David creates an appointment in Outlook for Thursday at 3:00 p.m., and he relates that to Janice's Contact record in Microsoft Dynamics CRM (see Figure 10.9).

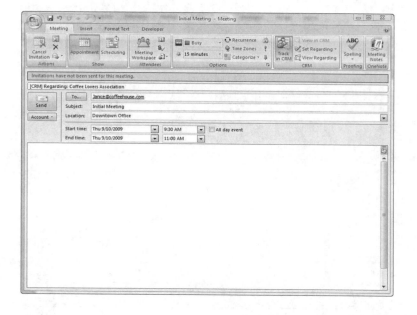

FIGURE 10.9
Associating an Outlook appointment to CRM.

David does a little research and discovers that there are a few other people associated with The Coffee House. He found Jack Wilkes, the CFO, by searching for The Coffee House on the Internet. He finds a couple of articles where Jack has been profiled, and he finds a Yellow Pages listing with a few primary contact people. David then adds these contacts to the account, as shown in Figure 10.10. He opens the Account and selects Contacts, New, and he enters the information that he has found. Figure 10.10 shows entering a new contact from the Account prospect. Because he first selects the Account and then Contacts, New, all the address details are automatically populated.

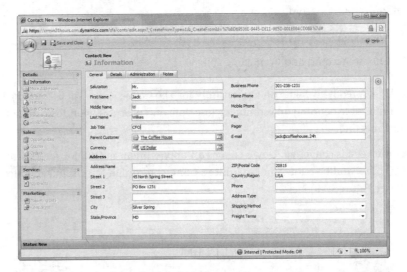

Figure 10.11 shows a list of all the new contacts that David entered and that are associated with the new Account, The Coffee House. Notice that the list is filtered and only shows contacts associated with The Coffee House.

David considers his options and decides that he wants to offer Janice and some of her associates a taste test of his product. He is not going to do this until after his first meeting with Janice, but by planning ahead, he can mention in his meeting the option for a follow-up. He also knows that there is a delicate balance between too few meetings and too many meetings. Using the sales process that he has configured in Microsoft Dynamics CRM, David has a well-used and rehearsed plan.

After each Activity in the sales process is completed, David completes the Activity (see Figure 10.12). This completion files the Activity away to history and date and time stamps it for future reference. David's appointment with Janice is an Activity, but he also needs associated Activities that help him prepare for his appointment.

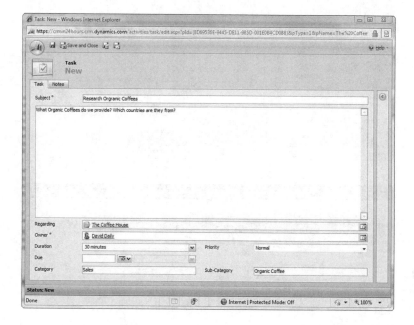

FIGURE 10.12
New task (activity): Check out Organic Coffee offerings.

He sets up a Task Activity to research which of the coffees that Semi-Roasted, Inc. provides are organic. He also sets up another Task Activity to research the most environmentally friendly coffee-producing countries and adds a note to double-check for the closest provider. Janice had mentioned that she tries to buy as much locally produced product as possible. Figure 10.13 shows the newly created task.

After David adds these two tasks, he runs to a meeting confident that he won't forget to prepare for the appointment he has with Janice now that he has captured the two things he wants to do before their meeting. Figure 10.14 is a list of all David's open tasks.

FIGURE 10.13
New task (activity): Check out
environmentally
friendly countries.

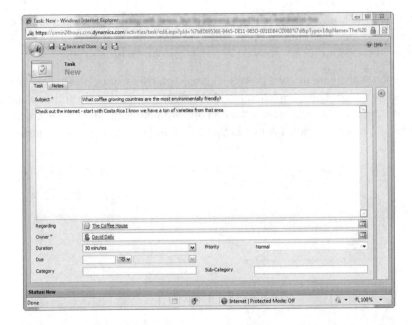

FIGURE 10.14
David's Open
Activities task
activity.

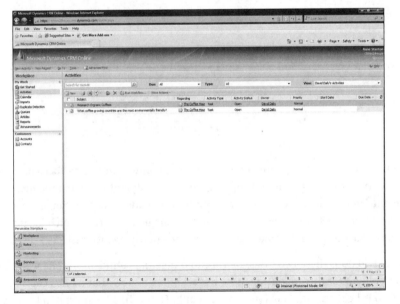

When David returns, he completes the first of the two assigned tasks. He can mark an activity as completed in three ways:

▶ From Outlook, check off the task as completed from the Outlook task list.

▶ From Microsoft Dynamics CRM, open the Activity and save as Completed (or Closed).

▶ From Microsoft Dynamics CRM, open the Activity and select Actions, Close Activity.

Figure 10.15 shows the detailed completed Task Activity. Completed Activities have a status of Completed and show up under all Activities and the history option associated with the Account. If you display all of David's Activities, you get Figure 10.17. If you choose the Account: The Coffee House and choose History, you get the Completed Activities associated with The Coffee House.

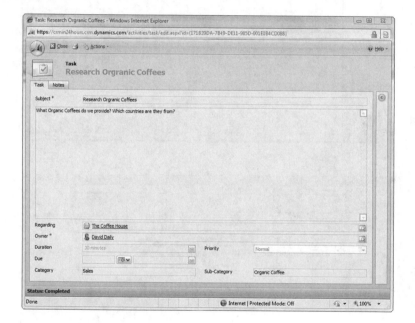

FIGURE 10.15
David's Open Activities task activity.

Options for Managing Activities

Microsoft Dynamics CRM provides different ways to manage your Activities. You can manage Activities from Outlook with Outlook Tasks synchronizing to Microsoft Dynamics CRM Task Activities. You can manage Activities from Microsoft Dynamics CRM, My Work, Activities. And can manage Activities from a specific Account by selecting the Account and then selecting Activities.

Did you Know?

David likes to manage his tasks in both Microsoft Dynamics CRM and in Outlook. He loves that he can mix and match how he keeps track of things (see Figure 10.16).

FIGURE 10.16
Activities display
with completed
activity.

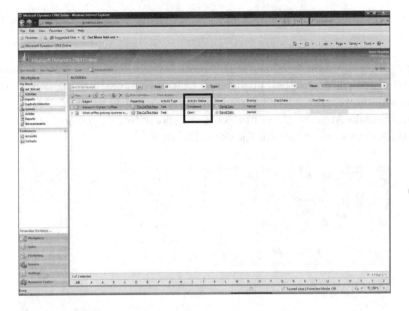

FIGURE 10.17
History display
from the
Account: The
Coffee House.

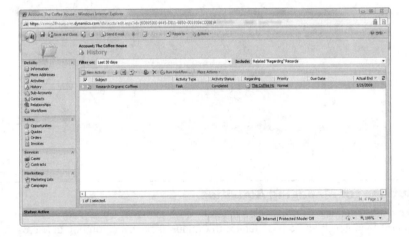

The Appointment

Thursday comes, and David is ready. He is looking forward to meeting with Janice
again and he feels confident that he has products that meet her needs.

David and Janice talk for a good hour. David spends a good amount of time listening to Janice's explanation of her business, goals, and needs. He asks a few questions
to support his internal efforts to ensure her company is going to be a good long-term
customer and that funds and budget are available, but in general, he mostly listens.

At the end of the meeting, David fills Janice in on the Semi-Roasted, Inc. philosophy that matches some of what she has mentioned, and he sets up a meeting for the entire team to try some of David's coffee and tea offerings. David specifically wants a chance to meet a few other people at the company so that he has good depth of buy in and some extra internal champions.

When David gets back to the office, he jumps into Dynamics CRM and prepares a follow-up letter using a template he has used in the past.

▶ Open the Account: The Coffee House.

▶ From the menu bar, select Actions.

▶ From the Action menu, select Mail Merge.

You will now see Figure 10.18.

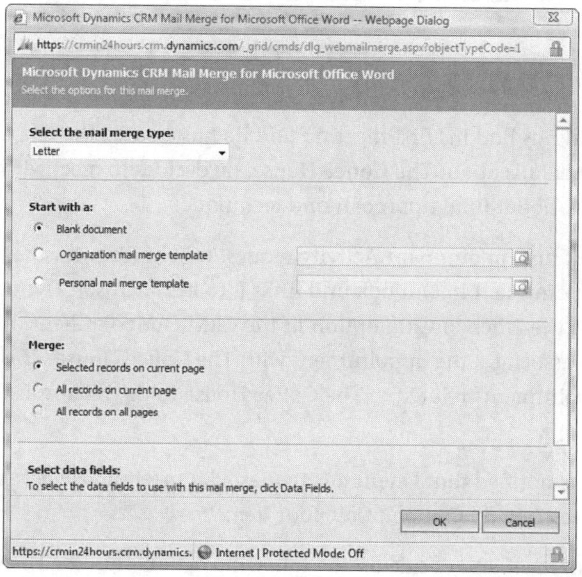

FIGURE 10.18
Mail merge follow-up letter form for Janice at The Coffee House.

David also realizes that he has a good chance at closing this deal within the next 60 days, and he decides to set up a new Opportunity with an estimated close date of July 31, 2009. He also calculates that the approximate revenue will be $1000/quarter and that this account is positioned for a long-term reoccurring revenue model if handled correctly. David creates the Opportunity as shown in Figure 10.19.

FIGURE 10.19
Create opportunity.

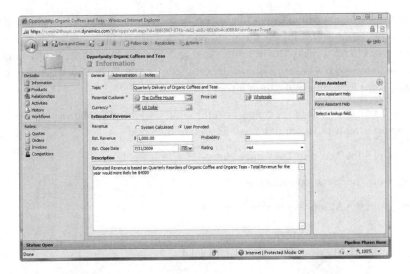

Final Planning

Now that David has had his first meeting and he has created the Opportunity and captured some details about The Coffee House, he decides to meet with his sales manager to talk about final approach and technique.

David sends out an Appointment Activity request to John Brown, sales manager. He creates this appointment in Outlook and links it to his Microsoft Dynamics CRM calendar choosing the Track in CRM option in the CRM Outlook Client. He also sets a regarding and associates the appointment with The Coffee House. This helps David to capture appointments related to The Coffee House in the Microsoft Dynamics CRM history.

John Brown gets notified that David has requested a meeting. He accepts, and the response updates David's Outlook Calendar item.

David and John meet and decide on the following action plan for The Coffee House:

1. The coffee/tea tasting

2. Follow-up call to the tasting offering a reference (or two)

3. Introduction to Mel Robinson, owner of This Little House of Cookies (an existing client from a neighboring state)

4. Follow-up call on how the discussions with Mel went and scheduling of the revenue meeting

5. A revenue meeting/discussion with Janice with some sharing of statistics related to potential profit that The Coffee house can generate from offering high-quality good-tasting coffee

6. Follow-up call to the revenue meeting to answer any unanswered questions

7. Close the deal meeting to sign final paper work and possibly an introduction to their new account/customer service representative

Now that the plan has been decided, David adds these items to his calendar and task list. They become activities in Microsoft Dynamics CRM (Outlook synchronizes from tasks and Outlook Calendar), which are dated with a pending date that balances all that needs to be done prior to July 31, 2009.

As the weeks go by, David completes each phone call, each appointment, and each task, resulting in a closed deal on July 31, 2009. After returning from his last appointment, David closes the Opportunity in Microsoft Dynamics CRM as a win, as shown in Figure 10.20.

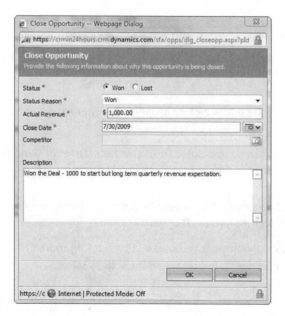

FIGURE 10.20
Closing the won opportunity.

Workshop

Semi-Roasted, Inc., also has a marketing department, which is run by Jackie Grand. Jackie is excited that David has closed The Coffee House because it is one of her favorite local restaurants. Jackie makes a point to introduce herself to Janice Fiddle-head next time she is in the restaurant. As they are talking, Jackie mentions that she is looking for a few new case studies for some of the marketing efforts she is working on. Janice jumps at the chance at some free advertising and volunteers to be written up as a case study for Semi-Roasted, Inc. Janice creates a new marketing campaign called Case Studies and defines a number of specific activities associated with this campaign. These activities include sorting and finding a list of happy existing clients, reaching out and talking with the clients, scheduling interviews with the clients who have volunteered, writing and editing the case studies, and sending a follow-up thank you gift. Janice has also been given a budget for these activities and she adds this to the marketing campaign.

Q&A

Q. *Does David need to use a VPN when he connects to the office?*

A. No. Microsoft Dynamics CRM builds in authentication and security through its design.

Q. *Can David associate a picture of Janice with her record in Microsoft Dynamics CRM?*

A. Yes. Pictures can be associated with records in Microsoft Dynamics CRM through a bit of architecture.

Q. *When an appointment is created in Outlook, what does that look like when synchronized with Microsoft Dynamics CRM?*

A. An outlook appointment becomes a Microsoft Dynamics CRM activity with a type of appointment. It displays on the activity views.

Quiz

1. Can David add one task to Outlook and a different task activity to Microsoft Dynamics CRM? What would his Outlook task list look like? What would his Open Activities list look like?

2. What does David do in Microsoft Dynamics CRM when he gets a new lead at the national coffee roasters event?

3. What are David's options for entering a new lead in Microsoft Dynamics CRM?

4. Why does David close Activities once they are done?

5. Can Jim Brown, sales manager, see David's Activities? Is this transparency valuable? Why?

Answers

1. Yes, David can add tasks to either Microsoft Dynamics CRM or Outlook. His task list will include all tasks.

2. He enters the lead as a new Lead entity (record type) in Microsoft Dynamics CRM.

3. One option for David is that he can enter leads through his mobile device using the Microsoft Dynamics CRM mobile client or a third-party mobile option. He can also use his laptop as long as he has Internet access or, if he is offline, he can use his laptop and sync with the corporate network later.

4. David closes Activities so that they are filed to history and removed from his active list of things to do.

5. Depending on how security is set up, Jim Brown can see David's activities.

Exercise

Create the marketing campaign that Jackie uses to keep track of her need to capture and create a number of case studies. What are other tools within Dynamics CRM that Jackie can leverage to make creating these case studies easier? Set up a marketing list, and then use this marketing list to invite people to participate in the case study effort. When people respond where do you capture their responses? Associate the responses to the marketing campaign.

HOUR 11

Configuring Your Interaction with Microsoft Dynamics CRM

What You'll Learn in This Hour:

▶ Basic Configurations

▶ Changing the Form

▶ Adding the Internet to a Form: The iFrame

▶ Attributes (Fields)

▶ Drop-Down Lists

▶ Views

In this hour, you will learn how to modify Microsoft Dynamics CRM to better fit your business needs. You will learn how to add new attributes (fields) to the data entry forms and modify existing attributes (fields). You will also learn how to move attributes (fields) from tab to tab. Finally, we will build up to including iFrames and adding form specific scripts to the system.

Basic Configurations

When it comes to designing the entry forms for getting data into Microsoft Dynamics CRM, Microsoft offers a robust offering. We start with making just a few changes and then expand out into the world of really changing a user's interaction with Microsoft Dynamics CRM without writing one line of code.

Figure 11.1 shows the default data entry form for an Account.

Every entity (record type) has a form and you can change a number of different things on these forms. You can add or remove attributes (fields), you can add or remove sections, and you can add or remove tabs. You can also modify the values of a drop-down list either by adding to them, changing them or deleting them. You can also add an iFrame. (We discuss what an iFrame is in later sections of this hour.)

FIGURE 11.1
Default Account
data entry form.

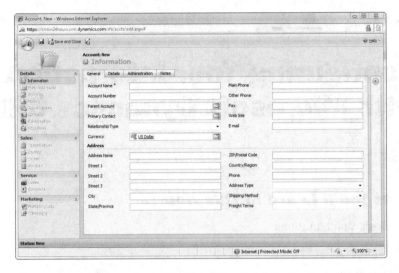

We are now going to change the look of this default data entry form by changing just one thing (the attributes [fields]).

Changing the Form

Forms can be changed. In the following section we will learn how to modify a form.

Removing Attributes

We will remove a number of attributes from the form shown in Figure 11.1.

To remove attributes and change the default form, you need to access Microsoft Dynamics CRM Settings, Customization. If you do not have this on your menu, you more than likely do not have the correct security privileges to perform this function. Talk with your Microsoft Dynamics CRM administrator.

1. Choose Settings.

2. Choose Customization.

3. Choose Customize Entities.

4. Choose Account.

You will now see a list of items that are related to the specific Account entity (record type). These include the core setup information, the forms and views functionality, Account attributes, a series of different types of relationships that can be created, and the Account specific system messages and error code descriptions. As discussed in earlier hours, an Account is an entity (record type) that is built from a number of attributes (fields). To modify the data entry form for an Account, select Forms and Views.

How Many Forms Can We Have for Each Entity (Record Type)?

For any given entity (record type), you can have only one form.

By the Way

Figure 11.2 shows the area where you select the Account form. Figure 11.3 shows the form as it looks when editing. Notice that you have a number of new choices, including a new Common Tasks pane.

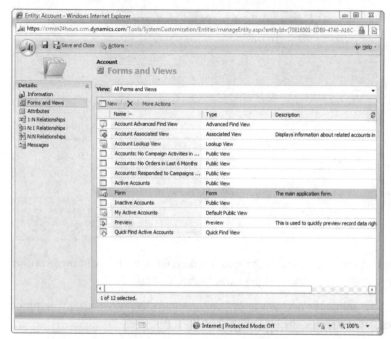

FIGURE 11.2
Choosing the Account form.

To remove an attribute (field) from the Account form, follow these steps:

1. Select the attribute (field) using your mouse. You can tell the attribute (field) is selected by the green box around the attribute. Notice that in Figure 11.3 the E-Mail attribute (field) is selected.

2. Once the attribute (field) is selected, you can remove it by choosing Remove from the Common Tasks pane. This process does not remove the attribute from the database, nor does it delete data.

Consider, for instance, a company that decides to only capture address information at the contact level. This has various disadvantages, but it is an example. It also decides that there is no email address associated at the generic company level, but it wants to leave its options open for later. To encourage the adoption of this business process, the company removes the Address attributes (fields) and the E-Mail attributes (fields) from the Account form. It does not delete the attributes from the database. If the place to enter data is not available, data will not be entered.

FIGURE 11.3
Changing the
Account form.

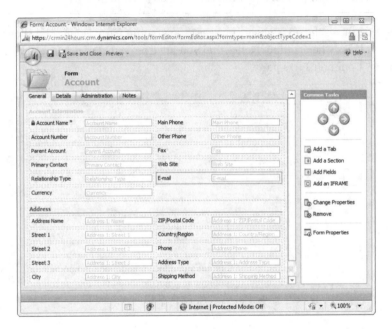

Figure 11.4 shows the exact same Account data entry form in edit mode minus the Address attributes (fields) and the E-Mail attribute (field).

Figure 11.5 shows the Account form from an interactive user perspective minus the Address attributes and the E-Mail attribute.

Moving Attributes

Now that you have removed a number of attributes, you might also want to move attributes around the form. We will move a number of attributes using the green arrows found in the Common Tasks pane. Figures 11.6 and 11.7 show the attributes (fields) moved to new locations.

Expanding the Section

One trick for expanding the section is to change the properties of an attribute (field) that is next to another attribute (field) from a one-column to two-column display. This pushes the other field down and as such potentially expands the section.

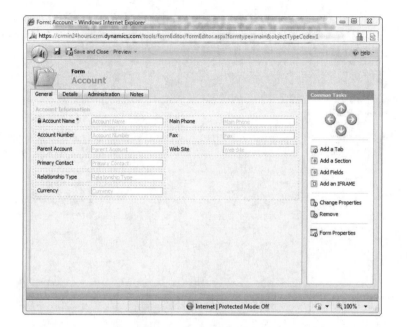

FIGURE 11.4
Remove the Address attributes: editing the form.

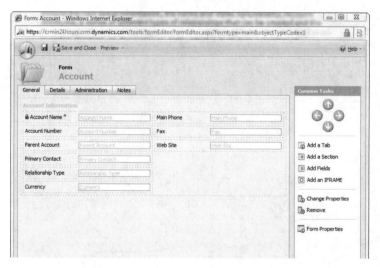

FIGURE 11.5
Remove the Address attributes: user perspective.

The green arrows can move attributes (fields) within a specific section, as follows:

1. Each tab within the form is made up of a series of sections.

2. By editing the properties of the specific attribute (field), you can move attributes from section to section and from tab to tab.

FIGURE 11.6
Move attributes
(fields): editing
the form.

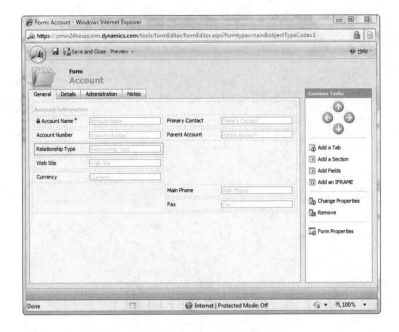

FIGURE 11.7
Move attributes:
user perspec-
tive.

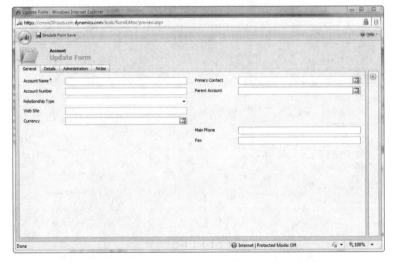

3. Select the attribute (field).

4. Choose Change Properties from the Common Tasks pane (see Figure 11.8).

5. On the first screen, look for Location (refer to Figure 11.8).

6. Choose the location for this attribute (field). Currency has been highlighted, and Change Properties has been selected.

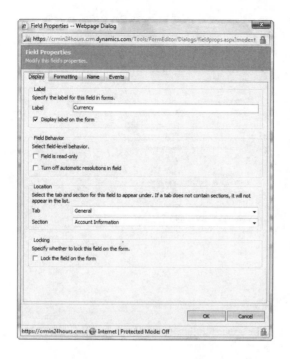

FIGURE 11.8
Move the Currency attribute (field).

7. The location for Currency will be changed to the Details tab.

8. Currency has been moved to the Details tab, but it has not been removed from the form.

Adding a Section

To add a section, do the following:

1. Choose Add a Section from the Common Tasks pane.

2. A section has to have a name, but you have the choice whether to display that name or not. Select a name, such as International Details (see Figure 11.9), and choose to display it.

3. In Figure 11.9, we add a section to the Account form's General tab to hold international details.

FIGURE 11.9
Add section:
International
Details.

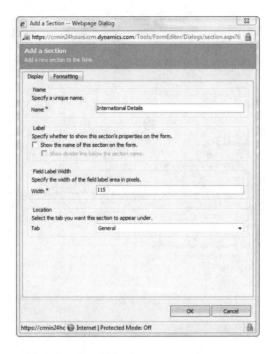

In Figure 11.10, we add and move attributes:

1. Move any attributes (fields) that are internationally oriented to the International section.

FIGURE 11.10
Add Fields
(attributes).

2. Choose the Add Fields (attributes) option from Common Tasks pane.

3. Turn on attributes (fields) that are international in nature.

The two attributes (fields) that we choose are Exchange Rate and Country. We have also moved Currency back to the General tab into the International Details section. Figure 11.11 shows the new international section of the Account Form.

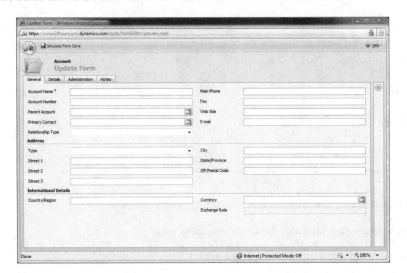

FIGURE 11.11
New International section on the Account form General tab.

Last Modified Section

The other section that I like to add, which is not a default section in Microsoft Dynamics CRM, is a Last Modified section. The Last Modified section can hold the system attributes (fields) Created By, Created On, Modified By, and Last Modified On. Figure 11.12 shows an example.

To add a new section called last modified do the following:

1. Add a Section.

2. Name the section Last Modified.

3. Add the existing system attributes (field names) Last Modified, Modified By, Created By, and Created On.

Adding a Tab

Attribute Limitation

Be aware that each attribute (field) can appear only once in the whole form and that you are limited to eight tabs.

By the Way

FIGURE 11.12
Last Modified
section.

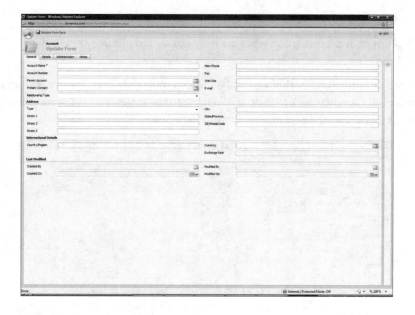

You can also add new tabs. To add a new tab, do the following:

1. Choose Add Tab from the Common Tasks pane.

2. Give the tab a unique name.

3. Choose OK, which saves the new tab with the entity form.

Now that you have the basics, you can use more advanced options when changing the look and feel of the Account form (or any form you decide to change).

Changing Columns Within a Section

Mr. Jack BlackHat decides that he does not want his display to appear in two even columns. He has a number of check box attributes (fields), and he wants to display these in four columns to get maximum use of the screen real estate. He wonders how to change this. To change this, Jack needs to do the following:

1. Create a new section.

2. Give the section a unique name.

3. Modify the layout of the section prior to saving. The section column choices are in Figure 11.13. Jack needs to choose Fixed Field Width and then four columns.

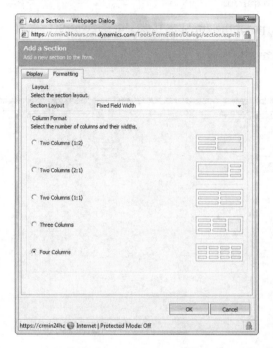

FIGURE 11.13
Section column choices.

Once Saved

Once the section is saved, the layout of columns cannot be changed unless you delete the section and set up a new one.

Watch Out!

After Jack creates the section as four columns, he can add fields (attributes) to this section. Jack has created a number of attributes (fields) to represent colors. Jack is a magician who makes balloon animals at parties, and he always asks his clients what their favorite colors are. Jack has added these color selections to the Account form. Notice that the choices in Figure 11.14 are all check boxes.

How Did Jack Add New Attributes?

You can only create new attributes from customize entities, Forms and Views option. To add new attributes, follow these steps:

1. Choose customize entities.

2. Choose Attributes.

3. Choose New.

4. Give the attribute a name.

5. Pick if it is required.

6. Choose a type for the attribute. (Jack chooses type BIT.)

7. Save the new attribute.

FIGURE 11.14
Check boxes.

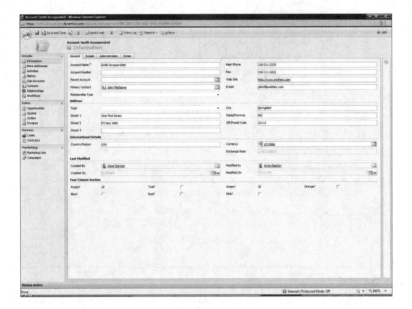

Bit Attributes (Fields) Format Options

You are not limited to check boxes if your attribute (fields) is of type Bit (Boolean). Your other choices are listed under Control Format and include check box, list, or radio buttons (see Figure 11.15, which includes the Control Format question that represents the formatting options for the Green attribute [field]).

This is a fun hour, because as you work through it the content, gets slightly more difficult with each section.

Adding the Internet to a Form: An iFrame

An iFrame is a frame that allows you to display content from other places within Microsoft Dynamics CRM or from the Internet, within an entity form in Microsoft Dynamics CRM. **iFrame** has an official definition, but if I told it to you, it would not support my intention of showing you how to add powerful content without getting lost in technical terms. For those readers who live and breathe technical terms, well, you either know what an iFrame is already or you can search for iFrame to satisfy that technical desire to add it to your vocabulary.

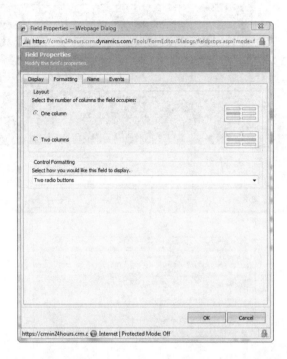

FIGURE 11.15
Bit attribute format options: radio buttons, check box, or list.

Jack BlackHat wants to search for content on specific accounts each time he is looking at the details of an account. He thinks that a tab that offers him some search capability would be wonderful. He is in luck: Microsoft Dynamics CRM supports this interest. lLok at Figure 11.16. We have created a new tab called Search, we have added a new section called Search, we have added an iFrame to this section, and in the properties of the iFrame, we have added Microsoft's new search decision engine's website (www.bing.com).

We have also changed the formatting of the iFrame to expand to use all available space and not have a border. These are two check boxes on the Formatting tab of the iFrame Properties sheet. Figure 11.17 shows the iFrame formatting property options.

Figure 11.18 is the final result. Sweet, right? You can use iFrames to display any web page within a form in Microsoft Dynamics CRM.

Are we having fun yet? Let's do more. We will dip our toe into a bit of programming, or at least we are going to visit the area of forms that programmers can have a ball with.

FIGURE 11.16
Bing iFrame
properties.

FIGURE 11.17
iFrame format-
ting properties.

FIGURE 11.18
The final iFrame showing Bing within Microsoft Dynamics CRM.

Form Properties

The form also has unique properties. Figure 11.19 hows the properties of the entire form.

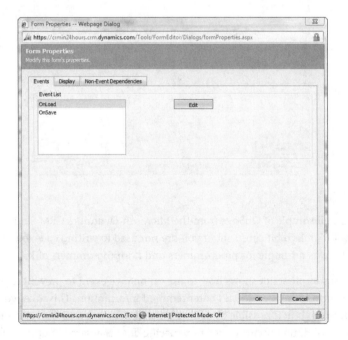

FIGURE 11.19
Form properties.

For any given form within the system (and each entity [record] has one form), you can run a script OnLoad or OnSave of the form.

To see where this can be done, follow these steps:

1. Select OnLoad or

2. Select OnSave and

3. Click Edit.

You can now enable the event using the check box and cut and paste in some script that you want to run OnLoad or OnSave. Figure 11.20 shows where you would paste in your script.

Here is a small sample of OnSave from the Microsoft Dynamics CRM Online help file. I agree that it looks a bit confusing if you are not used to writing code, but it works. It is placed here as a sample for programmers and nonprogrammers alike.

"This JScript sample script shows how to use an onSave event to prevent a user from saving the form if the user doesn't enter required information. This takes validation one step further than is possible by setting a field on a form as Business Required, because the validation occurs only when specific data is entered in other fields. The script has different behavior when the user clicks Save or Save and Close."[1] An example from Microsoft is shown in Figure 11.21.

FIGURE 11.21
Microsoft's sample OnSave script.

The form Properties sheet offers you OnSave and OnLoad areas for running scripts or calling small programs. The properties of an attribute (field) enable you to add an OnChange script to a specific attribute (field).

Default Attributes

A certain number of default attributes (also referred to as fields) come with the system, but you are not limited to just these. You can add your own attributes (fields) to capture data that might be specific to your company. After you create the attribute (field), you can circle back and update the form and add your new attribute (field) to any tab or section.

Optional Attributes

There are numerous attributes that exist within Microsoft Dynamics CRM that are not necessarily displayed on the initial forms.

Did you Know?

---

[1] *Microsoft Dynamics CRM v4.0 Help File (6,2009) retrieved from Online Help "Sample OnSave Event Script" at http://help.crm.dynamics.com/help/default.aspx?area=%2fTools%2fFormEditor%2fDialogs%2fevent.aspx&user_lcid=1033.*

Adding Attributes

To add or change attributes (fields), go back into the Customize Entities page.

Let's add some fun attributes (fields) to the contact entity to complement Jack Black-Hat's business model:

1. Choose Custom Entities.

2. Choose the entity you want to add attributes to.

3. Choose Attributes.

In Figure 11.22, you can see the list of default contact attributes. Some of them are already displayed on the form, and others can be used as needed. If the attribute that you want to create is not in the list, you can create it. When creating an attribute, you must make a number of decisions. We will create an attribute called Likes Magic? that will allow Jack BlackHat to mark each contact as either liking or disliking magic. This field has an answer that is one of two answers, Yes or No, so we are going to choose an attribute type of Bit. Figure 11.22 shows the list of default attributes for Microsoft Dynamics CRM. Figure 11.23 shows the first screen when creating a new custom attribute (field).

FIGURE 11.22
Default contact attributes.

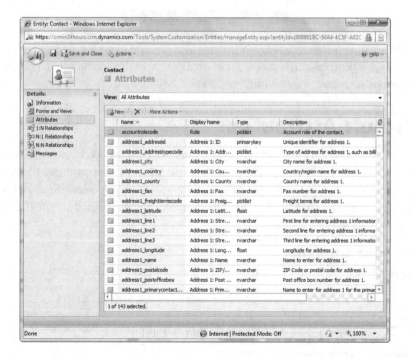

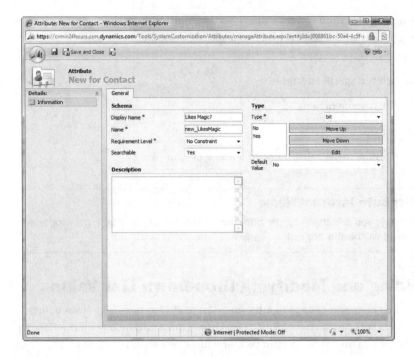

FIGURE 11.23
Creating a new attribute: Likes Magic.

Attributes can be of all different types. The Type field within the attribute is not only a drop-down list of choices, but when you make your choice the formatting of the actual details change based on the type you select. For instance, if you choose that the attribute you are adding is an Int (for integer), your formatting choices will include how many decimals and the maximum and minimum value.

Microsoft Dynamics CRM Architecture

Although mastery of adding attributes is possible, if you are going to add a number of attributes, I highly suggest that you read more about architecting Microsoft Dynamics CRM or talk with a Microsoft Dynamics CRM specialist before proceeding. The type of attribute and the creation of attributes impacts the entire Microsoft Dynamics CRM framework and database structure. A new attribute is not always the best architectural decision to solve a business need for a specific type of report or display.

Changing Names

Existing attributes (fields) can also have name changes. When you change the name of the attribute (field), the name on the form and the name in any associated views will also change. You cannot change the internal database name of the attribute, but you can change the display name of a specific attribute. To change an attribute name, follow these steps:

1. Select a specific attribute.

2. Select more actions.

3. Choose Edit.

4. Change the Display name to a name of your liking.

Attribute Internal Name

Although you are changing the attribute display name, the name that appears in reports will be the original.

Adding and Modifying Drop-Down List Values

The other common change to attributes is to modify or add drop-down values to attributes that are of type picklist. If we choose the Attribute role on the Contact entity, we can add to the default picklist values, as shown in Figure 11.24.

FIGURE 11.24
Adding to the drop-down listvalues.

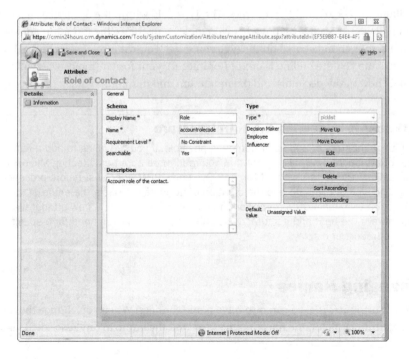

You now know how to change and modify a form and add and change existing attributes (fields). You can add drop-down values to drop-down attributes (fields), and you can create sections and new tabs on a form. You also have the power to add your new attributes (fields) to the existing form. You have also learned how to add a simple iFrame that serves up an external web page. These web pages could be a search engine or even a mapping application for easy access to maps.

Views

A list of system views is available on every entity (record type) that you select. System views include items such as My Accounts, Active Accounts, My Activities, Closed Activities, Leads Open Last Week, and more.

To create system views, le'ts start by looking at the Account entity (record type) system views option under customization. Figure 11.25 shows a list of the system views under Forms and Views associated with the Account entity. In addition to what you will learn about Advanced Find and creating Ad Hoc User specific views in later hours, let's review how you can modify existing system views and set up new system views.

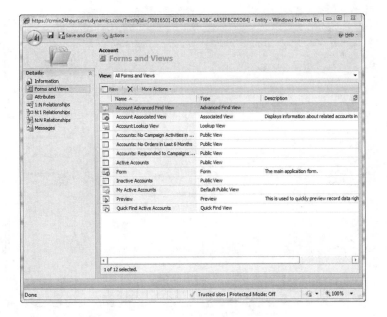

FIGURE 11.25
Forms and Views.

System Views

System views are available to all users who have access to your Microsoft Dynamics CRM system. You can have an unlimited number of system views per entity (record type).

Modify an Existing System View

To modify a view, follow theses steps:

1. Select the system view you want to change (Figure 11.26).

2. Choose a column.

3. Use your mouse to control the common tasks green arrows to move a column to the right or left.

4. Use the Common tasks, Add Columns to add existing attributes to the view.

5. Use the Common tasks, change properties option to change the width of the column you have selected.

6. Use Configure Sorting to select an attribute as the default sort.

FIGURE 11.26
Modify the My Accounts System View.

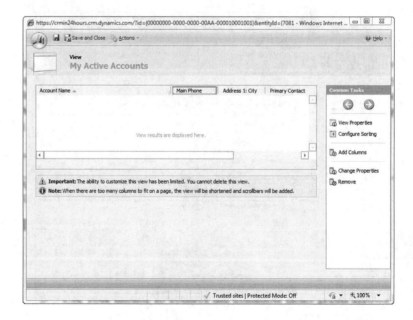

When you are modifying the My Accounts System view, you are changing the My Accounts view for all users. You might want to remove the columns that do not really apply to your business model, or you might want to rearrange the columns so that the most critical information on the accounts is listed in the first column.

When you use a view you can sort by any column by clicking on the column header, but a review and a change of the default sort saves a step.

The width of the column can also make a difference. If your business has long account names, ensure that the account name column is as wide as possible. On the other hand, if your account names are relatively short, shorten the account name column to take advantage of more screen real estate. Additionally, managing the white space adds more user friendliness to the display.

Columns that you select for your view are also columns of data that will appear in your interaction and use between Microsoft Dynamics Excel and Views of data. You will learn more about his in Hour 20, "Utilizing the Power of Microsoft Excel with CRM Data."

Adding a New System View

To add a new system view, follow these steps:

1. Choose customize entities.

2. Choose the entity associated where you want to create a new system view. Let's create a new view associated with the phone call entity.

3. Choose Forms and Views (See Figure 11.27).

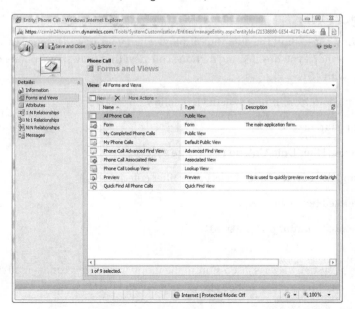

FIGURE 11.27
Forms and Views.

4. Click New and give your new view a Name and Description (see Figure 11.28).

FIGURE 11.28
Creating a New
System View.

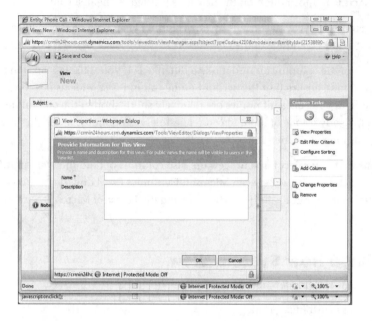

You can now proceed to select columns, adjust the width of those columns, and arrange those columns to your liking. After you finish, choose Save.

Adding a Filter

You might want to limit the data that displays when your new view is selected. For instance, perhaps you are creating a Phone call view that only shows phone calls that start with 401.

To filter the data in your new system view, follow these steps:

1. Edit your view.

2. Choose Filter Data Criteria (see Figure 11.29).

3. Using the power of query select your filter criteria.

4. Choose Phone Number.

5. Choose Contains and Enter 401.

Adding new system views is just a start to the many ways views can be used. For more details on creating custom ad-hoc views, see Hour 20.

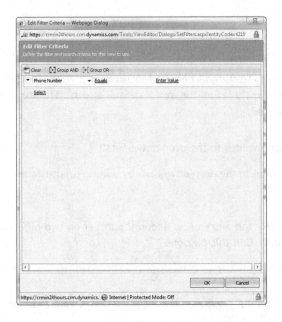

FIGURE 11.29
Filter Data
Criteria.

You have now changed your interaction with Microsoft Dynamics CRM and have added additional ways to interact with and display all the data that has been captured in the system.

Workshop

Jack BlackHat has a small business called BlackHat Magic, which offers magic performances to individual families for birthday parties, celebrations, and to large corporations for tradeshows and employee festivals. Jack uses Microsoft Dynamics CRM to track specific details on the contacts he works with and the families and companies who engage him. Jack has added a number of custom attributes to his version of Microsoft Dynamics CRM so that he can track the different color preferences of his contacts as well as the various associated birthdays, anniversaries, and special events. Jack also likes to remember everyone he meets, and so he spends extra effort to capture details that helps him remember his hundreds of contacts. These details include hair color, eye color, and favorite outfit.

Jack also keeps track of how different families are related to each other. He uses the Parent Account field within Microsoft Dynamics CRM to create a family tree type of association. Jack also uses the Microsoft Dynamics CRM relationships feature to capture associations between kids that play on the same sports teams and their parents so that he can pass out his business cards and ask for appropriate references.

Q&A

Q. *Are there attributes available to use that are not displayed on the default forms?*

A. Yes. Microsoft Dynamics CRM comes with a large number of attributes that might not be included on the initial default screens. These can be used as they are or renamed.

Q. *How do I add values to the drop-down lists?*

A. You add values to the drop-down lists by editing an attribute that is of type PICKLIST.

Q. *I want to offer the entry of an Account number on two different tabs in the Account form. Can this be done?*

A. No. Each attribute can only be displayed once within any given form.

Q. *How do I create a personal view that is not available to other users in the system?*

A. Use Advanced Find. For more details on using Advanced Find, See Hour 20.

Q. *Can I share a personal view with other people?*

A. Yes. You can create a personal view and share this view with a team.

Q. *Can I delete an existing system view?*

A. Yes, but this deletes it for all users of your Microsoft Dynamics CRM environment.

Quiz

1. What are three attributes that Jack needs to add to his Microsoft Dynamics CRM system? What type of attributes are these?

2. Do you see any example within Jack's business where an iFrame would prove useful?

3. How many forms does each entity have?

4. What needs to be changed on the form to allow for four columns?

5. Can you display an attribute more than once on any given form?

6. After you create a new system view, who has access to it?

Answers

1. Likes Magic? of type Bit, Favorite Color of type Picklist, and birthday of type DATETIME.

2. Jack BlackHat travels often. Easy access from within the account to one of the mapping applications, such as Live Maps, is extremely helpful.

3. Each entity can have only one form.

4. The properties of the section need to be changed to add four columns.

5. You cannot display an attribute more than once on any given form.

6. System views are available to all users of Microsoft Dynamics CRM.

Exercise

Add the attributes that Jack BlackHat needs for his BlackHat Magic company. Include attributes to track each critical event on the contact form and the details to help Jack remember each contact's unique features. These might include height, character, and eye color. In addition, create the color attributes of type Bit, and then add these to a section of the Account form. Set each attribute to a check box and display it in four columns.

Checkboxes Are Not Usually the Answer

Checkboxes are not the answer for a good number of business situations. There is a more historically appropriate solution in the use of activities. Discuss with your choices with an experienced Microsoft Dynamics CRM architect

HOUR 12

Contacts and Activity Capture

In this hour, you will learn about contacts and associated activities. Additionally, this hour gets into the details of relating contacts to each other and to other accounts.

Capturing Contact Information

The Contact information is captured through the contact form which is separated into up to eight different tabs. We are now going to look at the default tabs within contact.

General Tab of the Contact

As introduced in Hour 2, "The Basics: The CRM Functionality Vocabulary," a contact is a specific person. A contact also has related information, such as the activities a staff person might have promised to complete for a person and the relationships that a person has with other people and companies. Depending on your industry and business, and even your country culture and rules, various levels of detail can be captured about a specific person in the contact feature of Microsoft Dynamics CRM.

Contacts Are Not Always People

A contact does not have to be a person; it can be renamed just like any other customizable entity in Microsoft Dynamics CRM. If you want to get creative or if you are in a unique industry, you can rename and use contact for a piece of clothing, a farm animal, or a type of wine.

If we take a deeper look at contacts, there are a number of nuances of interest for discussion. For instance, I mentioned some business rule dependencies. Capturing details on a person is an area where it is not always about the technology. In certain countries, it is definitely not culturally accepted to track certain types of personal information within business electronic databases, such as personal habits, favorite hobbies, golf scores, and more. If you are configuring Microsoft Dynamics CRM for another company, you might want to check on some of these types of business and countries rules.

Figure 12.1 shows the default General tab of a contact entry.

FIGURE 12.1
Contact general details.

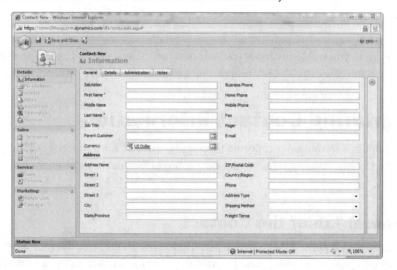

A note on salutation, and then we dive into the first area of core learning: the contact name.

Salutation

Salutation is a field to capture all the different terms that you would use when writing a letter or addressing someone other than by his or her first and last name. These can include Mr., Mrs., Ms., Dr., and more, depending on the country or style in which your company addresses their contacts. By default, the Salutation field is a text field, but if you have a long list of options, you will want to remove the default Salutation field and add your own that is of type Picklist to ensure a higher level of consistency in spelling and form over time.

Don't Let the Name Trip You Up

Notice that, in Figure 12.1, the name is displayed as three different fields: First Name, Middle Name, and Last Name. This format for capturing allows for sorting and for granular views based on having three specifically unique and yet related pieces of information. The system is also designed to offer a Full Name display if it has access to these three core data fields. There is also the option to totally skip this separation of name in exchange for Full Name only using a bit of Jscript to populate the required Last Name Field.

Job Title

Given that we are capturing information on a specific contact, one of the default attributes is the Job Title. As a default field in Microsoft Dynamics CRM, Job Title is an open text field. A user can enter any derivative of job title as fits. Again, if you want to control consistency of spelling and job title options, you might want to make this a drop-down list (Picklist attribute). On the other hand, in this day and age, you can come across some rather creative job titles, and you don't want to frustrate yourself or users if they want to add something creative.

Parent Customer

For any given contact, there is one parent customer. The parent customer relationship is a special one in Microsoft Dynamics CRM. Just as an account can have a primary contact, a contact can have an association to a specific account (or customer). The association to a customer is a lookup on the Account entity (record type). If the account doesn't exist, this field can be left empty or a new account can be entered at time of contact entry.

Currency

Every given contact can have a unique association to a currency from the currencies you have defined in Microsoft Dynamics CRM. Currency is a required field in the contact because it is used in many other places within Microsoft Dynamics CRM; although if you only have one currency, you can move it to a different tab and set a default.

Figure 12.2 shows the currency lookup.

Phone Numbers

Each contact has a place for five phone numbers and, by default, they are named Business, Home, Mobile, Fax, and Pager. There is also a sixth phone number that can be unique and is associated with the contact address. This sixth phone number is a delivery address phone number for reference to shipping forms that require a phone number. There are six default phone numbers, but that does not mean you can't add more or take away some that might not be useful. You can also change the phone-number format by creating new complementary attributes for extension and area code. You can also use a small set of code as an OnChange to the phone number attribute for formatting. For more information on OnChange, OnLoad, and OnSave coding, check out Hour 24, "Microsoft Dynamics CRM as a Development Framework."

Address and Addresses

The Contact form includes a primary address, but an unlimited number of addresses can be added for this contact using the More Addresses option in the left navigation pane. If you create the contact after selecting the account, the address will be prepopulated with the account address; otherwise, it will be blank. The primary address also includes an address name (which might be something like corporate headquarters).

Other fields worth noting include the Address Type (which includes Bill To, Ship To, Primary, and Other by default), Shipping Method, and Default Freight Terms. If you are a service industry and you don't ship product, you might want to turn off some of these fields through System Configuration, Customization, to offer a cleaner interface.

Details Tab of the Contact

Figure 12.3 shows the default fields on the Details tab.

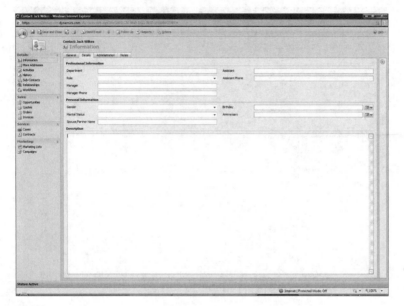

Description

The text in the Description field is limited to approximately 2,000 characters, so you want to consider how this is used. One use of the Description field is to summarize a general profile of the contact, or you can select the contact's profile off of a website and paste it into this space. The Description field should not be used for regular historical notes, because if used in this manner, a user might find they are running out of space.

Department

Department is descriptive only and is not used in other parts of the system. It can be helpful, however, when extending Microsoft Dynamics CRM or when creating ad-hoc reports.

Role

Role is a drop-down (Picklist) field supporting a user's interest in classifying the true role of the contact (for instance, the contact might be an influencer or a decision maker).

Administration Tab

Figure 12.4 shows the default fields on the Administration tab of the contact.

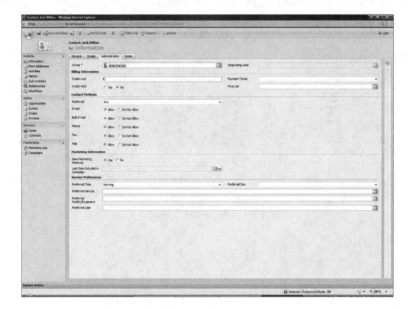

Owner

The owner of the contact impacts many things within Microsoft Dynamics CRM. It is a key field that helps to control data access and role oriented security. It can also be used to focus and filter data for views and reports. Every contact within Microsoft Dynamics CRM must be assigned an owner, and the owner of the contact must be a licensed Microsoft Dynamics CRM user of the system. This also applies to the owner of the Account. The owner of the Account and the owner of the Contact do not have to be the same.

For instance, perhaps you want to limit who has access to specific contacts. You can do this by assigning the proper owner to each of the contacts associated with an account and then configuring security to be owner specific. As you learned in Hour 5, "Security," many layers of potential security can be added to Microsoft Dynamics CRM.

Originating Lead

If you are using the Leads feature of Microsoft Dynamics CRM, and you convert a Lead to an Account and Contact, the originating Lead field will display the Lead record where this contact came from. You can use this link to look at Lead notes and activities as they relate to the contact.

Billing Information

If you integrate Microsoft Dynamics CRM with other Dynamics applications, such as the accounting software Dynamics NAV, Dynamics GP, or Dynamics AX, some of the billing information will be automatically populated. If your accounting software is not integrated with Microsoft Dynamics CRM, the billing information is a place to capture billing details that might be of interest to the sales team. In addition, if you are using Microsoft Dynamics CRM to create quotes, orders, and to-do invoices, the default price list defined on the contact will be the default price list used when creating quotes, orders, and invoices for this contact. If you are not using Microsoft Dynamics CRM for any type of accounting, you might want to remove these fields from the form.

Contact Methods

To help support antispam regulation and compliance with these regulations, Microsoft Dynamics CRM offers you a place to capture the marketing wishes of your contacts. When creating marketing campaigns, when sending email (including bulk email), and when doing mailings, Microsoft Dynamics CRM checks the settings on the contact and alerts the user of any mailing issues. For instance, if you set a contact to not allow email, Microsoft Dynamics CRM will not allow you to send email to that contact.

Marketing Information

As you learned in Hour 9, "Marketing Campaigns," Microsoft Dynamics CRM has a full-blown campaign management system that allows for detailed tracking of activity association to specific marketing efforts. When looking at specific contacts, you can see the last campaign that a specific contact was included in and you can set whether you want a specific contact included in future marketing campaigns.

Service Preferences

Service Preferences is a section associated with the scheduling and service functionality within Microsoft Dynamics CRM. If you are not using service and scheduling, you can remove these fields or this entire section from the form (although you might find some of the attributes [fields] useful). In terms of service, as you will learn in Hour 19, "Scheduling," scheduling is a detailed and robust function within Microsoft Dynamics CRM, but it is also quite particular when it comes to wanting specific details. If you plan to use scheduling, you definitely want to choose and set the right specifics on your contact with regard to preferred service, preferred equipment/facility, and preferred user. This will make using scheduling a lot smoother. Defining this within the contact when contacts are added also eliminates the need to go back and update all contacts with their preferred settings.

Notes Tab

Notes are available on many different entities, and you can capture notes on all or a subset of entities, but what you really want to consider is how these notes will be used. If you are looking to aggregate all notes from all entities into one central place, you will need either a report or a custom application or a third-party add-in to Microsoft Dynamics CRM. By default, Microsoft Dynamics CRM serves up notes as they relate to a specific entity (record type). There is definitely good reasoning behind this, but it also can trip you up. For instance, if I want to see all the notes and the total set of conversations between a specific contact and myself, choosing the Notes tab on that contact will show me a good running history, unless I also have contact-specific notes on an account or on an activity or on the opportunity.

You can keep yourself out of a disorganized situation by deciding on a good business process with regard to notes. You can also offer more freedom in note taking (ultimately capturing more corporate details) if you add in a Note display or report.

Figure 12.5 shows an example of the Notes tab with three captured notes.

Notes are also unlimited in terms of how many words you can type. You can have a long note or a series of short notes. You can also associate attachments with notes, although these attachments are more for historical reference than for long-term collaboration and editing. If you want a true document library where you can search, check out, edit, and check in documents, you really want to integrate Microsoft Dynamics CRM with Microsoft SharePoint. They make a natural partnership, and with a tiny bit of work (really tiny), you can have the correct SharePoint account-specific document library appear as a tab in the account or contact record of Microsoft Dynamics CRM.

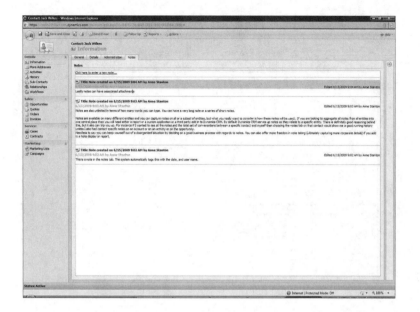

FIGURE 12.5
Notes tab.

For more information about integrating Microsoft SharePoint with Microsoft Dynamics CRM, talk with a local Microsoft Partner who specializes in SharePoint and Microsoft Dynamics CRM. As a parting thought on this subject: SharePoint is a natural for unstructured data and Microsoft Dynamics CRM as SharePoint's partner with structured data.

More on Notes (Where to Put Them)

If your teams are good at business processes, a simple rule of thumb could organize the free-form notes captured by all the different people within your organization. If each person at your company has a unique and creative style, however, you might want to leverage technology to summarize and organize the free-form notes captured.

One trick that is good to know and yet hard to figure out when configuring the system is that you can move the entire Notes section from the Notes tab to the bottom of the General tab. This move generally supports efforts to capture more notes. In general, people tend to stay on the first screen they arrive at unless otherwise motivated/trained to fill in information on other tabs.

Figure 12.6 shows the notes displayed at the bottom of the contact's General tab.

FIGURE 12.6
Notes moved to
the bottom of
the General tab.

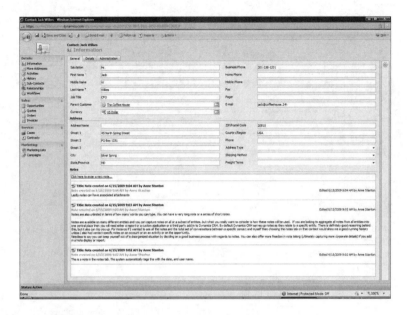

Related Contacts: Tracking Relationships

If you have many different related relationships that you want to track or if you want to capture the relationship that a given contact has to other contacts or accounts, you might want to take advantage of the relationship-tracking feature of Microsoft Dynamics CRM. The relationship-tracking feature offers you a chance to define relationship roles such as association and association member or vendor contact and reseller contact. The relationship-tracking feature of Microsoft Dynamics CRM is accessible from the left navigation pane of the Contact form, the Account form, and the Opportunity form.

Figure 12.7 shows the new relationship form as accessed from Contacts, Relationships.

Figure 12.8 shows the details of a completed relationship. In this example, Jack Wilkes is a member of the National Coffee Lovers Association.

You can even use the Microsoft Dynamics CRM Report Wizard to create a quick ad-hoc report that shows the relations you have created and defined. Figure 12.9 shows a report that includes all relationships that have been created.

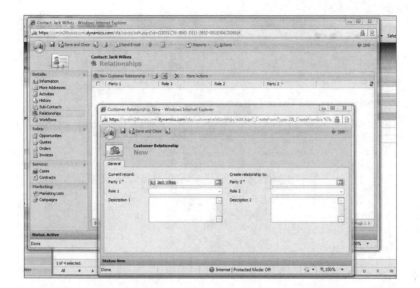

FIGURE 12.7
Add a new relationship.

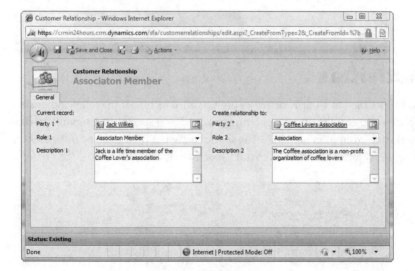

FIGURE 12.8
An added relationship.

FIGURE 12.9
Ad-hoc Relation-
ships report.

Activities

As you learned in Hour 2, activities are classified as one of the following: tasks faxes, phone calls, emails, letters, appointments, and as a special case service activities or marketing campaign activities. The special activities are discussed in Hour 9 and Hour 19. Figure 12.10 shows the full list of activity types.

FIGURE 12.10
Activity types.

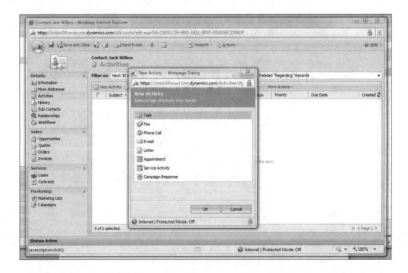

Each activity type captures a set of unique information and core details, and therefore each activity is slightly different, but they are all considered activities and are aggregated under the Activities entity views. This means that all activities can be shown under the activities view, and all your activities can be seen under the view My Activities (see Figure 12.11). We talk more about special types of activity views later in this hour.

Under Contact and Account, you have Activities and History. In these two areas, History is another name for completed activities.

FIGURE 12.11
Activities view.

Activities Are a Key Indicator

Activities are the key indicator for tracking who did what when within the system. When the Save as Completed option is chosen, an activity is locked into history and the system stamps it with a user, date, and time. This stamp allows you to view or report on the actual completed date and on the created date and last modified date.

By the Way

Activities: Type Tasks

Figure 12.12 shows the details of a task activity.

A task activity can be configured to synchronize with Microsoft Outlook tasks. This synchronization means that, if you check off the task as completed in Outlook, it completes the task in Microsoft Dynamics CRM. If you complete the activity in Microsoft Dynamics CRM, it shows up as completed in Outlook tasks. Activities of type Task are the only activities that synchronize with Outlook tasks.

In addition, you can associate an attachment with a task activity, as shown in Figure 12.13.

FIGURE 12.12
Task activity.

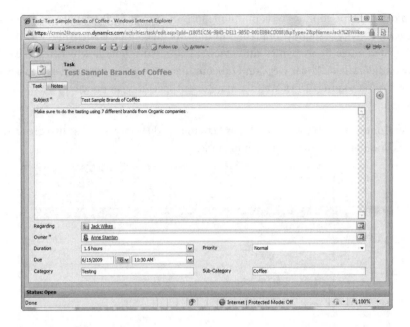

FIGURE 12.13
Task activity
attachment win-
dow.

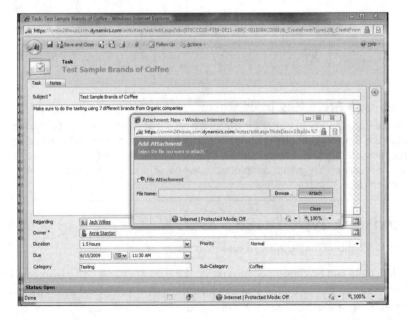

Attachments

Attachments are unstructured files of various sizes, and although Microsoft Dynamics CRM can be configured to limit attachments to sizes within a limit, you might want to discuss the risks and rewards of inserting attachments before building this feature into your business process.

Activities: Type Faxes

Figure 12.14 shows a Fax activity. Fax activities do not send faxes; they track that a fax was sent. In the Fax activity, notice that there are some unique fields, such as Fax Telephone Number, Recipient, Sender, and Cover Page. Fax activities do not synchronize with Outlook, but they can be viewed under the activities view (see Figure 12.15). You can also reach the activities view via the Activities folder in Outlook. As a clarification, the Fax activity is a classification that includes an area for you to indicate which number and to whom the fax was sent.

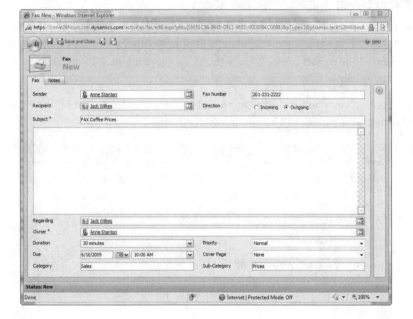

FIGURE 12.14
Fax activity.

FIGURE 12.15
Fax activity view.

Activities: Type Phone Call

If you create a new activity of type Phone Call after you have first picked the contact, the Phone Call activity will automatically populate with the contact's main phone number and the correct contacts for both the contact and the CRM user. Figure 12.16 shows an example.

In addition, if you change the outgoing and incoming Radio Button on the Phone Call activity, the names will be automatically inversed.

FIGURE 12.16
Phone Call activity.

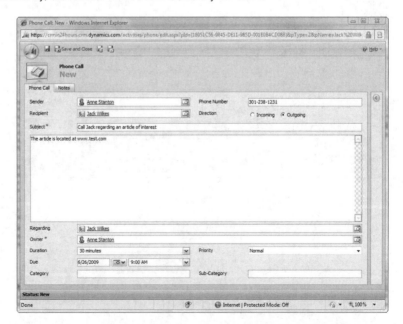

Activities: Type Email

Email activities are completed when tracking email from Outlook. However, from within Microsoft Dynamics CRM, you can create an email and save it to be sent later. You can also create an email and associate it with someone else so that the other person can send it when ready. Perhaps someone wants you to create a first draft and he then wants to do a final edit and send it. You can also create and send an email immediately. Emails created and sent from Microsoft Dynamics CRM are not tracked in Microsoft Outlook. This is by design. Figure 12.17 shows an email activity.

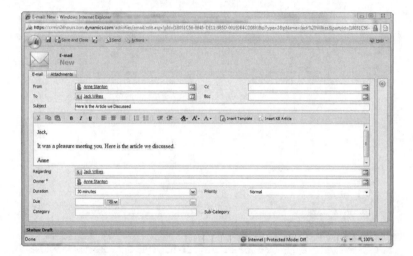

FIGURE 12.17
Email activity.

Email activities also have an option to allow you to format the email using Rich Text commands, insert a standard email template that might include data fields from Microsoft Dynamics CRM, or insert one of your Knowledge Base articles.

If you do want to associate an attachment with an email, you first need to save the email (you can save without exiting) and then associate the attachment to the created Email activity.

As you learned in Hour 9, you can also send emails as part of a Full Marketing Campaign or a Quick Campaign.

Emails that are tracked from Outlook, and emails that are sent from Microsoft Dynamics CRM would appear under the contact's History and under the staff members' activities. In addition, you can set a "regarding" within the email and associate it with another entity, such as an invoice, opportunity, or service case.

Activities: Type Letter

The Letter activity can track when letters are sent to a prospect or customer. The Letter activity is a classification that includes an area for you to indicate which address to send the letter to or which address the letter was sent. Figure 12.18 shows an example of an Activity of type Letter.

FIGURE 12.18
Letter activity.

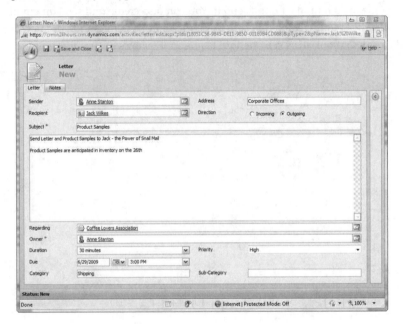

Activities: Type Appointment

The Appointment activity shows up on the Microsoft Dynamics CRM calendar in the Microsoft Dynamics CRM My Activities view. If you are synchronizing all appointments to Microsoft Outlook, they will also appear in your Outlook calendar. You can also selectively connect Outlook appointments to Microsoft Dynamics CRM from Outlook. When you do this, the items will appear as Appointment activities in Microsoft Dynamics CRM. See Figure 12.19.

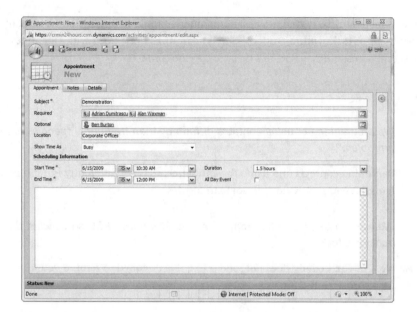

FIGURE 12.19
Appointment
activity.

Workshop

Janet has a boutique clothing store, and she uses Microsoft Dynamics CRM to manage her marketing efforts and relationships with her customers. Given that Janet's store is a boutique, she has a special relationship with some of her more loyal clientele, and Janet makes a point of remembering what they like. Janet captures each visitor who visits her store and who signs up for her regular mailings. Janet also uses Appointment activities to capture meetings for private showings of new clothing lines and to mark on her calendar her quarterly board meeting. Janet has rearranged the Contact form to fit her business model. She has created a new tab and a set of attributes to capture details, such as favorite clothing color sets, sizes, and notes on buying history.

Janet does not capture job titles on her contacts, but she does use much of the other information. She captures a home address, business address, and, if unique, a shipping address for each contact, and she makes sure to capture at least two phone numbers and (if possible) an email address. She also notes if one of her clients does not want to receive mailings or emails. There is a low tolerance in her audience for marketing material that is not requested.

Janet uses sub-contacts to capture details on each of her elite member customer's children. Janet plans to expand her children's clothing line, so having these details is helpful. (She always asks for permission before doing this.) When capturing children contact details, she includes the birth date.

Janet is incredibly busy and juggles many different to-do items. She keeps track of these items as tasks within Outlook. She synchronizes these tasks with Dynamics CRM and occasionally associates these to specific contacts.

Q&A

Q. *We are thinking of using contacts differently than traditional "people." Is this a problem?*

A. Renaming contacts and using the entity (record type) differently is not a problem; it is commonly done in some industries.

Q. *We want to be able to fax from Microsoft Dynamics CRM. Is this what the fax activity is for?*

A. No. The fax activity does not send a fax; it is designed to remind you to send a fax or track that a fax was sent.

Q. *We have a drop-down list for salutation. Can we change the type of the salutation field to a drop-down list?*

A. No. The salutation attribute (field) within Microsoft Dynamics CRM cannot be changed, but it can be taken off the form and replaced with your own salutation attribute (field).

Quiz

1. If Janet creates an activity of type Letter, will it show up in the Outlook Tasks list?

2. If you create and send an email from Microsoft Dynamics CRM, will it appear in the Outlook Sent folder?

3. Why is the owner of the contact so important?

4. Where would you recommend that Janet capture her notes on the buying habits of her customers? What about on the buying habits of the children? What are some of the advantages and disadvantages of your choices?

5. When will the system automatically populate the phone number of an activity of type Phone Call?

Answers

1. Letters will appear in Outlook tasks if Janet configures letters to synchronize with Outlook.

2. No. Mail sent from Microsoft Dynamics CRM does not synchronize back down to Outlook.

3. The owner of a contact is a key field for security and for views and reporting.

4. Buying habits can be captured within the notes of each contact. You potentially loose a summary view of all notes on the entire account, but with code or a third party add-on, there are options.

5. When you first select the Account and create a new activity of type Phone Call.

Exercise

Create two activities of each type and associate them with a specific contact. Create one activity from activities on the Workplace menu. Create the other activity after selecting a specific contact and then selecting Activity from the left menu of the Contact form. What happens differently when creating each of these activities in these two different ways?

Now, go to activity view and change the view type to each of the unique types. Notice how the views change based on the type of activity that you choose.

HOUR 13

Emailing from Microsoft Dynamics CRM

What You'll Learn in This Hour:

▶ Capturing an Email in Microsoft Dynamics CRM

▶ Sending One Quick Message

▶ Doing a Blast of Emails

▶ Dealing with Compliance to the Canned Spam Act

▶ Utilizing the Microsoft Dynamics CRM Outlook Address Book

▶ Configuring Email Based on Your Preferences

In this hour, you will learn about how email works within Microsoft Dynamics CRM. You will also learn how to capture email from the Microsoft Outlook world and associate that to records in Microsoft Dynamics CRM.

Capturing Email

Many of our conversations these days are captured in email, and yet we often don't manage to get these emails saved and associated with other company information. When only storing email in our personal Outlook folders, we lose the chance to categorize and associate emails with specific service cases, sales opportunities, and marketing campaigns. Microsoft Dynamics CRM resolves this issue by offering a number of configuration choices when it comes to email.

Choices include the following:

▶ **Track all incoming Outlook email in Microsoft Dynamics CRM:** This tracks all email for the specified user in Microsoft Dynamics CRM as email activities, and a link exists between all email-associated people in the To and From fields.

▶ **Track only incoming email that was sent in response to an email originally sent from Microsoft Dynamics CRM:** When email is sent from Microsoft Dynamics CRM, a tracking token is associated. When this email is responded to, Microsoft Dynamics CRM can link the response to the original via the tracking token.

▶ **Track only email related to your accounts, contacts, or leads:** Email that you send or that is sent to you is tracked if it came from an account, contact, or lead with a matching e-mail address within Microsoft Dynamics CRM for which you were designated as owner.

▶ **Manually track email you specifically choose:** You can manually track selected messages from Outlook in CRM using the Track in CRM option in the Microsoft Outlook Ribbon bar.

▶ **Track all email in Microsoft Dynamics CRM:** If you track all your email messages in Microsoft Dynamics CRM, they will be tracked as Microsoft Dynamics CRM email activities, and they can be accessed by anyone who has permission to view or work with your activities.

One Quick Message

You want to send a message from Microsoft Dynamics CRM. As you learned in Hour 12, "Contacts and Activity Capture," you can do this by creating a new activity of type Email. To send this quick email, follow these steps:

1. Select Activities.

2. Select New.

3. Select Email.

4. Look up and associate the recipient.

5. Add your email content.

6. Click Send.

Figure 13.1 shows how an email is sent directly from Microsoft Dynamics CRM.

Now, let's say you want to send a quick email from Outlook, and you want to track this email in Microsoft Dynamics CRM. To send this quick email, follow these steps:

1. Create an email in Outlook.

2. Click the Track in CRM button on the top of the email.

3. Click Send.

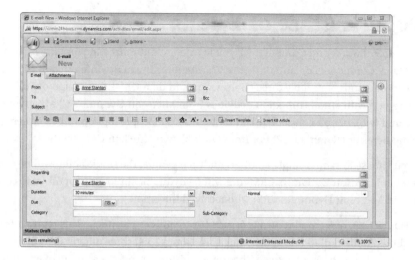

FIGURE 13.1
Email activity in Microsoft Dynamics CRM.

Figure 13.2 shows an email with the Track in CRM button in Microsoft Outlook. When sending an email or when opening an existing email, you have the option to select Track in CRM. This button also has the option to set a "regarding," which enables you to associate an email to more than just the sender and selected receivers. It lets you associate the email to other specific records in Microsoft Dynamics CRM.

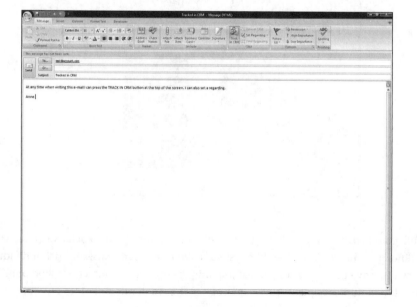

FIGURE 13.2
Outlook email.

Doing a Blast of Emails

In Hour 9, "Marketing Campaigns," you learned about marketing and the ability to do Quick Campaigns or Full Marketing Campaigns. If you are interested in tracking a blast of emails, you have three choices. You can do a Quick Campaign or Full Campaign with email campaign activities from Microsoft Dynamics CRM (options one and two), or you can send an email to multiple people (option three), either from Microsoft Dynamics CRM or from Outlook with Track in CRM selected.

If you choose to send a single email to multiple people, the single email will be captured in Microsoft Dynamics CRM and will be available for lookup on all valid contacts in Microsoft Dynamics CRM who received the email.

In Figure 13.3, one email record is associated to different contacts. This represents the sending of an email to multiple contacts. In Figure 13.4, three different email records are created, which are all exactly the same. This represents the sending of email from Bulk mail or Marketing Campaigns where a unique e-mail activity record is created for each and every person the e-mail is sent to.

FIGURE 13.3
Mail sent to multiple recipients.

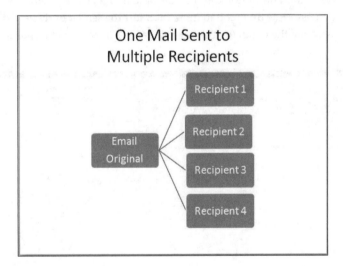

Bulk email creates and stores multiple copies of the same email, each associated with a different contact. This allows the system to capture the responses to each individual copy and save the responses against the unique e-mail and contact. Sending one email to multiple recipients saves one copy of the email and links it to multiple different people. If a recipient is not a contact within CRM, the contact's email address in the email activity record will be highlighted in red. All other email recipients who are contacts with valid and associated email addresses will appear in blue in the email activity record (see Figure 13.5).

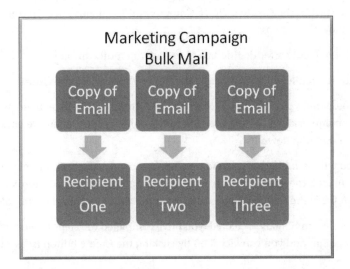

FIGURE 13.4
Bulk mail sent via marketing campaigns.

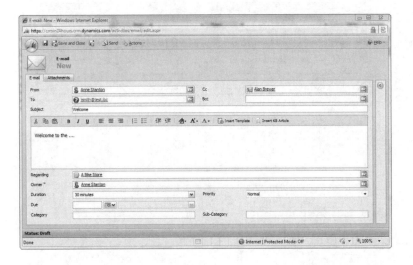

FIGURE 13.5
Email activity with an invalid contact email address.

To further clarify, in the first situation, if you delete one email, all other emails are retained. In the second situation, if you delete the email, it will not be available to any recipients.

Creating and Sending Bulk Mail from Quick Campaign

If you decide to do a bulk email from Quick Campaign, you have two choices. The first is to use Microsoft Dynamics CRM to create the email message that will be sent. Figure 13.6 is what the Create a Quick Campaign Wizard looks like. To complete the process, follow these steps:

1. Select or create a Marketing List to send your email campaign.

2. Choose Create Quick Campaign and follow the Campaign Wizard.

3. Choose the type of item that Microsoft Dynamics CRM will generate when the campaign is kicked off. Figure 13.7 shows our example, where we chose Email from the drop down list.

4. Create the email as seen in Figure 13.8. You can use Rich Text to make the email look the way you want, and you can insert Microsoft Dynamics CRM data fields that will populate when you create and kick off the campaign.

5. After the email body is created, you have completed the steps to prepare the campaign, and you can kick it off by clicking the Create button (see Figure 13.9).

FIGURE 13.6
Quick Campaign Wizard.

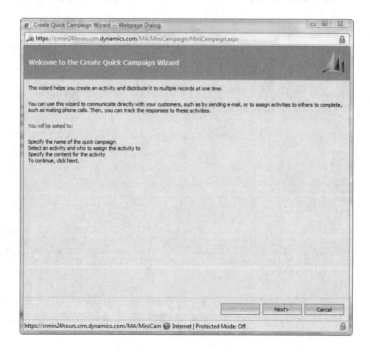

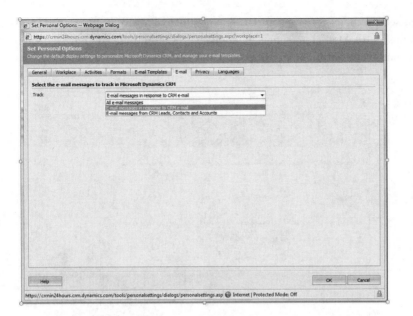

FIGURE 13.7
Select Email.

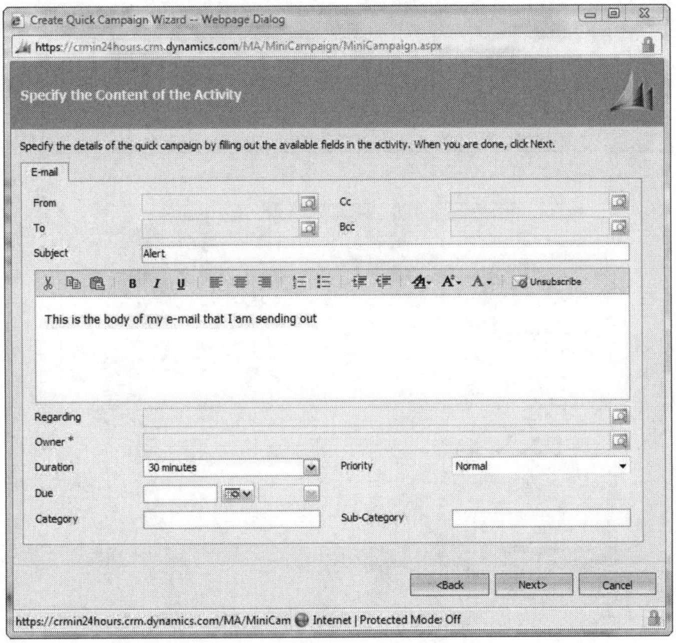

FIGURE 13.8
Create the email
body.

The second choice is to use Quick Campaign to do a Microsoft Word Mail Merge (see Figure 13.10). Mail Merge offers different choices than those you have when building the email from within Microsoft Dynamics CRM.

FIGURE 13.9
The Quick Campaign is prepared and ready.

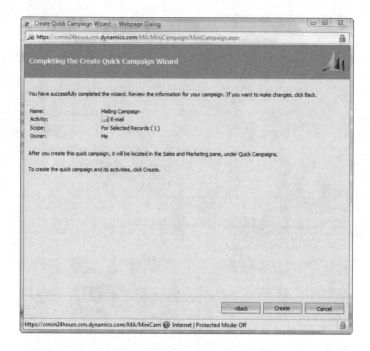

FIGURE 13.10
Mail Merge on List members.

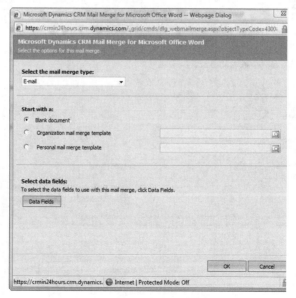

If you choose the drop down list to select the mail merge type, you have a number of choices as seen in Figure 13.11.

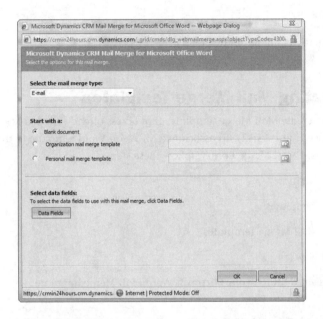

FIGURE 13.11
Select Mail Merge Type: Email.

You now want to proceed with creating a Quick Campaign mail merge of type e-mail.

1. Select either an organization email template or one of your own personal Mail Merge templates.

2. Select the data fields that you want to include.

3. Click OK. The Word Mail Merge template opens on your screen.

Creating Standard Email Templates

There are two different repositories of templates and options for creating email. These included an individual email template from your personal templates or an organizational template from the company templates. To create some standard organizational email templates that can be used by everyone on your team, you can do so in Microsoft Dynamics CRM by following these steps:

1. Select Settings.

2. Select Templates.

3. Select Email Templates.

4. Select New.

5. Choose Global.

6. Create the email template details.

Associating Mail Merge Templates

You can also create Mail Merge templates that access already created Microsoft Word templates (see Figure 13.12). To associate a Microsoft Word template to the Microsoft Dynamics CRM Mail Merge library, follow these steps:

1. Select Settings.

2. Select Templates.

3. Select Mail Merge Templates.

4. Select New.

5. Browse and attach your Microsoft Word Mail Merge template.

FIGURE 13.12
Associating Mail Merge templates.

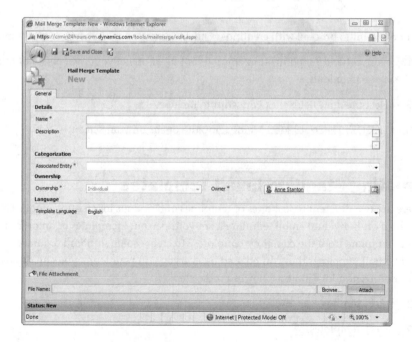

Canned Spam Act Compliance

As you learned in Hour 7, "The Account in More Detail," and Hour 12, you can mark individual accounts or contacts to prevent the sending of email.

You can also send bulk emails and track the responses from those emails, as you learned in Hour 9.

To further understand the Federal Trade Commission (FTC) Canned Spam Act and to ensure that your emails are in compliance with this Act, check the complete details at www.ftc.gov/bcp/conline/edcams/spam/.

Now that you have learned the ins and outs of emailing from Microsoft Dynamics CRM, you might want more, particularly as it relates to advanced marketing. If you want to do more, you will find third-party solutions to be ideal, and many plug right into Microsoft Dynamics CRM.

Microsoft Dynamics CRM Outlook Address Book

Microsoft Outlook has a concept called the Personal Address Book, which is what you see when you drill down on TO in Outlook. This is different than Microsoft Outlook Contacts. Microsoft Dynamics CRM offers a complementary personal Outlook address book with Microsoft Dynamics CRM data for use when choosing the "To" field when sending messages from Outlook. The Microsoft Dynamics CRM address book includes accounts, contacts, facilities/equipment, leads, queues, and users.

The Outlook address book is saved on the local drive of the Outlook user. If local data is of concern from a security perspective, you might want to discuss this external data with your Microsoft Dynamics CRM partner or you technology advisor.

Configuring Email Based on Your Preferences

Some configuration settings are unique to every user of Microsoft Dynamics CRM. One of these configuration options is the choice of how your Outlook address book is handled. Figure 13.13 displays the options.

These options are selected from the left navigation pane. Just look for the highlighted menu item called Personalize Workplace, and within that option, select the Address Book tab.

FIGURE 13.13
Email choices.

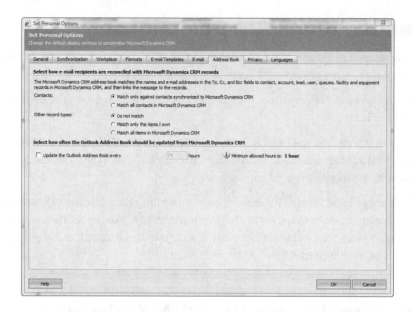

There is also an e-mail tab, which we showed in Figure 13.7. The tracking of email is worth thinking hard about as there are advantages and disadvantages to all email tracking options. For instance, consider the option to automatically track all emails. The benefit: The most robust capture of corporate intelligence is controlled by the system, eliminating human choice and error. The disadvantage: Personal email and email staff does not want tracked could be captured, tracked in Microsoft Dynamics CRM and seen by other Microsoft Dynamics CRM team members.

Workshop

A small medical practice called Just in Time Advice has just installed Microsoft Dynamics CRM. Just in Time Advice provides answers to common medical questions via the Internet and telephone. Questions that cannot be answered are referred to a local physicians network. Justin Brown is the CEO of Just in Time Advice. Justin wants to expand the number of physicians in Just in Time Advice's physicians network. Justin starts his efforts by using email to reach out to his connections from various previous positions. He reviews his contacts and selects 30 different people. He writes a personal email to each contact. The mail is written and then saved in Microsoft Dynamics CRM for future reference. The email is also set with a "regarding," which is the medical practice that exists in his database as Accounts that each physician is associated with.

Justin also asks his marketing coordinator, Mary Mill, to send out a bulk email to all contacts announcing a new e-newsletter. Mary uses a Quick Campaign to send this announcement.

Q&A

Q. *We send a lot of email. Does Microsoft Dynamics CRM track who has requested not to be contacted?*

A. Yes. Each contact can be optionally marked as *Do Not Send* or can be further refined and limited to *Do Not Send Bulk Email*.

Q. *Can we track the responses to emails that have been sent?*

A. Yes. You have numerous ways to capture responses to emails.

Q. *Some people at our company want all of their emails tracked and others want only selected emails tracked. Is this difference of choice an option?*

A. Yes. Tracking email is configured at the user level.

Quiz

1. What is one advantage to tracking email in Microsoft Dynamics CRM?

2. What are the three choices for tracking email responses?

3. When you send an email from Outlook and cc five contacts and you track it in CRM, how many copies of the email are saved in CRM?

4. What is one reason why you would not want to use the Microsoft Dynamics CRM Outlook address book?

5. What are Mary's choices when creating her announcement about the new e-newsletter?

Answers

1. Tracking email in Microsoft Dynamics CRM allows you to be more organized by association of e-mail to accounts and contacts.

2. Track all incoming Outlook email in Microsoft Dynamics CRM, Track only incoming email that was sent in response to an email originally sent from Microsoft Dynamics CRM, Track only email related to your accounts, contacts, or leads.

3. One copy of the email is saved in CRM.

4. There is a higher security risk when data is stored locally.

5. Mary can create an email activity and send it to multiple people or she can use the Quick Campaign feature of Microsoft Dynamics CRM to send a bulk mailing.

Exercise

Create Mary Mill's e-newsletter announcement email. To get started, set up a Marketing List for all active contacts. After the list is created, follow all the steps for creating a Quick Campaign using the Quick Campaign Wizard. Get creative when it comes to what you want to say in the email and insert some of the Microsoft Dynamics CRM fields. You can also insert a Microsoft Dynamics CRM email template.

HOUR 14

Word Mail Merge

What You'll Learn in This Hour:

- ► Creating and Managing Mail-Merge Templates
- ► Sending a Letter Created From a Template to a Lead
- ► Merging Contact Data into a Letter
- ► Merging Microsoft Dynamics CRM Data into a Microsoft Word Document

The ability to merge data from Microsoft Dynamics CRM into familiar tools, such as Microsoft Word, is a big plus for business professionals. This hour explores a topic that many business professionals struggled with before finding Microsoft Dynamics CRM. Workers often spent hours designing or creating business letters or complex Word documents each time their data changed or a new slightly different need arose. Using data stored in Microsoft Dynamics CRM and templates reduces the redundancy of always creating something new.

Microsoft Dynamics CRM can "work with what you have," by allowing much of the data from Microsoft Dynamics CRM to be merged into a template or different templates that then can be used to quickly create finished Microsoft Word documents.

Let's now look at the available templates and familiarize ourselves with our options.

Mail Merge Templates

Various management templates are available within Microsoft Dynamics CRM. For instance, several templates relate to major business building blocks (entities) within the software (quotes, letters, marketing events, and leads, to name just a few).

Figure 14.1 shows the gateway to templates, and Figure 14.2 shows a list of the templates that come with the system.

FIGURE 14.1
Settings, Templates.

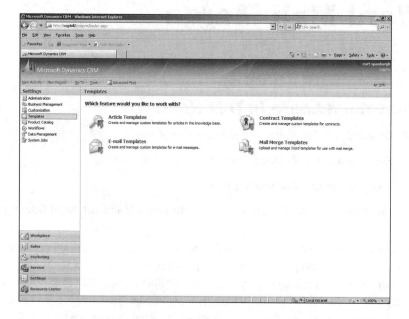

FIGURE 14.2
Default active mail merge templates.

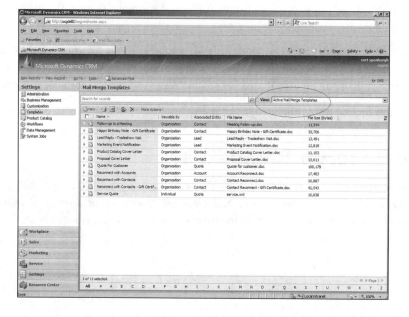

To reach templates, just follow these steps:

1. Choose Settings.

2. Choose Templates.

3. Choose Mail Merge Templates.

These templates were designed for both new and experienced users, and the list can be expanded as you get more comfortable with the application. In Figure 14.2, by default, the Word templates have the .doc extension (representing the Microsoft Word 2003 format). This extension gives the templates the most versatility for working with all versions of Word and backward compatibility with Microsoft Word 2003. It also allows them to work with Microsoft Word 2007.

The default system view when you select Templates is a list of All Active mail merge templates, which also includes any customized templates. Customized templates do not default to .doc. In Figure 14.2, you can see that the customized template filename differs from the default templates that come with the package. Customized templates use the current Microsoft Office XML format when they are created. There are two reasons for this. The first is that the Extensible Markup Language (XML) format is a new standard that is compatible with many other applications. The second is that the XML format is nonproprietary.

Other views, including the following, are also available to see all or a subset of available templates from this area:

▶ Active Mail Merge Templates

▶ All Mail Merge Templates

▶ Inactive Mail Merge Templates

▶ My Active Mail Merge Templates

All templates that you create and that are active are listed in the My Active Mail Merge Templates view (see Figure 14.3).

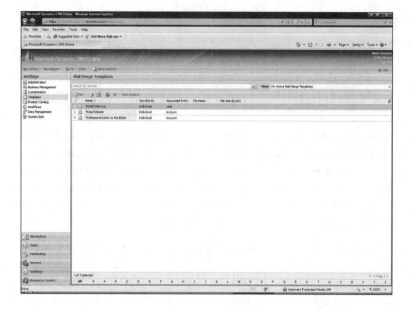

Creating a Template Using an Existing Word Template

To add an existing Microsoft Word XML template to Microsoft Dynamics CRM, choose New from the menu bar. Figure 14.4 shows what you will see. Basically, you take a standard Microsoft Word 2007 template in XML format and save this into Microsoft Dynamics CRM as a new Microsoft Dynamics CRM mail merge template.

Give your template a name that will make it easy to find and descriptive enough that others with whom you share it will readily know what it was designed for.

We are going to create a template that enables us to easily write business casual letters. We'll name it Business Casual Letter Template. Let's also associate this template with the Contact entity because it is meant for a specific contact.

Then, we will associate the Word XML template file created earlier to the template. Figure 14.5 shows the results of what we've done so far.

After you complete these steps, you can further edit the original XML file by taking Microsoft Dynamics CRM data references and inserting them into the Microsoft Word XML template by using the Data Fields button on the template screen.

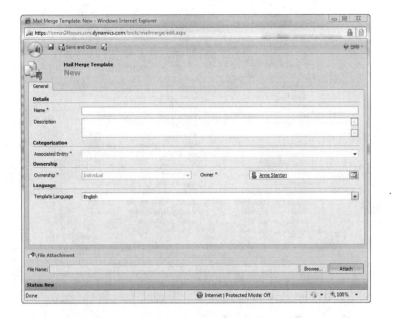

FIGURE 14.4
Creating a new mail merge template.

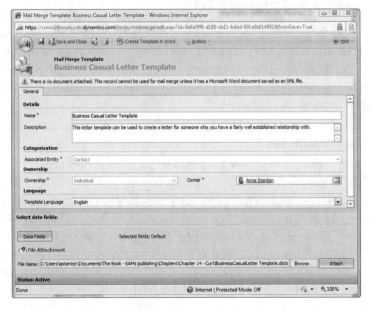

FIGURE 14.5
Mail merge template populated with answers.

After pressing the Data Fields button, a list of all available contact data fields (attributes) will display (see Figure 14.6).

By checking the check box next to each attribute, choose the extra data fields that suit your modifications. When you have done so, choose Save.

FIGURE 14.6
Available data
fields.

Managing Templates

Templates can be individual, shared, or available for everyone in the organization. Let's open up an existing template and look at some of our options for sharing and managing it. When you create a template, you are the owner of it by default. The new template is individual, available under My Active views, and not seen by others within the company.

Did you Know?

> **Deleting Templates**
> You can also delete or deactivate templates if they are no longer of use.

What if we create a template that everyone in the office will benefit from? You have the option to make this new template available to your entire organization. In addition, you can give even more granularity by selecting to assign the template to only one other Microsoft Dynamics CRM user in your organization. You also have the option to "share" the template with a team or list of users. Figure 14.7 shows the Assign Template option.

As shown in Figure 14.8, you can assign a template to a specific organization. The figure shows your options when you click the Assign button.

Now that you know how to associate an existing XML file so that it becomes a Microsoft Dynamics CRM mail merge template, let's look at the internal data fields of a specific template.

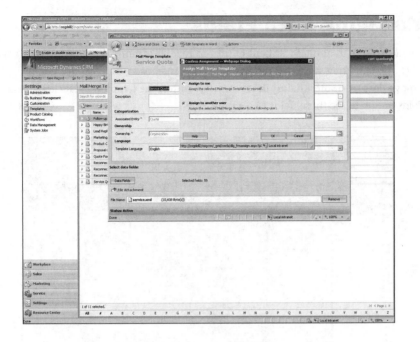

FIGURE 14.7
Assign a template.

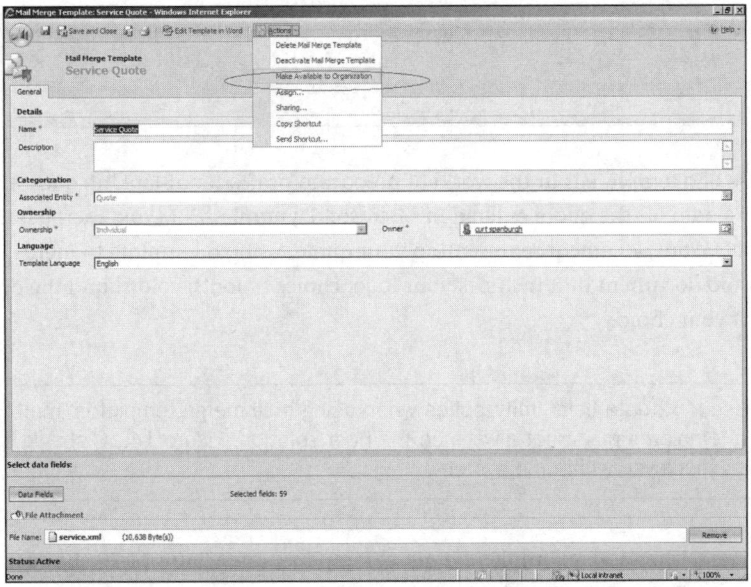

FIGURE 14.8
Assigning a template to an organization.

Managing Data Fields

Each Microsoft Dynamics CRM entity (record type) has many data attributes (fields). The basic templates have default attributes (fields) chosen, but you can add or remove data attributes (fields) that you want within the template. Just click the Data Fields option to see those fields (see Figure 14.9).

FIGURE 14.9
Data fields.

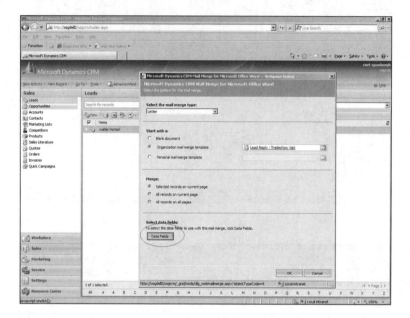

One use of a template is in the world of preparing professional-looking quotes. You can take data off the quote entered in Microsoft Dynamics CRM and merge it into a Microsoft Word document representing your quote, using a template to merge into a final word document that includes your logo, choice of fonts, colors, and the data fields of your choice.

Because a 62 data field limit applies when using mail merge templates, mail merge templates might not always be the best solution. Figure 14.10 shows the warning displayed within the system.

Figure 14.11 shows an example of a quote template, and Figure 14.12 shows the resulting mail merged quote. In the quote template, notice that you have a lot of commands and codes that look messy and can be fairly bewildering. These are Microsoft Word macro system codes that are used when you do the final merge.

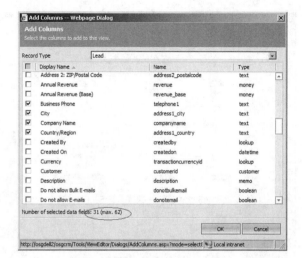

FIGURE 14.10
Note the 62-field maximum for customized templates.

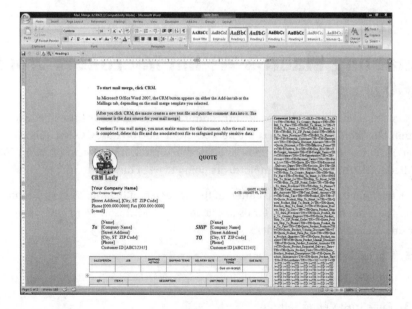

FIGURE 14.11
Quote template.

To use the template created, you actually go over to the Quote feature under Sales, Quotes. From the top of Creating a Quote, click the Word icon next to the words *Print Quote for Customer*.

After you get the hang of it, you can create numerous different quote templates in a variety of formats with a myriad of data fields. You can then share these quote formats with individual users or teams or change the value in Ownership to Organization and increase everyone's choices.

FIGURE 14.12
Quote.

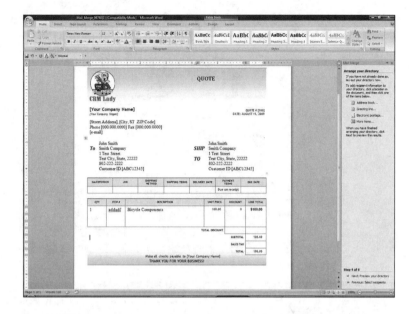

Enabling Macros Within Microsoft Word 2007

In some network environments, security administrators disable the use of macros within Microsoft Word to protect the network from macro viruses. Often, this is overkill, but we need to look at how to allow macros to work in Microsoft Word 2007 if Microsoft Dynamics CRM templates are going to be of any use to us.

Click the large Microsoft Office button at the upper left of the Microsoft Word interface. There are many controls for us to customize our Microsoft Word environment. We are interested in Trust Center:

1. Choose Word Options.

2. Click Trust Center.

3. Click Trust Center Settings.

4. Click Macro Settings.

We are interested in two settings:

▶ Disable All Macros Except Digitally Signed Macros

▶ Enable All Macros (not recommended, potentially dangerous code can run)

You security administrator will be happy to learn that the Microsoft Dynamics CRM macro is a signed macro. Therefore, you can choose the first option; you don't have to "discuss" the second option with the rest of the IT staff. Figure 14.13 shows the selection screen within Microsoft Word.

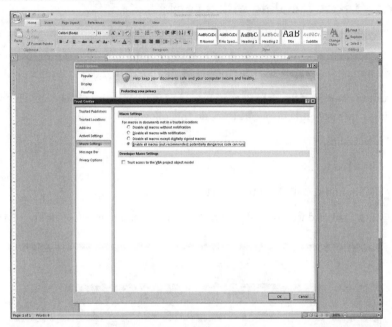

FIGURE 14.13
Enabling macros.

In addition, when you first work with a template, the macros are displayed and are technical looking. You need to get to the CRM button, as displayed at the top of the Word document. Figure 14.14 shows add-ins where you can find the CRM button to perform the merge.

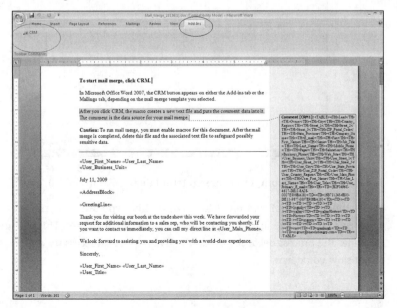

FIGURE 14.14
The CRM macro is digitally signed. You can find it under Add-Ins.

▼   **Try it Yourself**

Using a Letter Template with a Lead

Let's test run a merge using a template.

There is a lead in Microsoft Dynamics CRM whose name is Walter Horton. We want to send him a follow-up letter. (He stopped by our booth at a recent trade show.)

We want to use one of the default templates for leads to do this. To choose a default template and apply it to a specific lead, do the following:

1. Select Sales.

2. Select Leads.

3. Highlight a specific lead (Walter Horton).

4. Click the Word icon on the toolbar to start the mail merge (see Figure 14.15).

FIGURE 14.15
The Word icon starts the mail merge.

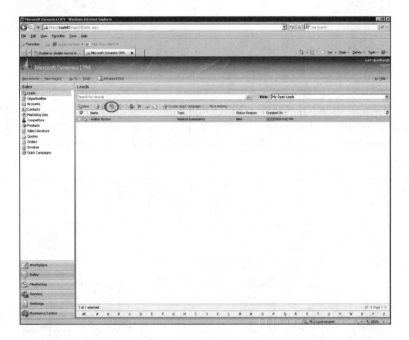

You then receive a prompt to choose a template (see Figure 14.16).

Notice that Microsoft Dynamics CRM is aware that you are using the Lead entity and so only the lists of templates for leads are displayed. This feature expedites the process because you don't have a lot of unnecessary options that might slow you down.

▼

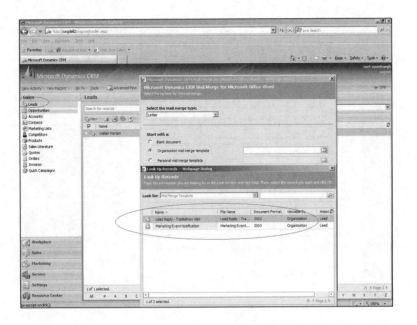

FIGURE 14.16
Select a template.

5. Choose a template from the list and click OK (see Figure 14.17).

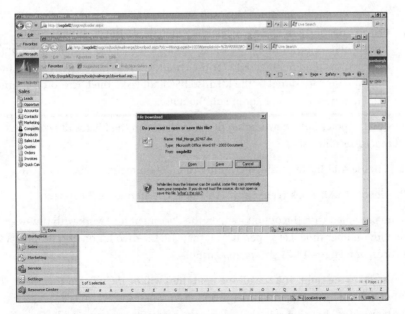

FIGURE 14.17
Starting mail merge.

When you start the merge, Microsoft Word opens, but it may look different from what you're used to (see Figure 14.18).

FIGURE 14.18
Opening
Microsoft Word
for a merge.

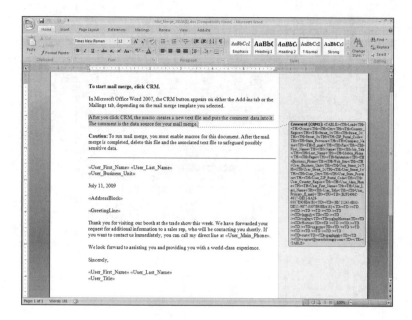

Here is what is happening: Microsoft Dynamics CRM is using a Microsoft Word macro to perform the merge. The data entered into the document can be understood as formatting from the template. Understand that the fields are referencing the data fields chosen for the template and, essentially, you are hooking into the data stored in the Microsoft SQL tables of the Microsoft Dynamics CRM databases. You can ignore all the noise.

Ignore all the potentially bewildering noise and just run the Microsoft Dynamics CRM macro, as follows:

1. Choose Add-Ins from the Microsoft Word Ribbon menu.

2. Choose CRM. The screens shown in Figures 14.19 and 14.20 appear.

You are presented with the option to open the document and work with it now or save it for another time. Let's open it. You then see the area for adding recipients to the document. Figure 14.21 shows an example.

If you scroll to the right, you see all the fields that will be included in the merge. The side bar offers many of the mail merge options in Microsoft Word. Let's preview the letter by making that choice in the lower-right area of the screen. The letter is displayed in Figure 14.22.

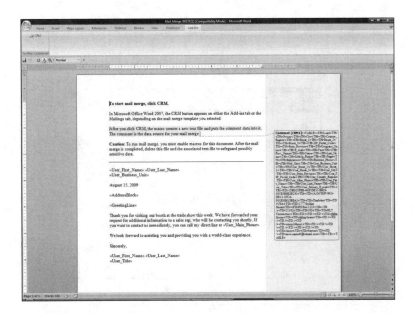

FIGURE 14.19
Mail merge document being created.

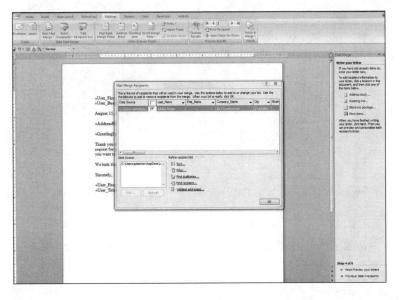

FIGURE 14.20
Mail merge document started.

Because this is the basic template, we might find this a bit lackluster for a business document. However, to spruce it up, you can always edit the document template to include a company logo and other text within the template itself or you can edit the document while in this process. Both options allow you flexibility.

Now, just choose the option to write the letter and you are done.

FIGURE 14.21
Adding recipients
to the
document.

FIGURE 14.21
Adding recipients
to the
document.

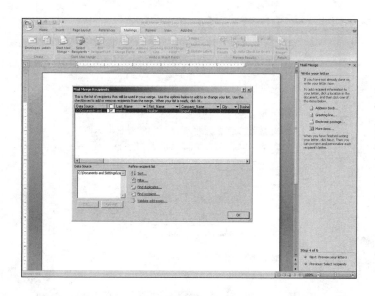

FIGURE 14.22
The letter.

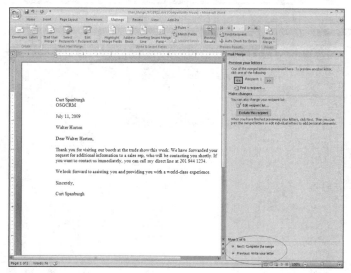

▼   **Try it Yourself**

Creating a Document with Merged Data from an Account

Now, let's work without a template to help clarify how Microsoft Dynamics CRM
works with Microsoft Word:

1. Select Sales.

▼

2. Select Accounts.

3. Highlight a specific account. (Figure 14.23 shows an example.)

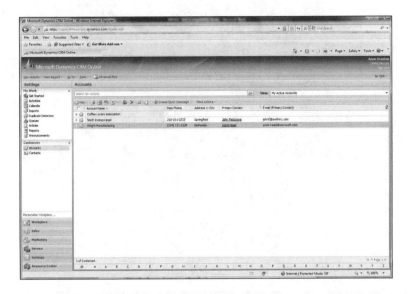

FIGURE 14.23
Creating a new document for an account with Microsoft Dynamics CRM data.

4. Choose the Microsoft Word icon from the menu bar.

You must now choose from a list of personal or organizational templates or create your document from a blank document.

5. Choose Blank Document (see Figure 14.24).

6. Click Data Fields and select the data fields you will use in your document.

7. Click OK.

8. Click Open to open the new document in Microsoft Word.

Figure 14.25 shows a blank document with the Microsoft Word macros enabled. You can now go below the line and add any number of data fields and various associated text or tables.

9. Type in any text that you want.

10. Choose Add-Ins.

11. Click the CRM button on the Microsoft Word Ribbon menu.

12. Select Mailings from the Microsoft Word Ribbon menu.

13. You can now use the Insert Merge Field to insert any of the Microsoft Dynamics CRM data fields that are of interest to your document (see Figure 14.25).

FIGURE 14.24
Creating a new
document for an
account.

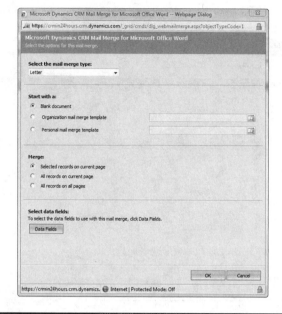

FIGURE 14.25
Insert mail
merge.

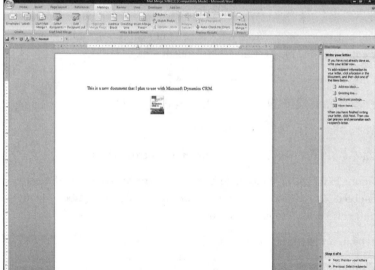

Match Fields

You can also use the Match Fields option to match Microsoft Word merge fields to
Microsoft Dynamics CRM merge fields. If you do this, you can use the Microsoft
Word wizards.

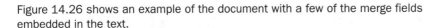

Figure 14.26 shows an example of the document with a few of the merge fields embedded in the text.

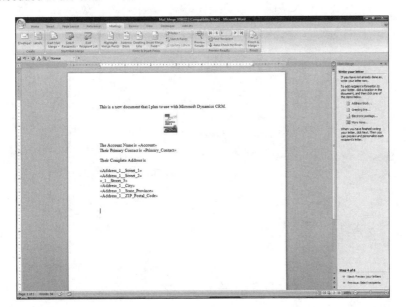

FIGURE 14.26
Word document with merge fields.

Try it Yourself

Using the Reconnect with Contact: Gift Certificate Template

As a final example, let's run through using one of the standard templates for a specific contact:

1. Choose Sales.

2. Choose Contact.

3. Highlight a specific contact.

4. Click the Microsoft Word button in the menu bar.

5. Choose Organizational Mail Merge Template.

6. Choose the last one in the list: Reconnect with Contacts: Gift Certificate.

7. Choose Selected Records on Current Page (see Figure 14.27).

FIGURE 14.27
Merging into an
existing tem-
plate.

8. Click OK.

9. The recipients are displayed, as shown in Figure 14.28. Click OK.

FIGURE 14.28
Merging into let-
ter.

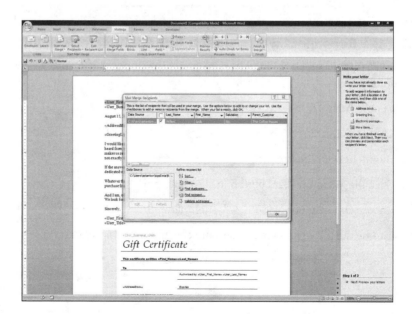

10. From the Mailings Menu option, choose Finish and Merge (see Figure 14.29).

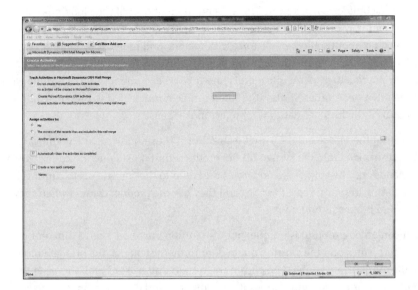

FIGURE 14.29
Finish and
Merge.

11. Choose Edit the Individual Document. The document then appears on the screen, and you can print, edit, or change it (see Figure 14.30).

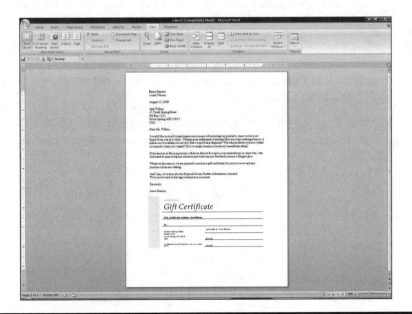

FIGURE 14.30
The end result.

Workshop

The bridge builder's architectural firm spends a great deal of time looking at potential sites for new bridges. When it looks at these sites, the employees gather a ton of unique data about soil types, distance, risk factors, and more. They enter all this data against an account that represents the site. The firm then uses Microsoft Dynamics CRM to put together all the site details into a Word document that is sharable with all the interested parties. It also uses Microsoft Dynamics CRM to prepare complex proposals if the firm decides that a project makes sense.

Given that the bridge builder's architectural firm is using Microsoft Dynamics CRM, it has also added into the system all the products that it uses and the contractors that it depends on. The employees add notes and data to the contractors to capture what each contracting firm specializes in, and they use the product catalog when they are preparing proposals and quotes.

Each generated proposal is unique, but also mostly based on 1 of 15 different proposal templates and the existing quote data in the system. So, the bridge builder's architectural firm uses the data within the system and a Word mail merge to the appropriate organizational proposal template to complete any proposal needs.

Q&A

Q. We have strict rules about Word macros at our company. Can the mail merge feature be used without enabling macros?

A. No. The Microsoft Word macros need to be enabled for mail merge to work.

Q. Does Microsoft Word 2007 make much of a difference? We are currently on Microsoft Word 2003.

A. Microsoft Word 2007 is the first version of Word to support the standard XML format. This format offers more flexibility and options with mail merging.

Quiz

1. Is there a way to see all mail merge templates in the system?

2. Does a default template exist for creating a letter?

3. Can I take my own Microsoft Word XML file and make it a Microsoft Dynamics CRM mail merge template?

4. What does the bridge builder's architectural firm need to do to set up its proposal templates?

Answers

1. Yes. You can use the All Active Templates view from Settings, Templates, Mail Merge Templates.

2. Yes. There are a couple of different default letter templates.

3. Yes. You can associate any Microsoft Word XML document with Microsoft Dynamics CRM.

4. The firm needs to save its existing proposal templates into XML format and then associate these to Microsoft Dynamics CRM.

Exercise

On your own system, set up a number of new mail merge templates. For instance, you can create a template for each of the major building blocks within the system, such as accounts, leads, contacts, opportunities, and quotes.

Now that you created some templates, use one or two of your new templates to see how they work.

Be patient, but be ready to be dazzled.

HOUR 15

Outlook Integration

What You'll Learn in This Hour:

▶ Synchronizing Data

▶ The Synchronizing Architecture

▶ Integration with Outlook Tasks, Calendar, and Contacts

▶ Mobility

▶ Troubleshooting Microsoft Outlook

Microsoft Dynamics CRM integrates to Microsoft Outlook in a number of different places. There are numerous choices when it comes to Outlook integration. In previous hours, we touched on a few of these. This hour examines the options that relate to data within the world of Outlook, data within the world of Microsoft Dynamics CRM, and data on your mobile device synchronizing to Outlook.

Microsoft Dynamics CRM for Outlook Options

Microsoft Dynamics CRM has many configuration settings, but only one set applies uniquely to each person. These unique settings are found under Set Personal Options, and Figure 15.1 shows the General tab within Set Personal Options.

To reach Set Personal Options within Microsoft Dynamics CRM, open Microsoft Outlook after the Microsoft Dynamics CRM Outlook client is installed. You will see a CRM option in the new CRM menu bar. From within this drop-down menu, choose Options.

FIGURE 15.1
Personal
options.

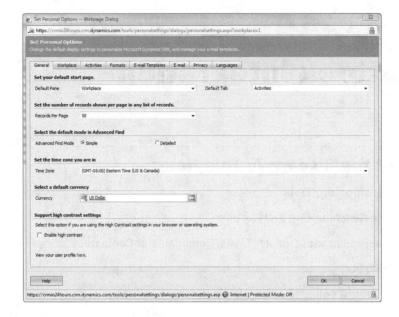

The Synchronizing Architecture

Within the world of Microsoft Dynamics CRM, you have a number of choices when it comes to where data is stored and what is shared between various potential repositories, including Microsoft Exchange, Microsoft Outlook, the centralized corporate Microsoft Dynamics CRM databases, and the local offline Microsoft Dynamics CRM Outlook client. Figure 15.2 shows a diagram indicating where data could possibly be located as it relates to the Microsoft Dynamics CRM Outlook Client.

Notice the word *possibly*. There is significant configuration choice with regard to this subject, as discussed in Hour 4, "Infrastructure Choices."

From a training perspective, all data is stored in the central Microsoft Dynamics CRM database on the server, with some temporary exceptions. Sometimes, users want access to data when they are not connected to the Internet, when they are out and about. Therefore, a subset of the master data needs to occasionally go offline (optional). In addition, in some companies, users are given control over which of their Outlook data is stored in the centralized database, so some data from Outlook is in both Outlook and Microsoft Dynamics CRM. There are advantages and disadvantages to each choice.

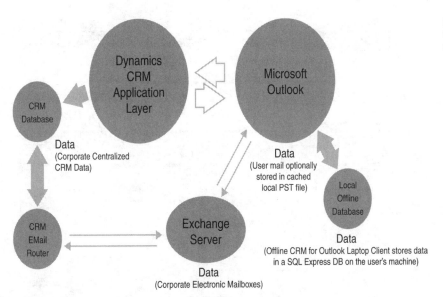

FIGURE 15.2
Where data is stored.

Synchronizing Data

When there is data in Outlook (such as Outlook Tasks, Outlook Appointments, and Outlook Contacts) that is also in Microsoft Dynamics CRM, there is reason to have these related, but you might not want to synchronize all the different pieces of data. The synchronization choices are defined under Set Personal Options, on the Synchronization tab, as shown in Figure 15.3.

Tasks

Microsoft Outlook tasks can be mapped and synchronized to Microsoft Dynamics CRM Task activities. If these two items are mapped, actions against one impact the other. This synchronization is so seamless that when you complete a task in Microsoft Outlook (by checking the Complete box), the activity in Microsoft Dynamics CRM is completed. In addition, if you add an activity in Microsoft Dynamics CRM of type Task, the task will appear on the Microsoft Outlook task list. If you follow the steps to close an activity of type Task in Microsoft Dynamics CRM, the task will be completed in Microsoft Outlook. Figures 15.4 and 15.5 show the tasks as viewed from Microsoft Outlook and Microsoft Dynamics CRM, respectively.

FIGURE 15.3
Set Personal
Options, Syn-
chronization tab.

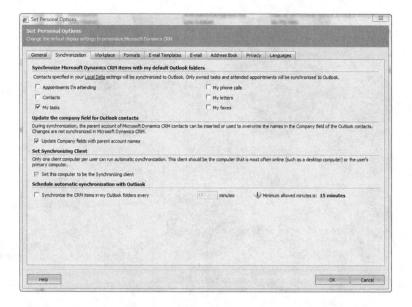

FIGURE 15.4
My Tasks
selected for syn-
chronizing.

To complete a task in Outlook, do the following:

1. Select Tasks.

2. Choose the task you want to Complete.

3. Click the check box to the left of the task.

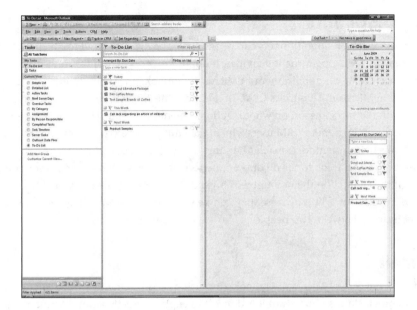

FIGURE 15.5
Microsoft
Dynamics CRM
activities of type
Task.

To complete an activity in Microsoft Dynamics CRM, follow these steps:

1. From My Work, select Activities.

2. Open a specific activity (double-click).

3. Select Actions from the top menu.

4. Select Close.

5. Choose Status (defaults to Completed).

6. Close the Window.

Watch Out!

Tasks

Only Task activities and, optionally, Phone Call activities from Microsoft Dynamics CRM synchronize with Task activities in Microsoft Outlook. Appointments and other types of activities do not synchronize to tasks, because they are related to other areas of Outlook.

Appointments

Microsoft Outlook appointments can be mapped and synchronized to Microsoft Dynamics CRM Appointment activities. If appointment synchronization is turned on, when you create an appointment in Microsoft Outlook, an Appointment activity is created in Microsoft Dynamics CRM. In addition, the Appointment activity is associated with the same person on whose Outlook calendar it originated. Thus, five different Microsoft Dynamics CRM users who are creating different appointments in their Outlook environment for possibly the same account have one place, Microsoft Dynamics CRM, to go to see all appointments associated with a specific account (but only if the contact on the account was invited to the appointment). Appointments have a special situation because they can be synchronized only if they relate to an appointment between two people.

Email

Email is the core of Microsoft Outlook. Capturing email from Outlook to Microsoft Dynamics CRM is so huge that it is difficult to explain exactly what a turning point this can be for some companies.

The communications between the teams and the clients or the teams and the prospects contain a wealth of insight into a company's relationships. This information is also a private conversation between two people. Needless to say, making these private communications more public may also be full of potential conflicts. Microsoft Dynamics CRM offers a couple of different choices for tracking email. From an Outlook perspective, you can synchronize all emails or you can choose which emails that you are composing or that you have received that you want to manually push from Microsoft Outlook to Microsoft Dynamics CRM. When you synchronize email, the email shows up in Microsoft Dynamics CRM as an Email activity. The email is associated with the sender and the receiver within the database. If either of these people is not a contact in Microsoft Dynamics CRM, the e-mail address will appear red in CRM, which indicates that it needs resolution. Figure 15.6 shows an email address in red.

Email also shows up with a red question mark in the view of all emails in Microsoft Dynamics CRM. Figure 15.7 shows an example.

The red email address can be resolved by doing the following:

1. Double-click the specific email address highlighted in red.

2. You immediately see the Resolve contact window (see Figure 15.8).

3. Resolve the email address by associating it to either an existing contact or creating a new contact and associate.

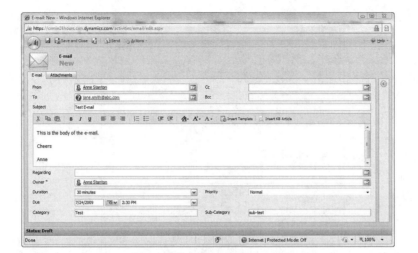

FIGURE 15.6
Microsoft
Dynamics CRM
unassociated
email address.

FIGURE 15.7
View of My Draft
Emails.

Deleting Outlook Business Rule

You can delete email in Outlook and it will not be deleted automatically in
Microsoft Dynamics CRM. This allows you to file and store email associated with
accounts and contacts and still keep your Outlook inbox small, clean, and neat.

Did you Know?

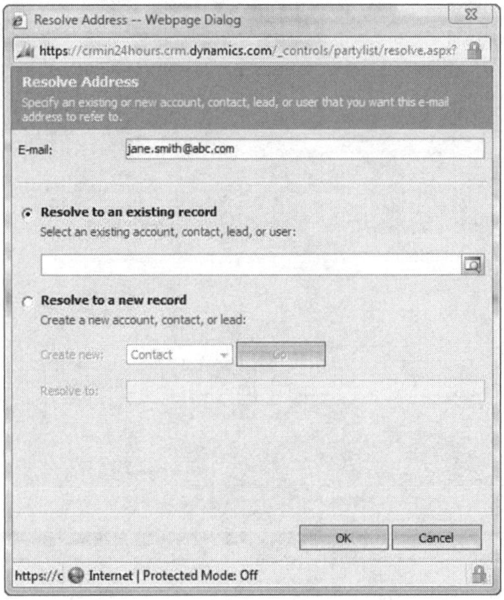

FIGURE 15.8
Resolving email:
Click the email
address.

Contacts

Contacts can be a tough subject, because many people actually use the Microsoft Outlook Contacts in their current daily business processes and, as such, they must *change* their habits and business process to take into consideration the new options with Microsoft Dynamics CRM. If you take Microsoft Dynamics CRM out of the picture and just think about Microsoft Outlook and contacts, Microsoft Outlook has a contact system that is represented in two different ways. I start from this baseline before introducing how the Microsoft Dynamics CRM Outlook client changes the picture with more choices.

Figure 15.9 shows the Microsoft Outlook Contact template. Notice that you have some core basic information, including name, title, address, email, addresses, and notes.

Figure 15.10 shows the Microsoft Outlook Contacts Address Book. This is the list of contacts that you access when you select and click the *To* field in a new email.

In Microsoft Outlook, you have some duplication. If you also synchronize your Outlook contacts to your mobile device, you have three places where your contact names reside. Wow! And yet it works. What happens when we introduce the Microsoft Dynamics CRM Outlook client? Microsoft Dynamics CRM offers three additional choices:

▶ Direct access to Microsoft Dynamics CRM central database of contacts via a Contacts folder right from within Outlook

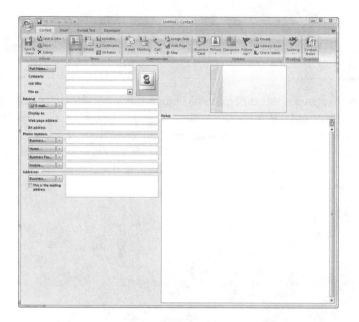

FIGURE 15.9
Microsoft Outlook Contact template.

FIGURE 15.10
Microsoft Outlook Address Book.

▶ A new Microsoft Dynamics CRM Outlook Address Book that complements the Microsoft Outlook Address Book and is available when you double-click the To field when sending a new mail message

▶ Synchronization and mapping between the Microsoft Outlook contacts and the Microsoft Dynamics CRM contacts

Synchronization

This synchronization is either all contacts in the main Outlook Contacts folder or individual selection of a specific contact.

Figure 15.11 expresses this concept that contacts can move from Microsoft Dynamics CRM to Outlook and then to a mobile device and back again. Understand that, in this example, the connection from Microsoft Outlook to the mobile device is specifically between Microsoft Outlook and the mobile device. Microsoft Dynamics CRM gets involved only because it is talking to Outlook. In the next section, we talk more about other mobile options.

FIGURE 15.11
Contacts synchronized.

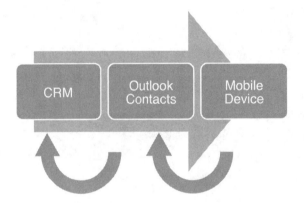

A key concept is that Microsoft Dynamics CRM synchronizes with the main Microsoft Outlook Contacts folder. If you create a second folder called Personal, you can move your personal contacts to this second folder. This prevents personal contacts from synchronizing to Microsoft Dynamics CRM. Be warned that it might also prevent synchronization to a mobile device.

Notice how, in Figure 15.12, there are three Outlook contact folders in addition to the main Contacts folder.

Another paradigm shift is that many companies that use Microsoft Dynamics CRM choose not to use Microsoft Outlook contacts. They get a piece of software for their mobile device, they use the Microsoft Dynamics CRM MobileExpress client, or they just stop using the Microsoft Outlook Contacts feature altogether. This is definitely a choice.

FIGURE 15.12
Contact folders
in Outlook.

Mobility

Microsoft Dynamics CRM lends itself to mobility, and Microsoft has recently released MobileExpress, as mentioned in earlier hours. One concept with MobileExpress or any of the mobility options for Microsoft Dynamics CRM is that if you can get to the web, you can access your Microsoft Dynamics CRM data in a form factor that fits on a phone. This type of option totally eliminates the complexity of moving or copying or synchronizing data between three places (the server, the laptop, and the phone). Data is stored on the secure corporate network, and access to that data is either via the Microsoft Dynamics CRM Outlook client, the Microsoft Dynamics CRM web interface via Internet Explorer, or a mobile client running on either a BlackBerry or Windows Mobile device.

The second concept in the world of mobility is to have a subset of the data copied to the mobile device and then resynchronized on regular intervals. This allows access to this data even when the Internet is unavailable, such as when you are on an airplane. A number of third-party companies offer this more complex offline capability, particularly with enterprise security, such as TenDigits (www.tendigits.com).

Keep in mind that Microsoft Dynamics CRM uses an authentication model that might not be compatible with the operating system or the browser that you use on your phone. In such cases, software specifically designed for Microsoft Dynamics CRM is usually required.

What to Watch Out For: Troubleshooting Microsoft Outlook

Given the complexity of moving data around between multiple places and the handling of this data (contacts) by many different applications, such as Microsoft Outlook and mobile synchronization, there are a few key things to watch out for.

If we also consider that Microsoft Outlook can be modified by many different applications and plug-ins, such as toolbars and other products, we have a number of variables. If you experience any difficulty with the Microsoft Dynamics CRM Outlook client, you might start with the Microsoft Dynamics CRM Development team blog to resolve some issues. The specific posts can be found at http://blogs.msdn.com/crm/archive/2009/05/29/troubleshooting-the-microsoft-dynamics-crm-client-for-outlook.aspx.

Microsoft has also upgraded and developed a number of tools to complement the Microsoft Dynamics CRM Outlook client software and help reduce and check for potential issues in a variety of environments. The tools are part of the installation of the Microsoft Dynamics CRM Outlook client v4.0, and they have options and preferences for troubleshooting.

You can get the tool at http://blogs.msdn.com/crm/archive/2008/01/22/introducing-mscrm-client-diagnostics.aspx.

Some of the areas that the Microsoft Outlook CRM tool helps to diagnosis are documented by Inetium on its helpful blog at http://blogs.inetium.com/blogs/tedh/archive/2008/12/22/microsoft-dynamics-crm-4-0-client-for-outlook-tidbits-and-asides.aspx.

These include the following:

▶ Address Book synchronization

▶ Outlook synchronization

And if you are using Outlook to send all CRM email,

▶ Send email

▶ Track email

▶ Automatic email tagging

▶ Offline data updates (for laptop/offline client)

You can also delete temporary Microsoft Dynamics CRM client files and create an output file for Microsoft. If you turn on client-side tracing, the files are located in the following areas:

- ▶ **On Vista:** C:\Users\username\AppData\Roaming\Microsoft\MSCRM\

- ▶ **On Windows XP:** C:\Documents and Settings\username\Application Data\Microsoft\MSCRM\

Other Resources

On troubleshooting the Microsoft Dynamics CRM Outlook client, The Power Objects team has a great blog post. It has expanded some of Microsoft's tips and added its own insight with supporting pictures (http://blog.powerobjects.com/2009/06/02/outlook-crm-client-troubleshooting-a-guide-for-the-rest-of-us/).

You might also find an eight-step guide to getting started with the Microsoft Dynamics CRM Outlook client interesting reading. To access this guide, go to the Microsoft Dynamics CRM Resource Center at http://rc.crm.dynamics.com/rc/regcont/en_us/live/articles/10stepstoOC.aspx.

Workshop

Jack Green is the CEO of an engineering company. His firm does a wide variety of sketches, drawings, inspections, and architecture for businesses all around his area. One of the goals that Jack has is to continually network at a variety of association meetings. He runs into numerous people whom he knows well, but occasionally, he finds himself talking with someone who he can't quite remember. Jack wants to be able to excuse himself and check his database of contacts and notes. To do this, Jack uses the mobile client for Microsoft Dynamics CRM. He can quickly search his contacts, and he has also set up a view to sort by a few key characteristics.

Jack also uses a combination of Microsoft Dynamics CRM and Microsoft SharePoint to organize and store the architectural drawings that are produced and their association to certain accounts. With enterprise search, he can quickly find any document needed without having to define account-specific folders.

Q&A

Q. *Outlook seems to take longer to load now that I have the Microsoft Dynamics CRM Outlook client installed. Why?*

A. If you are using a desktop machine, make sure that you have the Microsoft Dynamics CRM Outlook client for the workstation installed. Basically, the Microsoft Dynamics CRM Outlook client for the laptop needs to copy data continuously to a local database. You might also want to check your settings to ensure you are not downloading more than is needed.

Q. *I want to delete a bunch of contacts out of my Outlook folder. What happens in Microsoft Dynamics CRM when I do this to synchronized contacts?*

A. Contacts deleted in Outlook are not deleted in Microsoft Dynamics CRM. This also applies to email.

Q. *I have a limit on the total number of emails that I can keep in Outlook. Can I delete items from Outlook without deleting them from Microsoft Dynamics CRM?*

A. Yes. Any email that is synchronized with Microsoft Dynamics CRM can be deleted from Microsoft Outlook without impacting Microsoft Dynamics CRM.

Q. *I receive a number of attachments. What happens to my email attachments when I synchronize to Microsoft Dynamics CRM?*

A. Attachments can be stored with the email in Microsoft Dynamics CRM; however, they can accumulate and eat a lot of database space. Given this, larger Microsoft Dynamics CRM installations often have an alternative option for the storage of associated attachments, such as integration to SharePoint, which is a document library.

Quiz

1. What else can Jack use from his Microsoft Dynamics CRM system to help him remember details about different people he meets?

2. Mary wants to keep her personal contacts out of Microsoft Dynamics CRM and yet, she needs some of these key details at work. How can Mary keep her personal contacts separate if all contacts are synchronized?

3. Do you have to use the Microsoft Dynamics CRM Outlook client to access Microsoft Dynamics CRM?

4. Will Microsoft Dynamics CRM Phone Call activities synchronize with Microsoft Outlook Task activities?

5. Where do Outlook appointments synchronize?

Answers

1. Jack can use the Account feature of Microsoft Dynamics CRM to associate accounts with his contacts. He can then search by account or contacts.

2. Mary can create a new Outlook Contacts file called Personal. This personal file does not have to synchronize to Microsoft Dynamics CRM.

3. No. You do not need to use the Microsoft Dynamics CRM Outlook client.

4. Yes. Phone calls will synchronize with tasks if you choose to synchronize phone calls.

5. Outlook appointments synchronize with Microsoft Dynamics CRM Appointment activities. They do not show up in the Outlook Task list.

Exercise

Create a new Outlook folder of type Contacts. Move a couple of your contacts to this folder. What happens to these contacts? Can you associate these contacts to Microsoft Dynamics CRM? Now, try synchronizing a few email messages. What happens to email that has multiple recipients? Is this email available on each and every contact?

Workflow: Creating Simple Workflows

What You'll Learn in This Hour:

▶ What Is Workflow?

▶ Internal Alerts Based on Specific Criteria

▶ Using Workflow to Automate

This hour takes a closer look at the world of workflow and how workflow will help you automate simple processes. We touched on workflow a bit in earlier hours, specifically how it relates to the sales process. However, workflow can be used for much more. This hour is a primer and will help get you started working with the systems automatic creation features.

What Is Workflow?

Workflow is the automation of a process. The process automated is often associated with conditional statements, such as business rules that have multiple choices. Depending on the choice, an action can occur. For instance, if an email is received, then create an activity.

So, if a condition within a business rule is true and an action can occur, then workflow can empower the system to automatically do this action, such as create tasks, appointments, emails, or other activities. Workflow can also call small programs based on a set of conditions, and workflow can be designed to be extremely simple, such as identifying when an Account record is created. Workflow can also be designed to be quite complex.

You can have a personal workflow that streamlines your own tasks, or there may be workflows created that everyone in your organization uses so that processes are consistent.

Workflow can be about back-office processes or directly related and responsive to actions that a user might perform.

A few examples of workflow are as follows:

▶ When an opportunity is closed, send the sales manager an alert that indicates whether it was won or lost.

▶ When I enter a new lead, assign that lead to the appropriate territory manager.

▶ If a value is added to a specific attribute that is incorrect, send an email to the user to correct the value (or to their manager).

▶ If a client exceeds his credit limit, set that client's account to on hold.

▶ If an estimated close date has passed, send an alert to update or close the opportunity.

Key benefits of workflow include the following:

▶ Increasing efficiency

▶ Standardizing process

▶ Training new users on existing process

▶ Controlling well-established routine

▶ Improvement of existing process

▶ Audit trail

▶ Streamlining of steps

▶ Parallel processing to increase data throughput

▶ Increase in user adoption

▶ Improved internal communication and collaboration

The best way to learn about workflow within Microsoft Dynamics CRM is to set up a few.

Did you know?

> ### Shared Workflow Technology
> Microsoft Dynamics CRM uses the same Microsoft Windows Workflow Foundation that Microsoft SharePoint uses.

We will start with a few simple workflows. We then move to a slightly more complex workflow.

In Figure 16.1, we start the process by selecting Settings, Workflows.

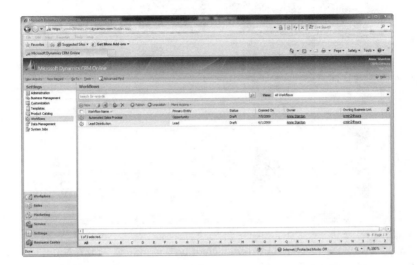

FIGURE 16.1
Settings, Work-
flow.

Access to Settings

If you do not have access to setting up workflows, talk with your Microsoft Dynamics CRM administrator to get your security role changed.

Watch Out!

Two workflows are listed, and we are looking at the common view window. Workflows can be unique to an individual, or they can be available to all users of the system.

Select New. Figure 16.2 shows the first screen you will see when setting up a new workflow. We are going to set up a workflow that sends an email alert when an appointment activity is created.

To create this new workflow, we need to choose a name and pick the correct entity (record type):

1. Enter **Appointment Alert Workflow**.

2. Choose Entity Appointment.

We are also going to create this workflow from scratch as opposed to using a predefined template. You can set up templates later in the process after you are using many different, yet perhaps closely similar, workflows.

FIGURE 16.2
Create a new
workflow.

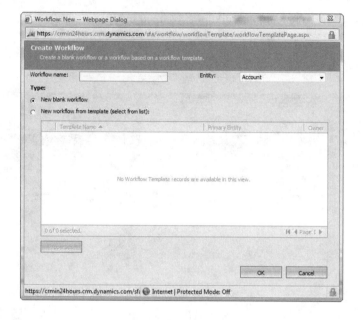

Figure 16.3 shows the second form when creating a workflow. At this point, we can indicate whether this is a workflow or a workflow template, and we need to choose the scope. In our example, we are going to create a personal workflow, so our scope is User. Our other choices include setting the access to this workflow to Business Unit, Child Business Unit, or Organization.

FIGURE 16.3
Defining work-
flow properties.

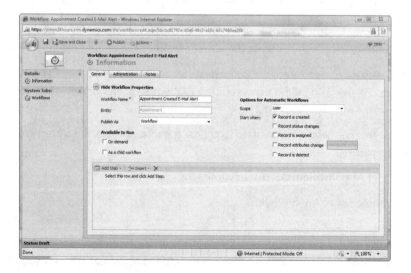

We indicated that we are going to create an alert when an appointment is created and, therefore, we can leave the default Start When (that is, leave it to start when Record is Created). The next step is to add the condition and the step. Figure 16.4 shows the condition statement.

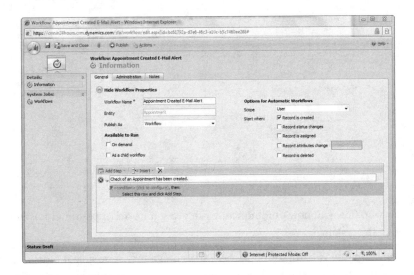

FIGURE 16.4
Adding a condition to the workflow.

1. Choose Add Step.

2. Choose Check Condition.

3. Add a description for the step.

4. We have added a description, but we have not added a step or an action.

5. Choose Add Step.

6. Choose Create Record.

7. Choose Email.

8. Select Set Properties to Edit and create the email.

Figure 16.5 shows a copy of the email template. Notice that there are a number of yellow fields, which indicate dynamic values that will be populated as the email is generated.

Now, save your workflow.

For the workflow to work, it must not be in draft mode. The new workflow must now be published. So, choose Publish at the top of the Workflow, Settings form.

FIGURE 16.5
Create a step to
create email.

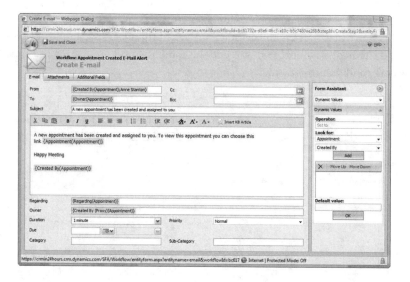

The new workflow will now automatically run every time an Appointment activity is created in the system.

If you are currently working through these steps on your system, give it a try. Create a new activity of type Appointment and assign it to yourself. In a minute or two, you will get an email alerting you to the fact that a new appointment was created.

Internal Alerts Based on Specific Criteria

What about a workflow that occurs when something else happens? We created a simple workflow to send an email when an Appointment activity is created, but perhaps there is something more critical. What if a company does not want to go after any sales opportunities of less than $100,000, because it thinks that these opportunities are not worth the expense that it takes to close them? Now, let's expand the scope to say that the sales force for this company is all over the world. It is hard to resist the temptation to go after a hot deal. Perhaps an opportunity has estimated revenue of $90,000, and all the salesperson has to do is make a few phone calls to close it. Do you think that salesperson is going to follow the company policy and walk away?

Microsoft Dynamics CRM's workflow can alert a few people when a new opportunity is added that is less than $100,000. Let's set up this new workflow:

1. Select Settings.

2. Select Workflow.

3. Select New.

4. Give the workflow a new name, such as **Opportunity Less Than 100,000 Alert**.

5. Select the Opportunity Entity.

6. Click OK.

7. Select Add a Step.

8. Select Check Condition.

Figure 16.6 shows where we are so far. We have created a new workflow for type Opportunity with this description.

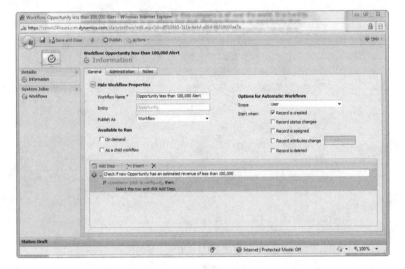

FIGURE 16.6
New workflow: Opportunity Less Than 100,000 Alert.

Now, we are going to set the variables associated with the condition. You will want to double-click the blue words that look like this: < condition>. Click to Configure.

Figure 16.7 shows the first screen for setting the condition. Notice that it looks almost exactly like the Advanced Find screen that you have seen in other hours.

In our particular case, we are inserting a condition that says that the opportunity estimated revenue is less than or equal to $100,000 and if this condition is true, then the system will send an email to the Big Boss. Figure 16.8 shows an example of an email that could be sent in this situation. Notice that you can use colors (for example, the word *alert* in red). You can also insert dynamic data fields, as shown here in yellow. These fields would be populated from the data in the created opportunity record.

Figure 16.9 shows the completed workflow. If our condition is false, we are not going to do anything, so we do not need to enter a condition and action if our original rule is false.

FIGURE 16.7
Insert condition.

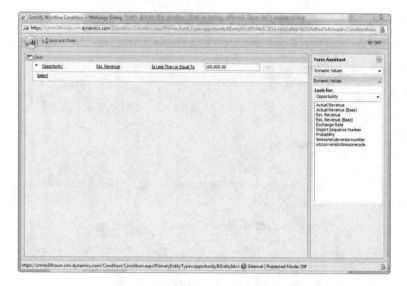

FIGURE 16.8
Sample alert
email.

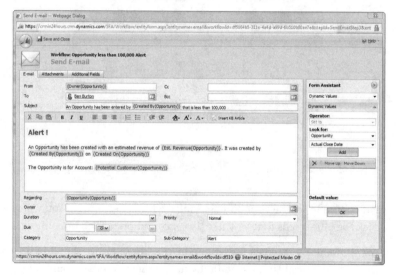

You do, however, have to publish the workflow for it to start working on the next
saved opportunity.

Watch Out!

Run OnCreate

Our new workflow is set to run OnCreate, and therefore, this workflow will not run
retroactively on already saved opportunities.

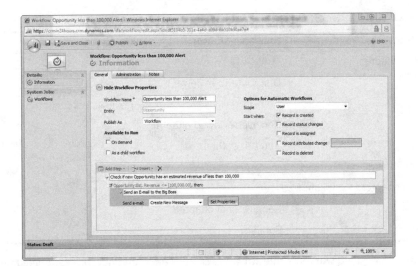

FIGURE 16.9
The finished
alert.

Setting Available to Run

You do not have to choose On Demand or Child Workflow for the workflow to run automatically upon creation of a new opportunity.

Using Workflow to Automate

We are still focusing on some fairly simple workflow rules. Rules that either have no condition or only one condition or if that condition is true they only do one thing. What about a more complex workflow designed to automate a complete process? We tackled the sales process in earlier hours, but workflow automation is not limited to sales. What if we have a process that requires three people doing things at different times to complete? Take, for instance, a simplified version of the process around completing one of these chapters. Each chapter has to be written, then reviewed, then edited for format and content, and then the reviews have to be signed off by the author.

The flow of information is shown in Table 16.1.

TABLE 16.1   Book Chapter Process

Author	Publishing Editor	Reviewer
Write chapter.		
	Distribute to reviewer.	
		Review chapter.
	Receive reviewed chapter.	
	Send to author.	
Confirm reviewer changes.		
Send chapter to publisher.		
	Receive final chapter.	
	Publish.	

Now, let's create a workflow that tracks these steps and, after a step is completed, it creates the next action for the appropriate person:

1. Choose Settings.

2. Choose Workflow.

3. Choose New.

4. Enter a name, such as **Book Chapter Process**.

5. Choose Task. (We are going to track a series of tasks, so our base entity is Task.)

6. Under Options for Automatic Workflow, we are also going to make this an organization workflow so that the workflow will kickvoff anytime someone creates a task that meets our conditions.

   Figure 16.10 shows our new workflow before adding any steps.

7. Set this to an On Demand (manual) workflow so that the user can start the write chapter process when they kick off their own process. Our other choice would be to set a condition that looks to see if a new task was created with either a specific subject line or a specific category or any other business-type rule that can be communicated through the data that the user would be entering.

8. Set Available to Run to On Demand.

9. Add a step.

10. Create a record. Make this a Task record.

11. Set the task to Write Chapter. The first step in our workflow will be to create the Task activity to write the chapter. We are going to give the writer three days to

complete this task. They can adjust as necessary, but we can use the system to set the due date as three days after the create date.

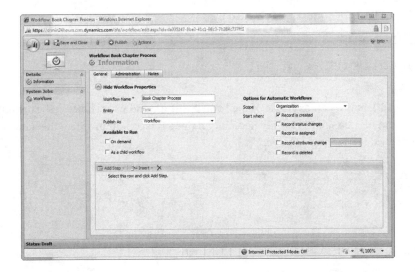

FIGURE 16.10
Book Chapter Process work-flow.

Figure 16.11 shows the configured task record. Notice the items in yellow.

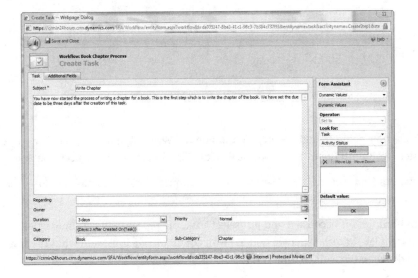

FIGURE 16.11
Configured task.

To create a due date of three days after the creation date, you can use the Form Assistant to the right of your form:

1. Place your cursor in the Due Date field.

2. In the Form Assistant, choose Operator 3 Days.

3. Choose After.

4. Set Look for To Task and Created By.

5. Press Add.

6. Click OK.

Figure 16.12 shows an example of the Form Assistant and your choices. The default value can also be set, but is only necessary if there is a condition where the data you selected would not be available.

FIGURE 16.12
Adding a dynamic data field.

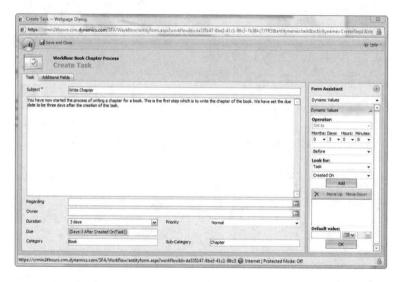

We are now going to add a wait condition on the Write Chapter (Task) to have the system wait until the task that was just created is completed by the user.

Notice, in Figure 16.13, that I selected Write Chapter (Task) as opposed to just Task as my variable.

This is important because if you just select Task, the process will continue when anyone completes a task. After we add the wait condition, we must add what the system is to do when the wait condition is met:

▶ Add a step.

▶ Add a stage.

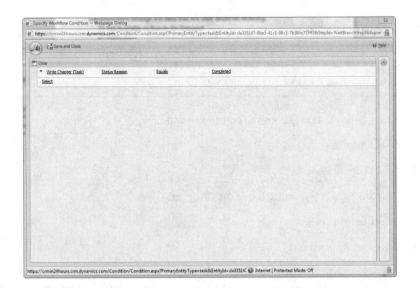

FIGURE 16.13
Write Chapter
(Task) condition.

The system will give you a warning that indicates that this particular workflow is more complex and that, if you add a stage in the middle, you must start the process with a stage. I added the stage Chapter Completed and renamed the automatically inserted stage to Write Chapter.

Figure 16.14 shows where we are so far. We have added two stages, one task, and one wait condition.

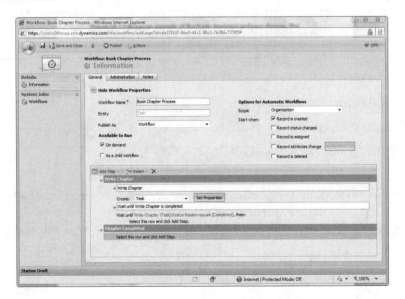

FIGURE 16.14
New stages on
the workflow.

Did you
Know?

Who to Assign To?

If you don't know who to assign a task to, you can use the Microsoft Dynamics CRM Queue feature and assign tasks to a queue.

In our example, we know who is going to do what.

We are now going to add the step to edit the chapter:

1. Select Add Step.

2. Select Create Record.

3. Give this step a name, such as **Edit Chapter**.

4. Select Create Task.

5. Select Set Properties.

When setting properties, you can assign the record to the specific publisher who will be doing the editing. In our example, we have only one publisher, so that makes it easier.

We are also going to create the draft email for the writer. The writer working off his own activity list will see the draft email and can then attach the chapter and send:

Create Versus Send

Notice that I choose to create a record and then choose email as opposed to choosing send email. The difference is that I am creating a draft email for the chapter writer.

1. Select Add Step.

2. Select Create Record.

3. Select Create Email.

4. Select Modify Email Properties.

Given that this is a more complex workflow, I am going to take a moment now to set up all the stages. I can then populate each stage with the proper set of steps. Figure 16.15 shows each of my stages defined. To define a stage, complete the following steps:

1. Choose Add Step.

2. Choose Add Stage.

3. Enter a description for the stage.

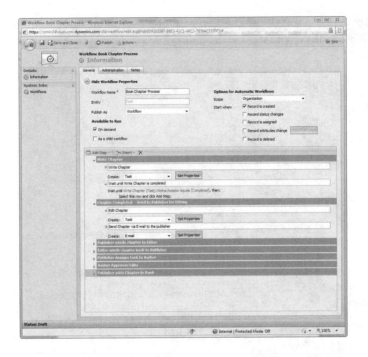

FIGURE 16.15
The stages of the Publish Chapter workflow.

Figure 16.16 shows the completed workflow. This workflow is a simplified version of what this process really involves, but it shows that multiple stages can be created for a process that is not related to sales. It also helps to show that each stage can have multiple steps and that tasks and emails can be assigned to other people. Workflows can be collaborative.

One of the goals of this hour is to get you started with workflow without overwhelming you. You want to increase your understanding of workflow slowly so that you can master an understanding of all the different parallel processes that can be kicked off.

Wait States

Pay particular attention to wait states within a workflow. A wait state will wait forever if the condition is never met. Needless to say, you can end up with a clogged process if you are not careful or if there is an error. Tracking down a clogged process is definitely no fun.

Watch Out!

Microsoft Windows Workflow Foundation tools are not only available in Microsoft Dynamics CRM. They are also available in other applications, such as Microsoft SharePoint and, as such, there are additional resources available related to architecting proper workflow functionality. Microsoft has a section on architecting workflow as part of the Microsoft Developers Center at http://msdn.microsoft.com/en-us/library/bb955348.aspx that is worth reading and mastering, but there are also more.

FIGURE 16.16
The completed
workflow.

Workshop

The Polar Bear Publishing Shop has a number of complex tasks that need to be completed in a certain order. Completion of these tasks is interdependent, requiring that one person do what he needs to do and then hand off to the next. The Polar Bear Publishing Shop wants to document and standardize some of these sets of tasks.

John Brown, CIO of the Polar Bear Publishing Shop, architects a set of processes. He first documents what the processes are and then lays these out in a business process diagram. After the process is validated and approved by his peers, John uses Microsoft Dynamics CRM to automate different sets. He sets up a workflow process for book binding and for editing and review. He also sets up the process around working with a particular set of vendors who supply paper and ink for his presses. John finds that Microsoft Dynamics CRM's flexibility allows him to review and redo processes on a regular basis.

John also uses the workflows he has designed as training tools. This reduces the classroom and e-learning requirements that would otherwise be needed for his staff.

Q&A

Q. *I want to emphasize my alert emails. Can I use different-colored text?*

A. Yes. You can use any number of text colors in the body of your email.

Q. *I have a process that involves many different people, and I don't always know to whom to assign a task. How can I set up this workflow?*

A. You need to use the Microsoft Dynamics CRM Queue feature, which allows you to assign an activity to the queue. More information on queues is covered in Hour 17, "Support Management." You can also use the team concept.

Q. *Can I use Microsoft Dynamics CRM without using the workflow functionality? We are just not ready to automate anything yet.*

A. Yes. You can use Microsoft Dynamics CRM without workflow, and you can add workflow when you are ready.

Quiz

1. When you are changing the properties of a task within a workflow, what do the yellow fields represent?

2. Why is it important to be aware of wait states?

3. What is an example of a process that could be automated with workflow?

4. What are three benefits of mastering and using workflow?

5. Where is a good place to learn more about workflow?

Answers

1. The yellow fields represent dynamic data fields that are populated when the task is actually created by the workflow.

2. Wait states have the potential to wait forever and so may cause a clogged-up workflow.

3. If a value is added to a specific attribute that is incorrect, send an email to the user to correct the value or to their manager.

4. Any three of the following:

   ▶ Increasing efficiency

   ▶ Standardizing process

   ▶ Training new users on existing process

   ▶ Controlling well-established routine

   ▶ Improvement of existing process

   ▶ Audit trail

   ▶ Streamlining of steps

   ▶ Parallel processing to increase data throughput

   ▶ Increase in user adoption

   ▶ Improved internal communication and collaboration

5. The Microsoft Developers center (http://msdn.microsoft.com/en-us/library/bb955348.aspx).

Exercise

Create some of John Brown's processes on paper or within Microsoft Dynamics CRM workflow. Take, for instance, the steps that John must go through to manage the ordering of a new supply of paper. He works with his CFO or the accounting department to first look at prices and to refresh the research regarding going rates and quality. He then needs to select both the quality and the price point that works for the company. He or a team member reaches out to the vendors for more information and real-time pricing, and then the order gets placed. When the order is received, the teams have to update inventory and store the new supplies.

HOUR 17

Support Management

What You'll Learn in This Hour:

▶ Setting Up Contracts

▶ Maximizing Support Profitability and Effectiveness

▶ The Subject

▶ Utilizing the Knowledge Base

We covered a lot of information in the last 16 hours; however, there is another department that can use Microsoft Dynamics CRM for specific non-sales-related needs. This includes everything that a typical support department might need to keep track of customer service, support contracts, incoming questions, and problems and solutions surrounding incoming calls. This hour delves into the world of support management using Microsoft Dynamics CRM.

What does a support department need? The functions within Microsoft Dynamics CRM that are key for a support department include contracts, cases, queues, the Knowledge Base, and scheduling. We cover scheduling in Hour 19, "Scheduling," so we touch on it only briefly here.

Contracts

A support contact consists of all the details of the agreement between your company and a client to provide support. The contract also includes management over what you sold to the client with regard to either the total number of calls, the total number of incidents (or cases), or the total number of support hours. Depending on how you offer support, the contracts feature of Microsoft Dynamics CRM can manage incoming use of services against a specific defined contract. Let's set up a contract to examine this further. Figure 17.1 shows where we need to go to get started.

FIGURE 17.1
Contracts.

1. Select Service.

2. Select Contracts.

3. Select New.

Figure 17.2 is the first screen that appears when you select New. Let's populate all the information in the next steps.

FIGURE 17.2
Contract Template drop-down list.

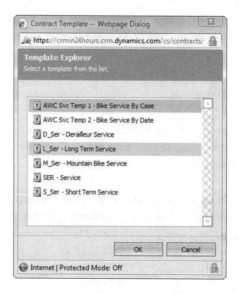

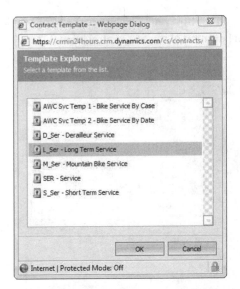

FIGURE 17.3
Creating a new
contract.

In our example, we start with a L._Ser - Long Term Service contract template, as shown in Figure 17.3:

1. Select L_Ser - Long Term Service.

2. Enter a name for the contract.

3. Choose a customer.

4. Choose a Contract Start date that the contract will be effective and when it ends. For our example, we have an effective date of June 30, 2009, and an end date of July 1, 2010. This does not necessarily have to be the create date. Contracts can be created and become effective at another time (perhaps the last day of the previous month, for example).

5. Choose the contract address or leave the address blank to use the customer's default address. The contract address can be any of the addresses listed under the Account More Addresses.

6. Confirm the billing information.

7. Now that the basics are entered, save the contract, but do not leave the screen. When you save the contract, you create the framework to associate other key Microsoft Dynamics CRM entities (record types) to the new contract (see Figure 17.4).

Now, we want to associate some specific products, prices, and other specifics that make up the bulk of the contract. This combination of prices, products, quantity, and more are referred to as contract lines, and contract lines can be accessed from the left navigation pane. Figure 17.5 shows the creation of the first contract line.

FIGURE 17.4
Creating a new contract, general details entered, contract saved.

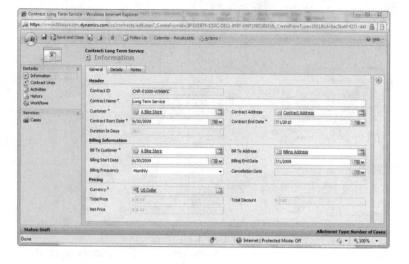

FIGURE 17.5
Creating a contract line.

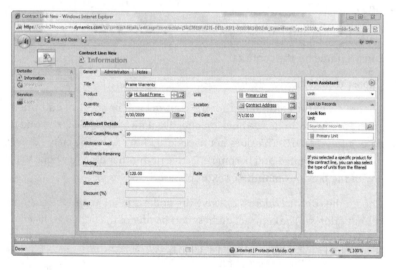

Watch Out!

Finance Department

Many times, contracts are part of the finance or accounting department's paperwork and finance creates them. The use of contracts in CRM is by the support department. There is a relationship in CRM between contracts and cases that can reduce the total allocated tickets or time on a contract.

Contract Lines

Contract lines make up the body of any given contract. They define what is covered under the contract terms.

1. Choose New.

2. Enter a title for the contract line. In our example, we are creating a contract line that covers the warrantee on a frame of a bicycle, so we used this as a reference.

3. Select the bicycle frame from the list of products.

4. Enter the quantity.

5. Enter the unit. Unit defines what quantity relates to. (For instance, a unit could be a box, an each, or a bundle.)

6. Enter the allotment details. The system will keep track of how many cases or minutes are used, but you need to enter what the contract covers.

7. Enter the price.

8. Save the contract line.

For any given contract, you can have an unlimited number of contract lines. After you add the contract lines, save the contract. However, to make the contract available for case or activity association, it needs to be marked as invoiced. Contract lines can include a set of service hours, a yearly maintenance and tune up, a number of phone calls to ask questions, and so on.

Associating Cases to a Specific Contract

You can also associate cases to a specific contract. You do this when you are working on a specific case and usually the person working the case is not the person who created the contract. The Case option under Contracts offers a view of all related cases.

When you associate a case to a contract, the data within the case can be used to reduce a set value within the contract. For instance, if you sell a service contract for 10 hours of service, you can have the system keep track of how many of the 10 hours have been used by the data within an associated case. You can also associate specific activities to either a case that is related to the contract or directly to the contract. Figure 17.6 shows the case form. Notice the area related to contracts.

Cases can be associated to a contract or to specific lines within a contract. In our example, we have associated the case to the specific contract and a specific contract line. In Hour 18, "Contracts, Cases, or Tickets and Capturing Time," we look more in depth at using cases.

FIGURE 17.6
Associating a case to a contract.

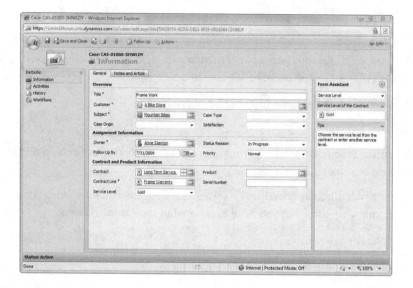

Maximizing Support Profitability and Effectiveness

Jumping away from the software a bit, let's consider how we might significantly increase the profitability of support. In so many situations, support and good customer service is a necessary expense, but it can also be a real profit center.

To maximize the profitability of support, you want to define what services you are offering. These could be different levels of telephone support or specific services that are performed in the office. You might also have some proprietary knowledge that is valuable. Take the time to really define and bundle these offerings. When you bundle the offerings, consider the following:

▶ What are you offering?

▶ What is the market value of these offerings?

▶ How should an offering be marketed?

▶ What terms can you use to classify and brand the offering?

▶ How can you differentiate the offering from your competition (particularly if the competition is offering a similar service for free)?

- If you were to list the offering on a price list, what would you call it?

- What skills are needed to provide the service?

- Are these skill sets of different values?

Each of these considerations can help you determine and sell a specific service. Customers will buy value and will pay a premium for something they need. You can also offer a certain amount of value-add for free; however, if you do offer something for free, make sure the client understands that they are getting a fixed amount of something for free. Don't forget to remind them occasionally with a letter that indicates how much they have used your service/product and how glad you are that they depend on you.

Consider, for example, the following service: unlimited tier-one support to help you refine and fine-tune and occasional solve your technical problems. Tier-one support can be a service offering that helps further define a specific problem. The tier-one team can be less experienced in a technology, but more experienced with capturing the finite details that make solving the problem easier. They can be used as a win for your own company and a win for the client. A client's easy questions are efficiently answered, and the problems are organized and data collected without the expense of spending hours with a tier-three support resource.

You now have two services you can sell:

- Unlimited tier-one support.

- Limited and more expensive, yet more efficient tier-three support. (Time is money to your company and to your client.)

When properly marketed and bundled, you end up with profit, and your customer ends up with an efficient and accurate answer to their problems from the right source.

The key concept to take away is that it is important to plan and design the services that you are offering. This is even more critical in this age of information, when information is a valuable asset. When information is shared, there is value in return. This value can be in dollars or in more information increasing the knowledge base and information asset pool.

As you work toward refining and defining your services, look at the Service Design Network. Its website is at www.service-design-network.org/. The Service Design Network was established in 2004 by Küln International School of Design, Carnegie Mellon University, Linküpings Universitet, Politecnico de Milano / Domus Academy and the agency Spirit of Creation.

If you are an information technology company and you are looking to bundle and market services more efficiently, there is a great resource on the ITIL home page at www.itil-officialsite.com/home/home.asp

There are other resources, too, but the key point is that marketing, branding, and selling can bring much needed profit and client satisfaction to your service offerings.

The Subject

Now, let's go back to talking about how Microsoft Dynamics CRM can help you organize and bundle these services. You face a small requirement with an impact within Microsoft Dynamics CRM: the configuration of subjects. Subjects are used in a number of different places within Microsoft Dynamics CRM. For instance, each case can have a related subject; and sales literature, products, and articles can have a subject. The subject tree should be set up with some thought, which supports both reporting and the general organization of a number of different areas of data.

1. Choose Settings.

2. Choose Business Management.

3. Choose Subject.

Figure 17.7 is where we get started defining our subjects.

FIGURE 17.7
Setting up sub-
jects.

In our example, we have already defined both parent subjects and child subjects. Creating subjects offers one way to organize entities within the system. Subjects, categories used in a hierarchical list to correlate and organize information, are used in the subject tree to organize products, sales literature, and knowledge base articles. In our example, we have a subject called Bikes, and we have child subjects of all the different types of bikes we work on. Via the creation of subjects, we can organize our cases by category of bike. We also get reporting by subject, which enables us to determine how many cases are being generated for what type of bike. We can then make business decisions based on such information, such as choosing not to carry the line of bikes that causes the most support.

Utilizing the Knowledge Base

The knowledge base is an area of Microsoft Dynamics CRM where you can both store your own knowledge base articles (KBAs) and manage the review process that creates your knowledge base articles. Look at Figure 17.8. One of the advantages of storing knowledge base articles within Dynamics CRM is that you can associate these KBAs with specific cases. If you use the Microsoft Dynamics CRM customer portal, you can also share these articles with your customers.

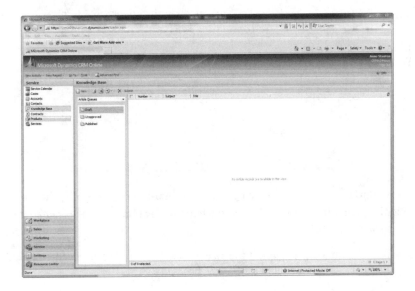

FIGURE 17.8
Knowledge base articles (Services, Knowledge Base).

One of the most frequently asked questions when it comes to the knowledge base is whether it's possible to associate a Microsoft Word document to a knowledge base article. When I hear this question, I try to explain that this breaks the model. The model is to organize data in structured, searchable templates. If I associate a Word document, I am not using a structured template, and I am bypassing the ability to search. If you would like a knowledge base of Word documents, you might consider integrating Microsoft SharePoint, which is built to manage unstructured data, such as Word documents and document libraries.

Notice that you have Draft, Unapproved, and Publish listed next to the left navigation pane. Support personal can write KBAs and then submit them for review. You can also build a workflow to support the effort. In addition, if you select New when starting to create a new KBA article, you have a number of template choices (see Figure 17.8).

Templates help your support department to capture information that is then placed in standardized formats. If we create a new KBA we are instructed to capture a title, subject, key words, a summary, and more comments (see Figure 17.9).

FIGURE 17.9
Template
choices.

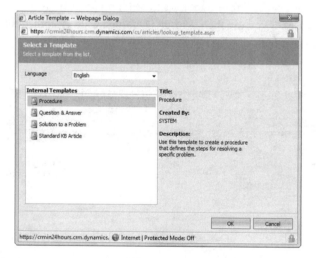

This standard format takes a bunch of different information and gathers it into a standard searchable library. Following the template, we have quickly created a new KBA (see Figure 17.10).

This is now a draft KBA. To submit this new article for publishing consideration, do the following:

1. Select Actions.

2. Select Submit.

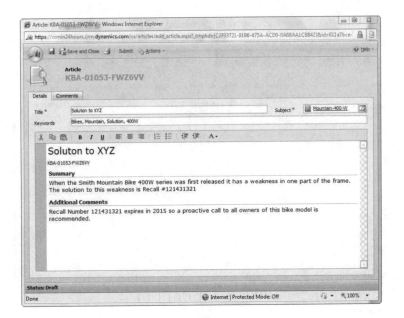

FIGURE 17.10
New draft KBA.

Once submitted, the article is in the Unapproved bucket. To publish the article, complete the following steps:

1. Select Actions.

2. Select Approved.

After the article is approved, it appears in the list of published articles and can be used as a reference throughout the company. Knowledge base articles can be associated to cases, for instance, or shared with clients through email.

Figure 17.11 shows the list of published KBAs.

FIGURE 17.11
Published arti-
cles.

Workshop

Technology Titans is a technology company that offers IT services. It sells service contracts based on number of cases (incidents), and it also offers ad hoc hourly billing.
Technology Titans sells products, too, and organizes its products in the Microsoft
Dynamics CRM product catalog. Technology Titans is particularly keen to utilize
Microsoft Dynamics CRM to keep track of how many cases are getting used by a variety of clients. To do this, it sets up service contracts in Microsoft Dynamics CRM for
each client. Each service contract is completed and then double-checked against its
accounting software to confirm that it has been billed. After the contract is set up,
the contract is activated. The teams are also trained that, to offer a service, they must
create a service case. Each service case created is associated to the appropriate client
contract.

Technology Titans also has a certain number recurring cases. The solutions to the
recurring cases are documented and saved in the knowledge base library within
Microsoft Dynamics CRM. The company reviews these knowledge base articles on a
scheduled basis to confirm that the information is still correct. It is also diligent
about not putting everything in the knowledge base area. It wants to save and store
only those items that recur regularly.

Q&A

Q. *We have the standard services that you might find at any technology company. How can we give these zing and the right marketing?*

A. The first step is to understand the value you are offering and your audience. Given that you are also a consumer of technology services, what would make you feel great about spending money on these services? I suggest that you would pay a lot for a real expert in a specific technology because you could learn and potentially resell some of this expertise?

Q. *Are subjects that important? We have not set up a hierarchy of subjects.*

A. Subjects offer a way to not only organize cases and associated literature and knowledge base articles, but they also potentially offer a reporting category for analytics.

Q. *We want to associate a Word document to a knowledge base article. Can we do so?*

A. No. By design, you cannot associate a Word document to a knowledge base article.

Quiz

1. Why does a contract have contract lines? What are they used for?
2. How does a case relate to a contract?
3. Is search available against knowledge base articles?
4. Name three areas to consider when bundling support services to sell.
5. Does the knowledge base section of Microsoft Dynamics CRM offer standardization?

Answers

1. Contract lines define the specific services or products covered by the contract.

2. A case can be associated to a contract, and the hours or incident that the case represents can reduce the total available incidents left.

3. Yes. There is extensive search associated with knowledge base articles.

4. Any of the items listed in this hour, but the following three could apply: What terms can you use to classify and brand the offering? What are you offering? What skills are needed to provide the service?

5. Yes. One of the key features of Microsoft Dynamics CRM knowledge base is the standardization of information into forms of information that are searchable.

Exercise

Using the workshop example about the Technology Titans, set up two different knowledge base articles for the company. Would "How to Configure Outlook" be a valuable addition to its library? Now, set up a contract for a new client who wants unlimited support. Should the Technology Titans offer 24x7 support coverage? What would be the cost of doing this right, with the right level of skilled labor? Can this service be profitable?

HOUR 18

Contracts, Cases, Tickets, and Capturing Time

What You'll Learn in This Hour:

▶ The Hierarchy of Contracts, Cases, and Time

▶ How Cases Are Used

▶ Proactive Versus Reactive

▶ Adding Workflow to Close a Case

▶ Queues

This hour spends more time on contracts and cases and looks at the concept of capturing time against activities in Microsoft Dynamics CRM. Microsoft Dynamics CRM is not designed with a timesheet and lends itself to capturing time on scheduled activities as opposed to a timesheet. However, a number of Microsoft partners offer timesheet timekeeping as an add-on product. If you want to capture time during the day on perhaps a subset of activities andcases; activities with duration might be for you.

The Hierarchy of Contracts, Cases, and Time

Figure 18.1 shows the hierarchy of how the entities (record types) relate to each other in the world of time capture. Time is captured on an activity in the duration field, and activities that are related to cases can map this duration into an actual case duration bucket. When a case is closed, time can be accumulated.

In Figure 18.1, the five-pointed star represents the capturing of time on a specific activity, and the seven-pointed star represents the potential of accumulation of actual time on a closed case.

FIGURE 18.1
Associated service entities.

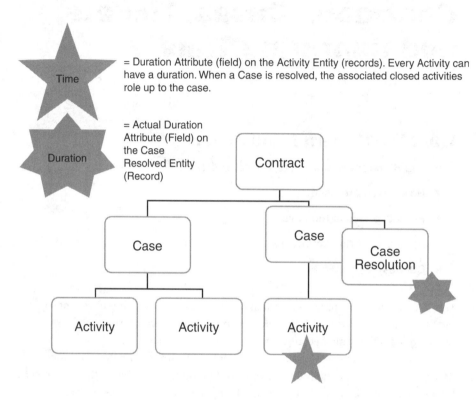

Time = Duration Attribute (field) on the Activity Entity (records). Every Activity can have a duration. When a Case is resolved, the associated closed activities role up to the case.

Duration = Actual Duration Attribute (Field) on the Case Resolved Entity (Record)

The general concept is that every activity can have a time duration and an activity can be associated to a case. When activities with a time duration are associated to a case, the case can be updated with the actual accumulated duration.

You can also capture a start and end time on each activity, and using the Report Wizard or a view or an export into an Excel pivot table, you can quickly see a list or picture of time for any given set of activities.

Having spent a good deal of time in time and billing software industry, I can tell you that this is only one type of time capture, and it is not the ultimate or only type of time and billing or practice management application. For instance, in the CPA niche, write-downs and write-down auditing would need to be incorporated; and in the legal niche, write-ups and write-up auditing would need to be incorporated. If we then expand further into the technology services industry, the extreme quick entering of time via a timesheet interface would be helpful when the phone is ringing off the hook. All of this is possible with some customization *and* you get full-blown customer relationship management software functionality, too.

Microsoft Dynamics CRM capturing a time duration against a specific activity and a total duration on a case is powerful, but it does not necessarily meet all industry needs by default. Without customization (some of which can be done fairly quickly), you will not have the efficient timesheet that other time-tracking systems might offer.

Before you start reinventing the wheel when it comes to taking Microsoft Dynamics CRM smoothly into a deep and focused time and billing application, check with a couple of independent software vendors who have fine-tuned the application for specific industries. Take, for instance, CRM4Legal, Dynamics Methods, Axonom, Customer Effective, and other partners who have added timesheet and advanced service billing functionality. Ah, but I digress.

Let's get back to really looking at the capturing of time within Microsoft Dynamics CRM without customizations. Figure 18.2 shows the time-oriented fields within a Task activity.

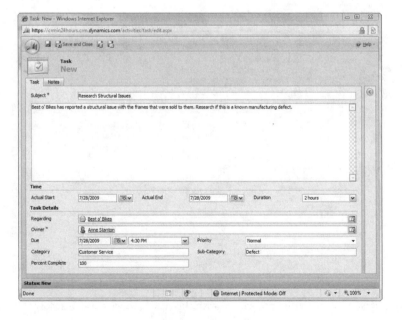

FIGURE 18.2
Task activity, duration entered.

In Figure 18.2, we have added a two-hour duration on July 28, 2009. This duration can be reported on, viewed, or exported with relationship to a contact or account. Now, let's associate this new activity to a case. You can create a case and then an activity, you can create a case without any activities, or you can create an activity and then associated it to a new case.

To associate this activity to a case, complete these steps:

1. Choose Services.

2. Choose Case.

3. Choose New.

4. Add all the information for a new case and save and close.

5. Choose Activities.

6. Find your activity.

7. Open the activity.

8. Add the case to the Regarding.

Figure 18.3 shows an example of the new case, Figure 18.4 shows a list of the associated activities, and Figure 18.5 shows the specific activity.

FIGURE 18.3
New case.

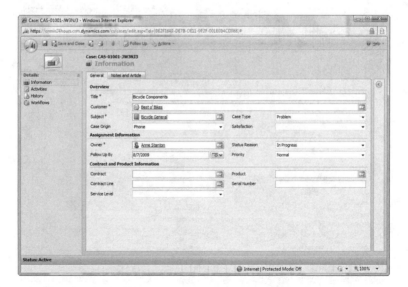

Now that we have activities associated with the case, can we close or resolve the case?

1. Choose the case.

2. Open the case.

3. Select Actions.

4. Select Resolve Case.

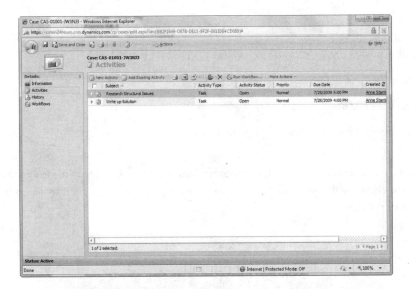

FIGURE 18.4
Activities related
to the case.

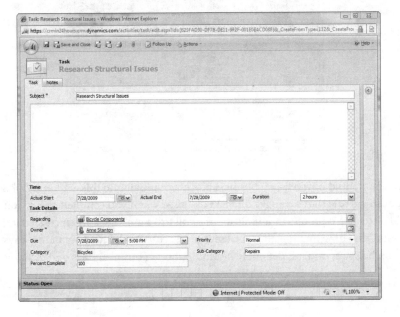

FIGURE 18.5
Specific activity
details.

Figure 18.6 shows what happens when you try to resolve a case with open activities.

FIGURE 18.6
Resolving a case
with open activi-
ties.

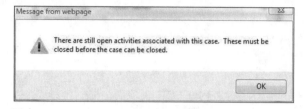

You have two choices. One, you can close each activity as follows:

1. Open the activity.

2. Select Actions.

3. Select Save and Close to close the task.

Figure 18.7 shows the screen that appears when you choose this way of closing. Your second choice with regard to closing is to close a task when you save it by using the Save and Close option.

FIGURE 18.7
Closing a task.

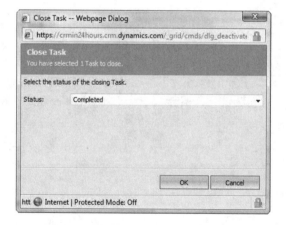

Have you noticed how nicely a business process would fit into this explanation? Such as a business rule that says save all tasks as closed when you complete them. You could also have a process that indicates that all tasks are closed when created if they are capturing time and the official close is at the case level. There are many ways that this can be spun, and it is definitely a combination of business rules and technology.

How Cases Are Used

Microsoft Dynamics CRM allows for rename, and cases are often renamed to tickets. This change is quick, easy, and has a very low impact. To change the name of case, do the following:

1. Choose Settings.

2. Choose Customization.

3. Choose Customize Entities.

4. Choose Case.

5. Change the display name Case to **Ticket** and Cases to **Tickets**.

Rename the Views

You might want to rename your views, too, given that their names will still contain the word *case*. While you're renaming things, click Messages. Double-click each message and replace "case" and "cases" in each message.

Watch Out!

6. Save.

7. Publish.

8. Exit all the way out of Microsoft Dynamics CRM.

The next time you enter Microsoft Dynamics CRM, cases will appear as tickets. Figure 18.8 shows the screen where you would rename case to ticket.

Notice, in Figure 18.9, our former case entity (record type) is now called a ticket, even in the left navigation pane.

What are other ways that cases (or tickets) are used? Cases can be used to keep track of a subset of activities. A case can be used to accumulate time and reduce the time sold as represented on a contract, and a case can be used to track the beginning, the middle, and the end of a problem or complicated question.

Cases can represent an RMA (a return of a defective product), where the RMA number is associated to the case, the resolution and replacement of the "item" are tracked as associated activities or orders, and the final resolution is wrapped up on close.

FIGURE 18.8
Rename case to ticket.

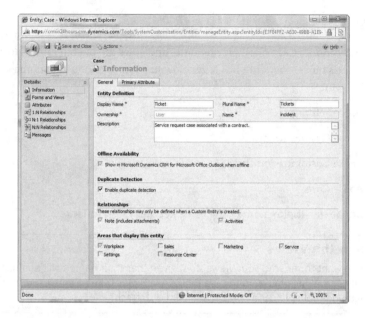

FIGURE 18.9
Left navigation menu shows ticket.

Proactive Versus Reactive

If you are constantly planning your schedule and proactively creating tasks, phone calls, and appointments that need to be completed, Microsoft Dynamics CRM is fantastic for capturing the time associated with these activities. When you complete the activity, you add the time and complete the activity. In addition, if you are proactive, adding the layer of case works well. You can proactively create a case when you become aware of an issue, and you can then plan out what needs to be done to close the case (for example, associate needed tasks, phone calls, appointments, and emails).

On the other hand, if you live in a highly reactive world, then for each time item that you want to capture, you first create an activity, add the details (including the time), and then save it as completed. You can also create a case and immediately close the case or create a case and create activities and assign them to other people. This opens a case and pushes it out for completion in a reactive and distributed manner. The monkey comes in the office, a tracking hat is assigned, and it is then split and distributed to the rest of the team.

Adding Workflow to Close a Case

When major functions occur, such as the closing of a case, they create great opportunities to have the system react with some automation. Consider, for instance, a need to alert the customer that their case has been closed. With data from the case, an email can be put together that includes details from the case. Figure 18.10 shows a sample email. Notice that the case number and the subject have been included in this email template.

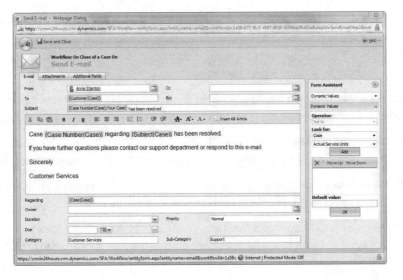

FIGURE 18.10
Email upon the close of a case.

When does this email get sent? This email gets sent when there is a change in the case and the status of the case is set to resolved. In our example, the email is sent from a specific service person and sent to the customer associated with the case. In many companies, I have also seen a user set up with a support email alias. In that case, this type of email would be sent from support@....

The workflow to check the status of the case on change and to send an email if the status is equal to resolved is a workflow with two steps. Figure 18.11 shows this workflow.

FIGURE 18.11
Close a case,
send email.

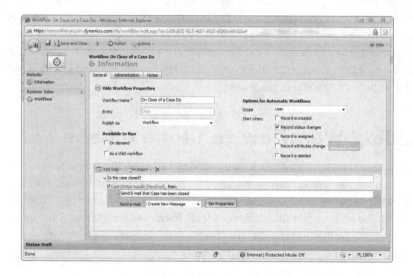

Notice that the options for automatic workflow are set to on Record status changes, as opposed to when the record is created. We are capturing when a case changes and then reviewing the change with a condition statement to check to see whether the change resulted in the status being set to resolved.

What is another situation where you might want a workflow on a change to a case? Here are some examples:

▶ When a case closes for a high-profile client, send an email or create an activity to the internal support department manager or the CEO for a personal follow-up.

▶ When a case includes a value in the Follow-Up By field, schedule an activity to follow up for the appropriate support person or the incident manager.

▶ When a case changes and the status changes to high priority, create an appointment with a due date. The appointment would synchronize to Outlook and pop up an alert at the set time.

▶ When a case is resolved and the satisfaction level is very dissatisfied, kick off a special workflow process called Turning Around a Dissatisfied Customer.

The list can get even more interesting if you add a few layers or a bit of code. For instance, consider the following examples:

▶ When a case closes, send an email to the client that his case is closed and include three questions. When he responds to this email, capture the response and update the case with his input to the specific questions.

▶ When a case is updated, check whether there are any associated activities and if these activities are open. If the activities are open and it has been a certain amount of time, determine who the owner of the activity is and alert his manager.

▶ When a case is updated, determine whether there are any other open cases for the same customer. If there are, check whether the subject has similar words that might indicate a possible duplication.

Now that we managed to get through 18 hours and we have touched on how support might use Microsoft Dynamics CRM, we can't leave support without spending a bit of time talking about the use of queues in support.

Queues

Queues allow you to assign specific tasks to a bucket of pending items as opposed to a specific person. What this means is that you can assign an activity to a queue. A queue can be a department, such as the support department, or a subset of people, or a generic place where everyone checks to see what is pending.

To create a queue, follow these steps:

1. Choose Settings.

2. Choose Business Management.

3. Choose Queues.

4. Choose New.

Figure 18.12 shows the beginning of setting up a queue, and Figure 18.13 shows the setup of a queue with data entered.

After the queue is created, how does it get used?

FIGURE 18.12
Creating a new
queue.

FIGURE 18.12
Creating a new
queue.

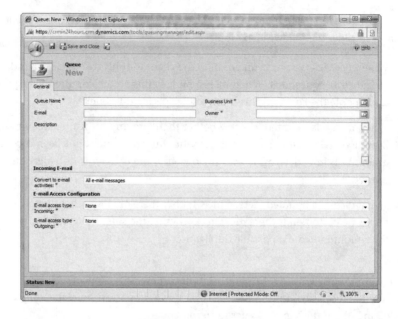

FIGURE 18.13
Queue created.

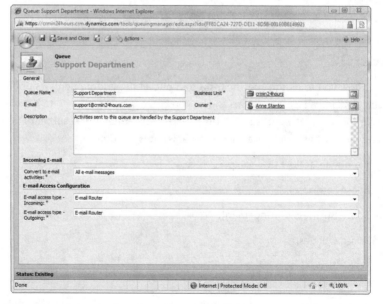

1. Select Workplace.

2. Select Queues.

You can open an activity that already exists, and you can reassign this activity to a queue, as shown in Figure 18.14.

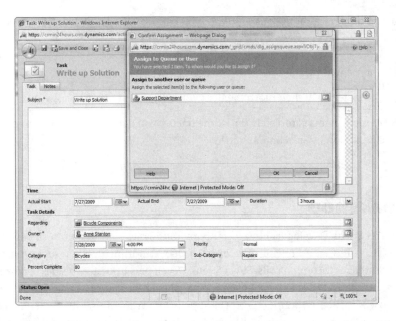

FIGURE 18.14
Assigning an existing activity to the support queue.

You can also have all email that is sent to support@crmin24hours.com end up in the queue. In our example, the email address is the email address we associated to the queue when we created it. This is another way that items can get into the queue.

What happens when we want to move activities or emails out of a queue? Figure 18.15 shows the populated support queue as reached through My Work, Queues. Nothing in the queue is assigned or in progress.

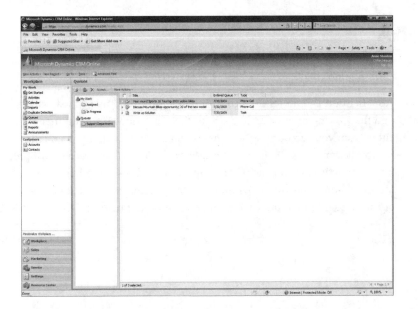

FIGURE 18.15
The support queue.

To accept an item from the queue so that you can work it, do the following:

1. Highlight the item you are interested in.

2. Choose Accept.

3. The system will then move the item you selected into In Progress.

4. To move items completely out of the queue, you can assign the item to a specific person by selecting Assign.

Workshop

The Silver Streak Developers have a company that writes software for town governments. They have a number of developers, a Q&A department, and a support department that takes incoming calls. Silver Streak Developers also have a sales department that sells their software to town governments all over the country. Silver Streak Developers use Microsoft Dynamics CRM. The support department uses all the service components of Microsoft Dynamics CRM. Each of their clients has a support contract that is either a Gold or Silver level. The Silver level offers 24 incidents equally, approximately 24 calls a year, and the Gold level support contract offers 50 hours of service. Customers of Silver Streak can send email to support@silverstreak.com, and a support person accepts this request from the support queue as soon as he is available. The support person creates a case, associates the email, and tracks all that he does to resolve the problem. When the problem is resolved, the support person closes the case.

Q&A

Q. *We want to capture all our time and then bill it. Can Microsoft Dynamics CRM handle this?*

A. Yes. Microsoft Dynamics CRM can support capturing time against activities and the viewing of these activities with their duration. Time can then be billed either from your accounting software or via an invoice that you enter in Microsoft Dynamics CRM against a service product. If you need robust project billing, practice management, write-up/down auditing, or other features, look for an add-on to Microsoft Dynamics CRM or integrate a practice management or time and billing or project billing application to Microsoft Dynamics CRM.

Q. *We do not use the term cases at our company. Instead, we use the term tickets. Can we rename cases to tickets?*

A. Yes. The case entity can be renamed to ticket or incident or any other word that better fits your industry niche vocabulary.

Q. *We use RMAs and need to track when a product is returned under an RMA number. How well does Microsoft Dynamics CRM handle RMAs?*

A. The structure of Microsoft Dynamics CRM actually works extremely well for the management and handling of RMAs.

Q. *We have all our legal contracts set up in Microsoft Word. Can we associate a Word contract to the contract feature of Microsoft Dynamics CRM?*

A. No. File attachments cannot be associated to contracts in Microsoft Dynamics CRM. Okay, this is not really correct; yes, you can associate the Word contract to a saved note associated with the contract entity, but I do not recommend this because Microsoft Dynamics CRM is not designed to be an incredible document library for unstructured data. For associating unstructured data, such as Word documents, to Microsoft Dynamics CRM, I suggest you look into the incredible integration points for Microsoft SharePoint.

Quiz

1. Identify two places where time can be captured.

2. How are contracts related to cases?

3. Why would you want to use a queue?

4. If you are a proactive person, is it fairly straightforward to capture time on your activities as you complete them?

5. Name two ways to close an activity.

Answers

1. Time can be captured on an activity, and time can be captured on a case.

2. Cases can be associated to a specific contract, and the time on the case can reduce the available time on a contract.

3. Queues allow you to assign activities or send email to a generic bucket, such as a support queue or a support email address.

4. Yes. When you complete your planned activities, you can add the duration when completing.

5. You can save the activity as closed or you can use the Close Activity option on the Action menu.

Exercise

Set up the Gold and Silver contract that the Silver Streak Developers use with their customers. In addition, set up the support queue. Now that the contract and queue are created, create some new activities and assign them to the queue. Now, try to send an email to the queue's email address. How about a case? You can create a case and assign it to the contract you just created.

HOUR 19

Scheduling

What You'll Learn in This Hour:

▶ Viewing and Managing Schedule Conflicts

▶ Setting Up Scheduling

▶ Defining Staff Availability

▶ Defining the Resources, Equipment, and Locations

This hour focuses on scheduling people, places, groups, shared facilities, and equipment. This is a robust subject worthy of deep thought and consideration. If scheduling is a core piece of your business, set aside extra time to master this subject.

Scheduling in General

Microsoft Dynamics CRM offers the ability to schedule, find conflicts, assign people, and handle the juggling of in-demand equipment and locations, such as conference rooms and training facilities.

Before we dive into scheduling, let's set some context. Some features and functions within Microsoft Dynamics CRM are more complex than others. The silver lining is that these complex functions complement more complex long-term functionality.

Scheduling is one of these more complex features, particularly when it comes to getting it all configured. So, in this hour, you will first learn about how scheduling works and all the great things you can do with scheduling, and then we will get into the key areas of Microsoft Dynamics CRM that need to be set up for scheduling to work smoothly.

Getting Started with Scheduling

The world of Microsoft Dynamics CRM scheduling uses the term *service* as a specific item. A service is made up of a number of unique variables, including various associated resources, times, and durations. If we fine-tune our earlier definition in context of service, scheduling can organize and manage service teams, service people, service appointments, service activities, and associated needed service equipment.

Service Calendar

The Service calendar is a unique centralized calendar for service activities and appointments that is configured and displayed in a manner to support conflict resolution and filtering. Service activities will also show up on the specific staff member's assigned calendar as accessed from My Work, Calendar.

Service activities are unique items that apply to the management of service-specific activities. They are not the same as your more standard activities of type Appointment. One way to think of a service activity is as a supersized and more complex appointment.

The Service calendar is located on the Service menu:

1. Select Service.

2. Select Service Calendar.

When you open the Service calendar, you will immediately see a list of all resources within a left menu bar. These resources consist of all Microsoft Dynamics CRM users and other resources that were created, such as groups of users, equipment, or facilities. What displays in the left navigation pane is controlled by the Type drop-down menu option on the top of the calendar. Figure 19.1 shows the initial Service calendar.

| **A Programmers Option** |
| You cannot customize the Service calendar or change the default view with the application. However, with a bit of programming expertise, you can edit the ISV.Config file (such as an XML configuration document used to update the navigation structure of Microsoft Dynamics CRM Online, including adding custom buttons, tabs, and menus to entity forms) to change the colors of the time blocks. |

Items that are scheduled on the Service calendar include service activities and appointments. Before you can schedule a service activity, you need to create the service activity. After you create the service activity, the system immediately gives you the option to schedule it.

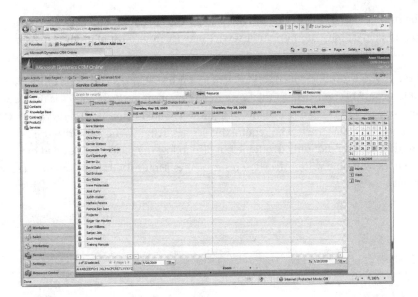

FIGURE 19.1
Service calendar.

Creating a Service Activity

To create a new service activity, follow these steps:

1. Select New (See Figure 19.2).

2. Select Service Activity from the top of the Service calendar display.

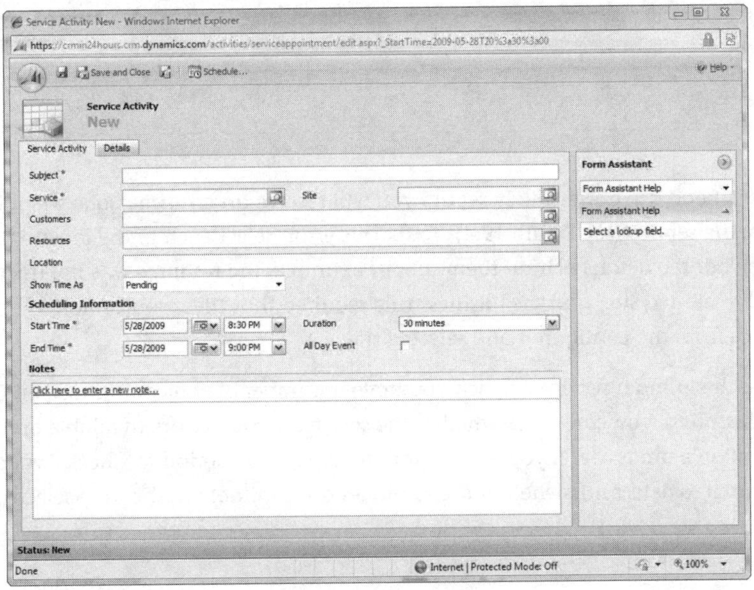

FIGURE 19.2
Service activity.

The subject field of the service activity is required. This field can be used as a category to help classify this particular service activity from a list of many other similar service activities.

Perhaps you want to create a service activity for inspecting a corporate office. Your subject could become Inspect the Corporate Headquarters. Your service is the standard service you created in system configuration called Inspection. Customer or Customers are the customers who require this service activity. The Resources are resources that are not only available but also follow the business rules and are resources available within the chosen site or sites. Figure 19.3 shows the saved service activity.

FIGURE 19.3
Saved service activity.

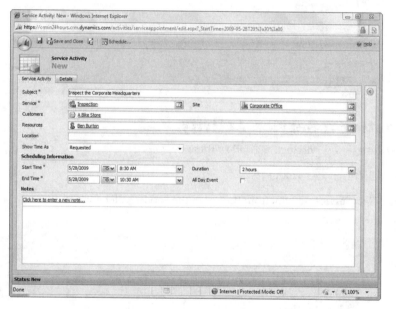

If all the fields are not properly set up, you will receive an error message when trying to save the service (see Figure 19.4). To fix this error, select each of the lookup items and look at the details behind them. In our example, the resource was not associated with the selected site, and the business rule required that the resource had to be a resource from the configured and selected site.

When scheduling a service activity, you have a number of choices to consider. During scheduling, you can check whether the selected resources are available and what the available times are. If you enter a specific time, your option to Check Available will search to determine whether the resources are available at the time selected. You will be presented with a list of available options that you can then select from for scheduling. Figure 19.5 shows a list of available times.

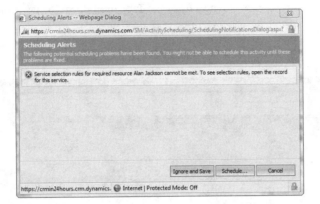

FIGURE 19.4
Service Activity Creation error.

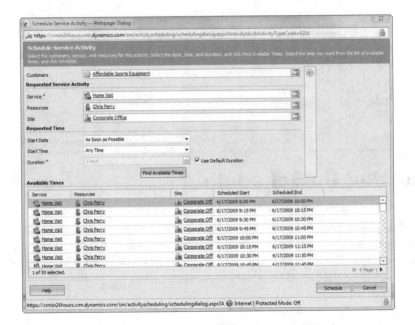

FIGURE 19.5
Scheduling a service.

Viewing and Managing Schedule Conflicts

After service activities are created and scheduled, you can use the Scheduling calendar to check for conflicts:

1. From the Scheduling calendar, choose your view.

2. Click Show Conflicts. Conflicts in people's schedules show up in the calendar with a red box around them.

3. Choose view service activities from the Type drop-down to view conflicts between specific service activities.

4. Confirm that Show Conflicts is turned on (see Figure 19.6).

FIGURE 19.6
Scheduling con-
flicts.

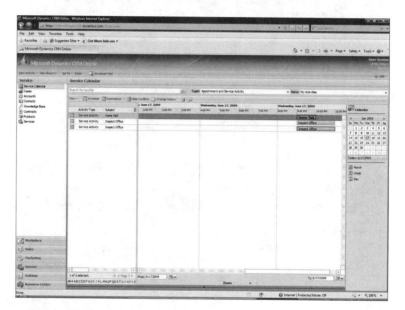

Setting Up Scheduling

Setup does not have to be done more than once, and for those working with a Microsoft Dynamics CRM partner, part of your project might be finalizing and configuring the scheduling functionality of Microsoft Dynamics CRM. If it is not, this section goes through each section of Microsoft Dynamics CRM system configuration that needs to be configured for scheduling to work smoothly.

Defining Staff Availability

The first step in setting up scheduling is to double-check and configure staff people's work hours. To do so, follow these steps:

1. Choose Settings.

2. Choose Administration.

3. Choose Users.

4. Choose a specific user.

Now, from the left menu bar, select Work Hours (see Figure 19.7).

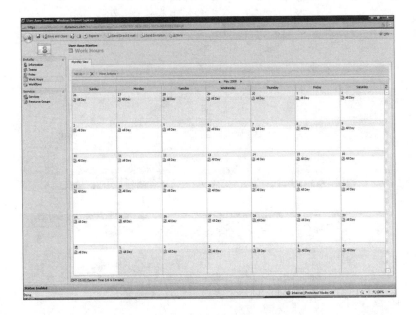

FIGURE 19.7
Work Hours cal-
endar.

Figure 19.7 is a display of Work Hours as it would appear when first accessed. To configure Work Hours, follow these steps:

1. Select Setup, as shown in Figure 19.8.

2. Drill down on the blue words Work Hours.

In Figure 19.9, I entered my work hours as 7:00 a.m. to 5:00 p.m., with an hour lunch.

The point of adding in work hours for people you want to schedule is that, once configured, scheduling becomes much more intelligent. If you try to schedule me during my break, the system will understand and warn you.

In Figure 19.10, you can now see that, as of May 23, 2009, I have new work hours. Spend some time adding some unique work hours to your system for practice. Consider this as your warm-up and stretching exercise for the following sections.

FIGURE 19.8
Specifying the
work hours.

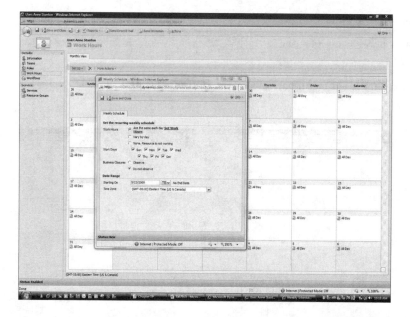

FIGURE 19.9
Entering breaks
and hours.

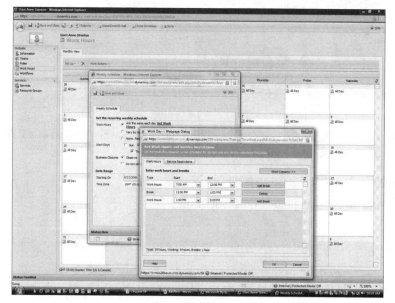

Defining the Resource Groups, Equipment, and Locations

After the staff is correctly configured for scheduling, the other items referenced from the scheduling functions need to be set up. Let's tackle resource groups. Resource groups are made up of a combination of users, equipment, facilities, and teams. To set up a resource group, follow these steps:

1. Select Settings.

2. Select Business Management.

3. Select Resource Groups.

4. Click New.

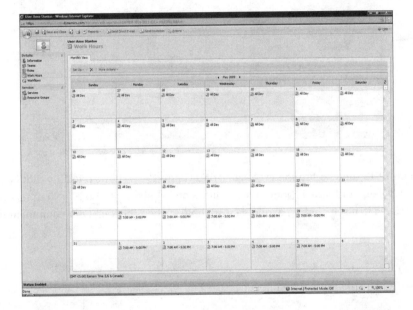

FIGURE 19.10
The newly config-
ured work hours.

Figure 19.11 shows a resource group. When creating a new resource group, you are selecting from users, facilities, equipment, and teams, so if you are going to create groups that include facilities and equipment and teams, take a minute and set these up as well.

Setting Up Facilities and Equipment

To set up Facilities and Equipment, follow these steps:

1. Select Settings.

2. Select Business Management.

3. Select Facilities/Equipment.

4. Click New.

FIGURE 19.11
Resource
groups.

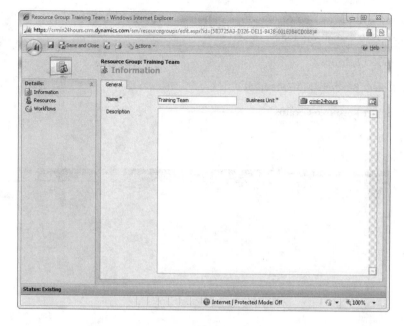

Figure 19.12 shows a brand new facility, and Figure 19.13 shows a facility that has already been configured. Notice that facilities and equipment also have a number of associated items, including available work hours (when the facility or equipment is

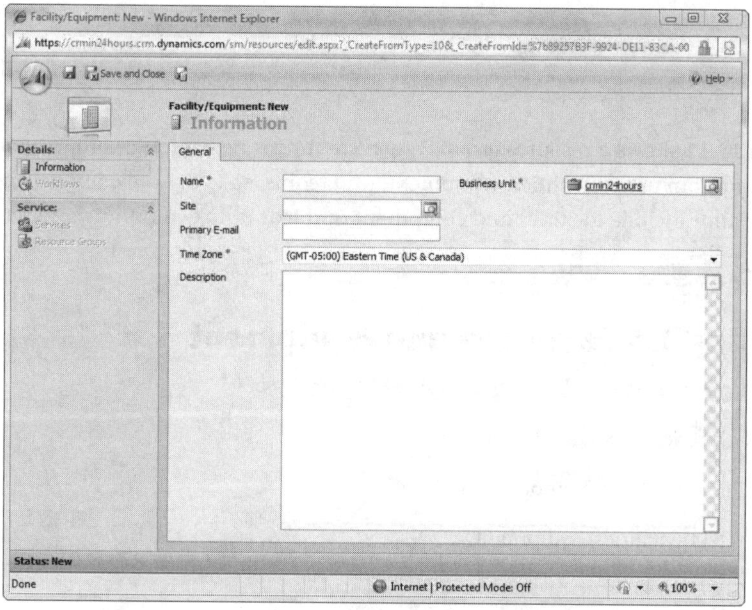

FIGURE 19.12
New
facilities/equip-
ment.

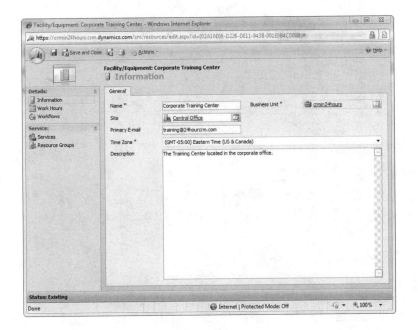

FIGURE 19.13
Configured
facility.

available for scheduling) and services, which also need to be configured. (Did I mention that configuration is a bit mind-bending?)

The configured facility is a training center associated with the corporate headquarters. Resources associated with this facility can include a specific team of staff members, training materials, equipment (such as a projector), and more.

Set Up Services

To set up services, follow these steps:

1. Choose Settings.

2. Choose Business Management.

3. Choose Services.

4. Click New.

Figure 19.14 shows the first tab of creating a new service. When you create a new service, you define associated required resources, a default duration, a default status for when the service is applied to a specific schedule activity, and the scheduled activity creation interval.

FIGURE 19.14
Creating a new
service.

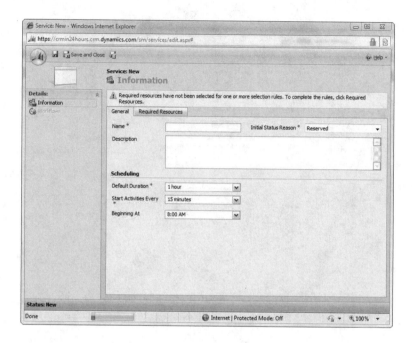

Figure 19.15 shows the second tab of creating a new service form. This form is more difficult, but you can master it. The system is looking for a few variables to associate with some business rules. First, when adding this service to a schedule, where are resources found? From what site are they drawn? By clicking the word *site*, you can choose the total number of sites to look at and how many resources to select from that site. Figure 19.16 shows what the entry looks like.

Choose one resource from the same site. In our example, we will associate this rule with the corporate training center, and there is only one corporate training center and it is not located at multiple sites.

In Figure 19.17, we associate a resource group of trainers and determine that, when scheduling this service, a person must choose three trainers out of a group of five different people (users).

When we select the specific people (users) and go to save, the system asks if these particular people (users) should be saved and associated to a resource group. In Figure 19.17, I said yes and gave the group a name of trainers. See Figure 19.18 and Figure 19.19 for more visibility.

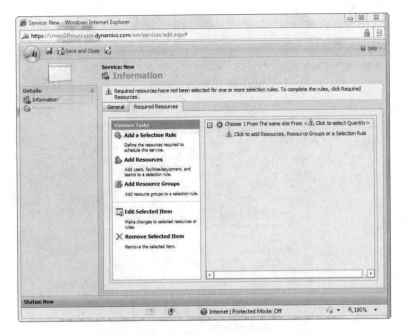

FIGURE 19.15
Assigning resources to a service.

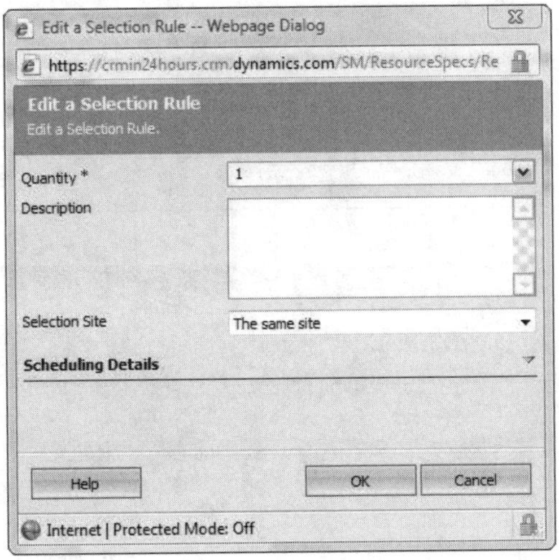

FIGURE 19.16
How many resources are there, and from where?

Now that you created one service, take some time to set up a few more services. Examples include the following:

▶ **Service: An onsite visit to fix something**: Ask yourself what is being fixed? Who and what skills do they need to fix it? What tools are needed? Where are the tools located? If your company has a service truck that includes an inventory of tools, for instance, then scheduling either the truck or an associate tool might be of interest.

▶ **Service: A demonstration**: It requires a special demonstration laptop, a projector, a sales engineer, and a salesperson.

▶ **Service: A cleaning service**: It requires cleaning supplies, a company-owned vacuum cleaner, and a cleaning person.

FIGURE 19.17
Other resources.

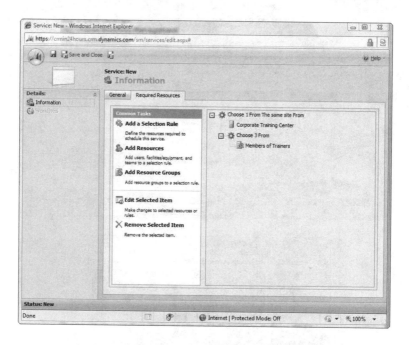

FIGURE 19.18
List of users.

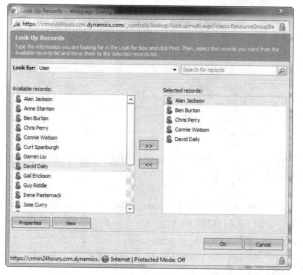

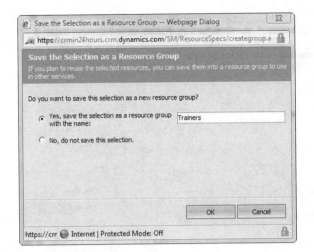

FIGURE 19.19
Saving the list of users as a resource group.

Figure 19.20 shows a list of services.

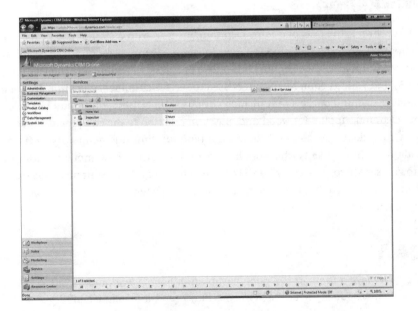

FIGURE 19.20
List of services.

You can deactivate a service, but you cannot delete it. Therefore, you want to carefully consider what services you want to create before you create them.

In summary, Figure 19.21 shows the specific settings in Settings, Business Management that need to be configured for scheduling to function properly. The items are highlighted in yellow.

FIGURE 19.21
System Settings,
Business Man-
agement: Sched-
uling setup
items.

Workshop

Carla Brown is the CEO of a large cleaning business with a staff of 200 people. Her
company, Corporate Cleaning Inc., specializes in cleaning corporate offices all over
the city. Corporate Cleaning Inc. has a fleet of trucks, including one rug-cleaning
truck, and various equipment that is used to service customers (vacuum cleaners,
bundled cleaning buckets that include various rags, brushes, and small brooms,
and cleaning supplies for wood and glass). In addition to the equipment needed to
service its clients, Corporate Cleaning has both full-time and temporary staff. In
addition, it has students who work hourly, mostly during the summer months. Carla
Brown uses Microsoft Dynamics CRM to keep track of all 200 staff members and
their associated equipment, assigned vehicles, and when staff is unavailable to work
at a client site.

Q&A

Q. *We have a team of five people who often handle work orders out in the field.
Can scheduling keep track of who they are visiting and when?*

A. Yes. Microsoft Dynamics CRM's scheduling functionality allows the tracking of
who is where and when, and who needs to be where and when.

Q. *Can resource groups have more than just people associated to them?*

A. Yes. Resource groups can include people, facilities, and equipment.

Q. *We ran into numerous errors when trying to use scheduling. What is happening?*

A. More than likely, you have not completed the configuration for Schedule, and all the pieces that you need for your schedules are not available.

Quiz

1. What is unique about a service activity?
2. Do you have to set up work hours if you are not using scheduling?
3. What items are scheduled on the Service calendar?
4. Can you delete a service?
5. Name three different things that can be scheduled.

Answers

1. The service activity has additional attributes (fields) that are scheduling oriented. One way to think of a service activity is as a supersized and more complex appointment.
2. No. You do not need to set up work hours if you are not using scheduling.
3. Items that are scheduled on the Service calendar include service activities and appointments.
4. No. You cannot delete a service.
5. People, equipment, and facilities.

Exercise

Set up the equipment and ten of the staff resources that Carla Brown uses in her business. Create the carpet-cleaning truck and a few staff resources, including at least two students whose schedule are different than 9 a.m. to 5 p.m. Set up a student, Jackie Tee, who works only on Tuesdays and Wednesdays from 5 p.m. to 12 a.m.

Configure the rest of the requirements for scheduling based on Carla Brown's business model. After scheduling is configured, schedule Jackie Tee to clean a specific office every Tuesday evening from 6 p.m. to 9 p.m. and a different client's office from 9 p.m. to 12 a.m.

HOUR 20

Utilizing the Power of Microsoft Excel with CRM Data

What You'll Learn in This Hour:

▶ Exporting the Right Data Using Advanced Find

▶ Exporting a Static Worksheet

▶ Exporting a Dynamic Worksheet

▶ Exporting Data for PivotTable Analysis

▶ Adding Outside Data

▶ Reusing and Sharing Your Spreadsheets

Now that you understand how to enter data in Microsoft Dynamics CRM, it's time to learn how to get that data out. In this hour we will cover using the power of Microsoft Excel to work with data from Microsoft Dynamics CRM.

Key Concepts and Caveats

There are many reasons you need to analyze data. Microsoft Dynamics CRM makes it easy to specify criteria for which records to include, and then export the list to a Microsoft Excel worksheet or PivotTable. After the data is in Excel, all the power of Excel is there to analyze your data. When you're ready to export a list of data to Excel, Microsoft Dynamics CRM will offer you two basic choices: static or dynamic, and table or PivotTable. A static spreadsheet has no connection to Microsoft Dynamics CRM after it is created. The data is extracted and saved, and a user can't tell that it was created from Microsoft Dynamics CRM. A dynamic spreadsheet on the other hand retains its connection to Microsoft Dynamics CRM. It will refresh the included data from Microsoft Dynamics CRM when it is opened, and it maintains the data security that exists within Microsoft Dynamics CRM Security.

Here is more detailed information you need to know to make the decisions.

An export to a Microsoft Excel spreadsheet can either be static or dynamic.

▶ A **static spreadsheet** is a snapshot of the data at the moment you created it, and it does not change when data in Microsoft Dynamics CRM changes. Static spreadsheets are great for one-time tasks and for capturing data at the end of a reporting period. They are also useful when you need to present the data to someone who is not a Microsoft Dynamics CRM user.

▶ A **dynamic spreadsheet** is connected directly to Microsoft Dynamics CRM data. When data in Microsoft Dynamics CRM changes, the data in the dynamics spreadsheet also changes. Dynamic spreadsheets are useful if you want to do the work to design the spreadsheet once and then analyze or share the data as the data changes.

Because of the security built into Microsoft Dynamics CRM, the data in an exported spreadsheet only includes records that the person who exports the data has permission to see. This is a key difference between the two types of spreadsheets:

▶ In a static spreadsheet, anyone who opens the spreadsheet can see the data, whether or not they have access to Microsoft Dynamics CRM. This means that you need to be careful if you create a static spreadsheet with confidential data: Anyone who can open the file can view the data.

▶ In a dynamic spreadsheet, only Microsoft Dynamics CRM users with the right security can view the data. When the spreadsheet is opened, users are prompted to refresh the data. Only data they have permission to see is included. This means that one dynamic spreadsheet can be used by many people, so someone with more Excel experience can design a complex PivotTable or worksheet, and each user can use it to analyze his own data.

Excel has two ways of presenting data: tables and PivotTables. Either can be turned into a chart:

▶ Tables are a flat way of viewing your data using rows and columns.

▶ PivotTables are interactive: They are designed for the viewer to experiment with alternative ways of looking at the data.

Every time you export to Excel, Microsoft Dynamics CRM asks you to make a choice between exporting to a worksheet (table) or a PivotTable. Figure 20.1 shows the difference between these two formats.

FIGURE 20.1
Excel worksheet
and an Excel
PivotTable.

This hour doesn't make you an expert on Microsoft Excel; instead, it focuses on how
to get the information into Microsoft Excel.

Required Software

If you use CRM Online, to export to dynamic spreadsheets or PivotTables, you
must also use the Microsoft Dynamics CRM Outlook client. This is available as a
free download for all Microsoft Dynamics CRM users.

Watch
Out!

Finding Your Way in Microsoft Dynamics CRM

You need to know where the Advanced Find button is and where the Export to Excel
button is. These buttons are in the same spot no matter at what entity (record type)
you are looking. Figure 20.2 shows the location of these buttons.

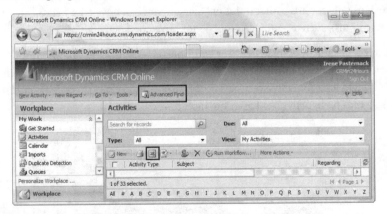

FIGURE 20.2
Location of
Advanced Find
and Export to
Excel buttons.

Exporting the Right Data: Using Advanced Find

If you're not exporting the right data, no fancy Excel trick will get you useful information. To get the right data, you'll need to learn how to use Microsoft Dynamics
CRM Advanced Find to do two things:

- ▶ Filter data to exactly the data you want

- ▶ Display all the columns you need

▼   **Try it Yourself**

Limiting the Data Displayed

When exporting to Excel, you can limit the data you export or you can export all data and filter it in Excel once the data is there. The approach you take will vary, depending on the amount of data you have and on the specific analysis task you're working on.

Here's how to limit the data in Microsoft Dynamics CRM before you export.

Did you Know?

> ### Using Advanced Find
>
> The easiest way to use Advanced Find is to go to a pre-existing view that is close to what you want and then click Advanced Find. This defaults to that existing view and offers you the chance to modify it, because most of the Advanced Find criteria you need will already be defined.

From anywhere in the product, click the Advanced Find button to open Advanced Find.

To limit the data displayed, select the primary entity (record type) to search and then specify **search criteria.** You can have criteria on the entity (record type) you are searching, such as only records with a status of Open, or you can have criteria based on related entities (records), such as entities (records) that have open activities associated.

You can be specific in your search. For example, if I was getting organized for a business trip to businesses with zip codes starting with 980, I could use the query shown in Figure 20.3 to look for active contacts that I own that are in a zip code beginning with 980 that have activities due in the next four weeks.

FIGURE 20.3
Query showing active contacts in zip code 980*.

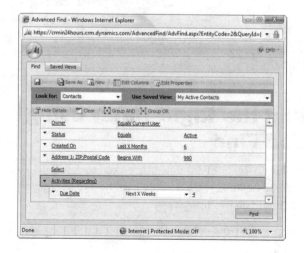

There are several things to notice about specifying criteria. First, notice that each criteria line has three possible parts:

- **Field to search**: For example, in the second line, you're looking for records that have a Status field with Active as the value.

- **Operator**: In the third line, the operator is Last X Months, and in the Value column, you specify the number of months.

- **Value**: Displayed in the third column. If the operator includes the value in it, such as the "Equals current user" operator in the first line, no separate value part is displayed.

Second, notice the shaded area labeled Activities (Regarding). This shaded bar indicates that any criteria below it are from different entities (record types). In this case, the criteria are from the Activities entity (record type), and I'm looking for activities due within four weeks that are associated with the contacts.

By searching for criteria from multiple entities (record types), you can find exactly the data you need.

You need to know a few details about specifying criteria:

- You can group criteria:

  - **Group AND**: Specifies that all the grouped criteria must be true

  - **Group OR**: Specifies that only one of the grouped criteria must be true

- You can add multiple values in one criterion. These are processed as an OR; if a record has any of the multiple values, it will be included in the results.

In Figure 20.4, notice the little arrow next to each criteria row. Select it to see the options.

After you select a row, you can group it with other rows. Figure 20.5 shows the two City clauses grouped together.

If you are selecting criteria from a list, multiple values can be separated by a semicolon. Figure 20.6 shows grouped criteria.

FIGURE 20.4
Select or delete
a criteria row.

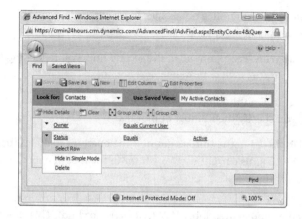

FIGURE 20.5
Grouped criteria.

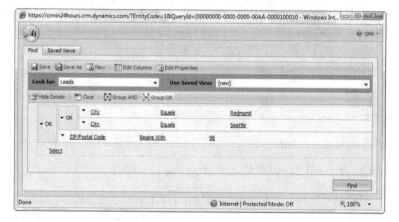

FIGURE 20.6
Enter multiple
values in one cri-
terion.

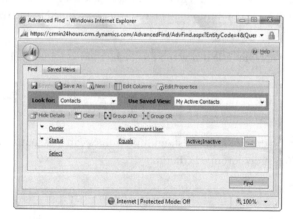

Task: Displaying the Exact Columns You Need

How you specify columns depends on which export method you choose:

- ▶ For static worksheets, select columns in Advanced Find before exporting.

- ▶ For PivotTables, select columns in Advanced Find first or click Select Columns in the Export dialog box.

- ▶ For dynamic worksheets, select columns in Advanced Find or click Add Columns in the Export dialog box.

First, we'll look at how to select columns in Advanced Find.

For example, perhaps you are preparing print mailing labels for a selected set of Lead records collected from a tradeshow.

From the Leads area, open the Open Leads view and click Advanced Find. Add your criteria for Lead Source.

Then, click Edit Columns, Add Columns to add the columns necessary for a mailing. Figure 20.7 shows the Add Columns dialog.

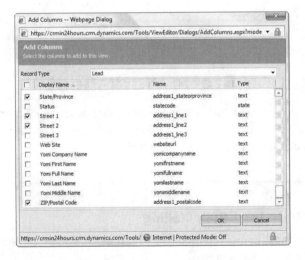

FIGURE 20.7
Select additional columns to display.

Click OK to select the Lead columns. Then, click Add Columns again, but this time, in the Record Type drop-down list, select a type of record (noticing that you can select from the main record type you already picked or from related record types). Select the Owner record type, select the First Name column, and click OK.

Data From Multiple Record Types

You can select columns from multiple record types to include in the output. For example, if you are exporting leads, you can include the name of the source campaign, or the name of the referring account.

The order of the columns in the Advanced Find results is the order that the data will be displayed in Excel, so you might decide to reorder the columns using the green arrows, shown in Figure 20.8. While you're at it, delete any columns you don't need in your spreadsheet. Don't worry about sorting; that's easier to do in Excel after you export your data.

FIGURE 20.8
Reorganize or remove columns.

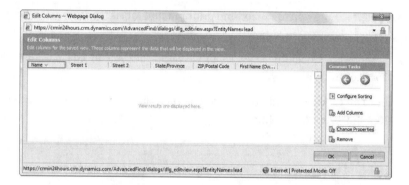

Exporting a Static Worksheet

Now that you have exactly the data you want to analyze in your Advanced Find results, it's time to export the data to an Excel spreadsheet. A common use of this is to organize mailing information for a bulk mailing.

▼ **Try it Yourself**

Exporting Data for a Bulk Mailing

After you have the columns you need, such as name, and address information for mailing labels, follow these steps:

1. Click the Export to Excel button.

2. Exam is the choice of options.

3. Select Static Worksheet with Records From This Page, or select Static Worksheet with Records from all Pages in the Current View. (This depends on what records you want in the spreadsheet.)

Figure 20.9 shows all the choices possible when you export to Excel.

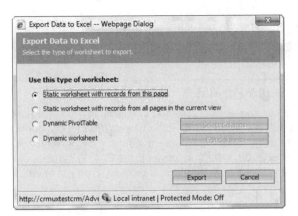

FIGURE 20.9
Select the type
of Excel file to
create.

Don't Panic on Message

When you click Open, don't panic when you get the dialog box shown in Figure 20.10: It will happen every time you open an Excel file you exported from Dynamics CRM. Dynamics CRM actually exports an XML file that Excel knows how to open. Save the file and then open it.

You'll see a dialog box prompting you to open or save the file.

FIGURE 20.10
Warning about
file type.

When your data is in Excel, the column header will show you when the data is from a related record type. For example, the First Name (Owner) column comes from the Owner record type.

Figure 20.11 shows you the output in Excel.

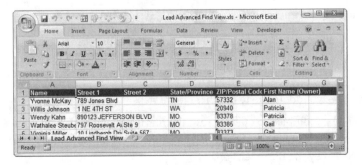

FIGURE 20.11
Source of data
displayed in col-
umn heading in
Excel.

Now that the data is in Excel, you can do a Mail Merge to Microsoft Office Word to print letters or labels. You can even sign each letter with the lead owner's first name, because you included that in the columns you exported.

By the
Way

Select the Right Format

When you save any spreadsheet created by exporting from Microsoft Dynamics CRM, by default, it is saved in XML Spreadsheet 2003 (*.xml) format. When you save it, if you're using Excel 2007, save it in format Excel Workbook (.xlsx), or if you're using Excel 2003, save it in format Excel 97-2003 Workbook (.xls). This will prevent you from getting a warning message every time you open the spreadsheet.

Exporting a Dynamic Worksheet

If you want to create a spreadsheet that you can reuse as data changes in Microsoft Dynamics CRM, create a dynamic worksheet. A dynamic worksheet updates the contained data from Microsoft Dynamics CRM each time you open it. This is helpful when you want to put some time into formatting a worksheet, and don't want to have to redo this work each time new data is added. It's also an essential feature if you're creating a dashboard that shows current data whenever it is viewed.

Task: Exporting Data to Chart

To export data to a dynamic spreadsheet,

1. Start from an Advanced Find view that includes all the records you want to export. For example, you might want to see a chart showing opportunities grouped by size, so you could start by exporting the My Open Opportunities view.

2. Select the Dynamic Worksheet option. Notice that the Edit Columns button becomes available.

3. Click Edit Columns.

4. Select and order the columns you want in your table.

5. Click Export after your columns are set.

Before you see your data, there are three more steps:

▶ You'll be prompted to open or save the file. Go ahead and open the file, and click OK when you see the message that the file is in a different format than specified by the file extension.

▶ With some versions of Excel and some operating systems, you might see a message "Security Warning: Data connections have been disabled," and no data will be visible. If you receive this message, click the Options button and select Enable This Content.

▶ If you are using Microsoft Dynamics CRMOnline, the first line of the spreadsheet will say "To view and refresh dynamic data, Microsoft Dynamics CRM Outlook Client must be installed."

If you have the Microsoft Dynamics CRM Outlook client installed), click the Data tab, then click the Refresh from CRM button.

After you have the data exported, you can use Excel to create whatever charts you need. Each time you open your worksheet, the data will refresh from Microsoft Dynamics CRM, or you can use the Refresh from CRM commands on the data ribbon to refresh the data.

Figure 20.12 shows a dynamic spreadsheet with the Refresh from CRM ribbon.

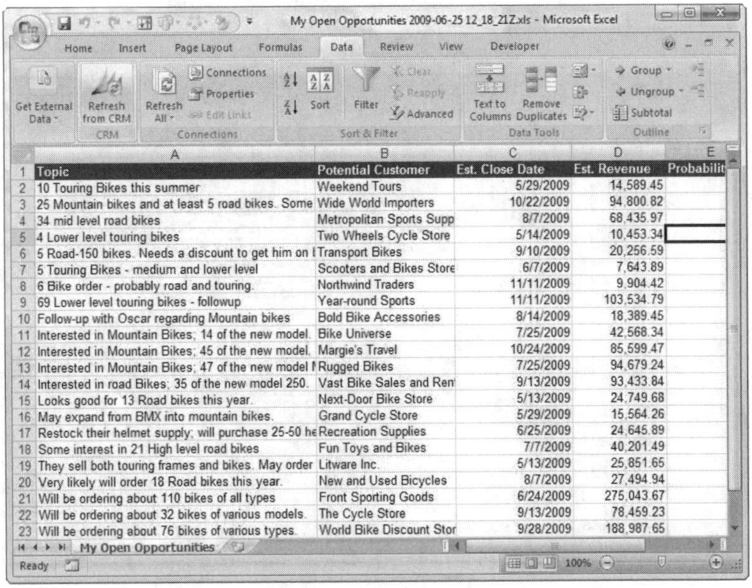

FIGURE 20.12
Refresh from CRM on the Data ribbon in Excel.

Exporting Data for PivotTable Analysis

Dynamic PivotTables provide a way to slice and dice your data in different ways to quickly discover patterns.

Task: Exporting a Dynamic PivotTable

By default, all the columns in your view will be available to use in your PivotTable. If you want more columns, you can either add them to your view before you export or click the Select Columns button.

When you open the exported file, you'll see your standard blank PivotTable, ready to select the data to pivot. To select the data to pivot, do the following:

1. In the security message, click Options to enable viewing the content.

2. On the Data tab, click Refresh from CRM.

You are now ready to explore your data using the PivotTable.

Two sheets are created for each PivotTable: Sheet1 contains the PivotTable, and the second sheet contains the raw data used by the PivotTable.

In Figure 20.13, by pivoting on the estimated close date and estimated revenue, you can see the projected income.

FIGURE 12.13
PivotTable for opportunities.

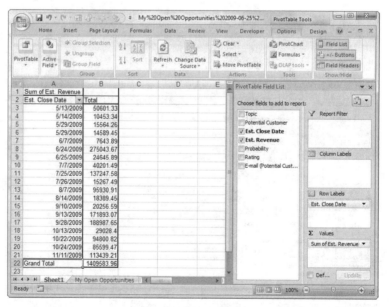

Now, you're free to use Excel to analyze and format your data, knowing that the work you put into getting it just right will be usable each month as you forecast revenue from your opportunities. Figure 20.14 shows the example PivotTable turned into a PivotChart.

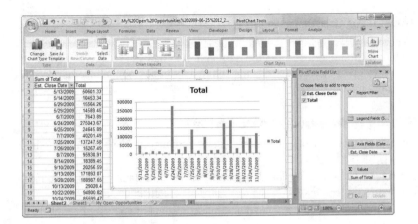

FIGURE 20.14
PivotChart for
opportunities.

Adding Outside Data

After you have a spreadsheet or PivotTable saved, you might want to connect the data in it to data in another spreadsheet or database. You can do so by using the advanced features of Microsoft Excel, which support establishing a data connection to another data source from the new Excel worksheet. This chapter's focus is on Microsoft Dynamics CRM, so the advanced features of Excel are not outlined.

For example, your department might have a budget model in Excel. You could connect it to your opportunities to assess whether you are on track to meet the budget numbers.

Reusing and Sharing Your Spreadsheets

To make your Excel file available to other people, you have several options:

▶ Add the Excel file to Microsoft Dynamics CRM as a report. This report can be available for you or for other people in your company. (See Hour 21, "Reporting and Query Basics.")

▶ Email a static or dynamic spreadsheet to other people or save it in a shared file system.

▶ Put the Excel file on an intranet site, such as a SharePoint dashboard.

Accessing the Data

Remember, if you email or save a dynamic spreadsheet, only other Microsoft Dynamics CRM users can see the data in it. And they might see different data when they open it, because they will see results based on the records that they have permission to see.

Making It Your Own/Customizing

The following tasks typically require system administrator or system customizer security roles:

The columns that are displayed in Advanced Find by default can be customized. This changes the columns for all users in your organization.

New system views can be defined and made available to all users.

A Microsoft Dynamics CRM dashboard can be created using dynamic Excel spreadsheets and added to Microsoft Dynamics CRM as a report or as a web page.

Using a Dashboard

There are many possible ways to make a dashboard. Which you choose depends on the needs of your company, such as how frequently you change what information you want to monitor, and whether the dashboard is used by all users or just a few. If you do not have the Excel and other tool knowledge in your company to create a dashboard, ask for help from a Microsoft Certified Dynamics CRM partner.

Workshop

John Brown, the sales manager from Hour 10, "Entering Data as a Salesperson," is getting ready for his quarterly meeting with the CEO. He wants to analyze patterns in how opportunities are won or lost in his territory so that he can clearly communicate to his boss, and so that he can improve the results of his team. He creates a custom view in Advanced Find and exports it to an Excel PivotTable. After experimenting with various pivots, he finds one that clearly shows the data and turns it into a PivotChart. He fusses with the details to make it look exactly how he wants it for his PowerPoint presentation. The chart shows the three top factors in successfully winning opportunities, with the main factor being a response to the lead within 24 hours.

John saves his dynamic PivotTable in Microsoft Dynamics CRM as a report so that he can use it on a regular basis, and he embeds it into a PowerPoint presentation.

His boss gives great feedback about his presentation and asks him to make it available to all the sales managers in the company. He shares the spreadsheet with the other managers and the CEO and decides to share it with all the salespeople. Because of the way data security is set up in the company, when each sales manager views the report, he sees just his own territory's data. When the CEO views the report, she sees the data for the entire company. When each sales representative views the data, all he sees is his own data.

Because the point of analyzing data is to learn what to do differently to improve results, the sales managers get together to determine best practices based on what they learned. They decide to implement a new sales process using workflow to make sure that the recommended procedures are followed. A simple workflow is implemented that sends an email to the manager if a lead hasn't been followed up within 24 hours.

Q&A

Q. *When I share my dynamic spreadsheet with my manager, why does she see different numbers than I do?*

A. Each person who opens the spreadsheet sees data that matches records that she has permission to view in CRM. If she can see more records than you, more records will be included.

Q. *If I'm using Microsoft Dynamics CRM Online, why do I need the Microsoft Dynamics CRM Outlook client to export dynamic spreadsheets?*

A. Microsoft Dynamics CRM Online won't offer you the option of dynamic worksheet or dynamic PivotTable unless the Microsoft Dynamics CRM Outlook client is installed.

Q. *How many record types can I export at once?*

A. In any Advanced Find view, there is one primary record type. You can include columns from related record types. So, you can have data from many record types displayed, but only if they relate to the primary record.

Quiz

1. What type of spreadsheet should contain confidential information: static or dynamic?

2. For which types of export do you need to select columns in Advanced Find before clicking the Export to Excel button?

3. Why should I save the Advanced Find view I used when exporting the data?

Answers

1. A dynamic spreadsheet contains data that you have permission to view in CRM. After data is in the static spreadsheet, anyone who views it can see the data.

2. This isn't relevant for PivotTables, because you have to specify where you want the data when you open the file. If you're exporting a static or dynamic worksheet, organizing your columns in advance is important only if you plan to reuse the Advanced Find search, because you can always reorganize the data in Excel.

3. Saving the view lets you know what the criteria were for the records in the spreadsheet. It also makes it easier to do the same or a similar export again.

Exercise

In your Microsoft Dynamics CRM or a demo version, export contact records to Excel to do the following:

▶ Create an Advanced Find search that includes just the columns you need to create mailing labels.

▶ Create a PivotTable that you can use to analyze the city and state where your customers come from. Determine whether the percentage for each state is the same in each month.

HOUR 21

Reporting

What You'll Learn in This Hour:

▶ Finding and Using the Default Reports, Including Running Them on Specific Records

▶ Writing Your Own Reports Using the Report Wizard

▶ Adding Other Files, Such as Excel Workbooks as Reports

▶ Organizing Your Reports to Make Them Easy to Find and Use

▶ Sharing a Report with Other Users, or with All Microsoft Dynamics CRM Users at Your Company

▶ Additional Reporting Options if You're Using On-Premise Microsoft Dynamics CRM

▶ Tips for Efficient Use of Reports: Changing the Default Filter, Renaming Reports, Setting Permissions, and More

When we use the word *reports*, we mean formatted presentations of data, with information either grouped or charted. A report is typically used for getting a quick overview of patterns in your data so that you can make a business decision, or for communicating performance to other people, such as capturing end-of-quarter results.

Microsoft Dynamics CRM comes with 24 predefined reports. Depending on how much Microsoft Dynamics CRM has been customized for your organization, these reports may or may not be useful for you.

Microsoft Dynamics CRM also comes with a Report Wizard that makes it easy to create your own reports that include charts/tables for presenting your data.

Reporting

Reporting is one area where there are significant differences between Microsoft Dynamics CRM Online and On-Premise. Several features are available only to On-Premise users, such as the following:

Modifying the default reports

Scheduling snapshots of reports to run at specific times

Creating your own reports using Microsoft SQL Server Reporting Services or other ODBC reporting tools and adding them directly into Microsoft Dynamics CRM as a report

The default reports are divided into four categories:

▶ Sixteen sales reports show information about accounts, competitors; quotes, orders, and invoices; neglected accounts and leads; sales history and pipeline; activities and product data by account or by contact.

▶ Three marketing reports show information about campaigns and lead source effectiveness.

▶ Four service reports show a summary of cases, information on neglected cases, service activity volume, and top Knowledge Base articles.

▶ One administrative report shows data on Microsoft Dynamics CRM users such as name, title, phone numbers, and Microsoft Dynamics CRM security roles.

Defaults

The default reports use the default names of record types and fields in Microsoft Dynamics CRM. Any customizations, such as renaming cases to tickets (or adding, renaming, or removing fields), will not show up in the default reports.

One of the first tasks when you're planning to use Microsoft Dynamics CRM is to evaluate the default reports and determine what additional reports are necessary.

By defining what reports you need, you'll also think through what data you need to capture. For example, if you want to track opportunities by sales stage, you have to make sure your sales process tracks sales stage.

Running Reports

To get started with reports, you need to know where to find them, the basic anatomy of a report, and understand which security roles can do which report-related tasks.

Finding Your Way to Microsoft Dynamics CRM Reports

There are three ways to get to reports:

▶ From the workplace:

1. Click Reports.

2. Select Workplace.

3. In the left navigation pane, click Reports. All the default reports are available from this location.

▶ From a view of records:

1. Click the Reports button on the menu bar for the view for reports that make sense for the records being viewed.

Some reports, such as Sales History, only make sense when run on all the records. Others can be run on one or a group of records.

▶ From a record:

1. Click the Reports button on the menu bar of the record for reports that make sense for the current record.

Figure 21.1 shows the options when you click the Reports button from the Active Accounts view. Only reports that make sense for accounts are displayed.

FIGURE 21.1
Reports menu, shown from a list of Account records, with two accounts selected.

You'll be offered a choice of how to run the report (see Figure 21.2).

FIGURE 21.2
Choices for
which records to
include in a
report.

When you select The Selected Records, the report will run on just the two records you highlighted. Click Run Report to see the results.

Figure 21.3 shows the Report menunfrom within a record. When you select a report this way, the report is run just on the open record.

FIGURE 21.3
The Report
menu, shown
from within a
record.

Anatomy of a Report

Each report has a default filter that contains predefined criteria for which records to include. Typical default filters include limiting the results to records owned by you or to records modified in the past 30 days.

When you run a report, the Report Filtering Criteria screen is displayed before you see any data so that you can modify the filter. This lets you change the filter every time you run a report. The less data that is in a report, the faster it will run, so use the filtering criteria to limit the data to just what you need to see.

The report filter uses the same user interface as Advanced Find. For each criteria row, you enter a field name, an operator, and a value. Figure 21.4 shows a typical default filter, specifying records that have been modified within the past 30 days.

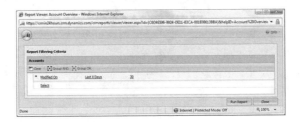

FIGURE 21.4
Report-filtering criteria.

After you run a report, it's helpful to know the filter criteria used to generate the report. This is handy before printing the report, because it ensures when you look at the printout later, you can still tell what's included. Figure 21.5 shows the summary for the previous filter.

FIGURE 21.5
Expanded filter summary.

If the default filter doesn't match how everyone in your organization typically uses a report, your system administrator or system customizer can change the default filter.

Navigating in a Default Report

Most of the navigation to explore a report is at the top of the page, including buttons to page through the report and a search box to search for data in the report.

Many reports have grouping or display options at the top. When you run a report, the default grouping or display option will be used. You can select another option and click View Report to refresh it. Figure 21.6 shows these options for the Account Summary report.

FIGURE 21.6
Grouping and
display options.

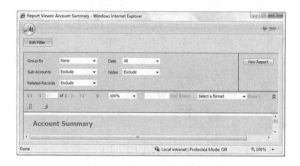

No Save Button

There is no Save button on a report for saving the data in the report. In Figure 21.6, notice the box for selecting a format. You can export a report to other formats, such as PDF and web archive, and save these files. These formats are useful for capturing specific results at a specific time period.

Exporting from a report to Excel exports a formatted report. This is typically not useful for analyzing the data with Excel.

Viewing Data in a Default Report

If a default report includes a chart, click a section of the chart to see the data behind the chart section. Figure 21.7 shows a chart produced by the Activities report.

To see all data used in the chart, click Show All at the bottom of the chart. There is no easy way to get back to the chart; you'll need to rerun the report.

In the table of data, click any record to go right to the full record in CRM.

Who Can Do What with Reports?

Several permissions control who can do report-related tasks. These are defined in your Microsoft Dynamics CRM security role:

▶ All default security roles give all users permission to run reports. When a person views a report, she can only see data on records that she has permission to view.

▶ All default security roles give all users permission to create a new report with the Report Wizard for their own use.

Report Layout

The layout of reports is not changeable by report users. The orientation, page size, font, and contents are predefined.

Organizations that use the On-Premise version of Microsoft Dynamics CRM can have a system customizer modify these aspects of default reports, but the layout cannot be modified for reports created by the Report Wizard.

Watch Out!

▶ Most default security roles do not have permission to make reporting changes for all users at a company, such as adding a report for all users, renaming reports, or changing the default filter for default reports.

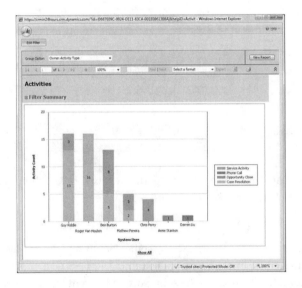

FIGURE 21.7
Activities report.

There are two types of reports, organization-owned and individual-owned:

▶ Organization-owned reports are visible to all the Microsoft Dynamics CRM users in your organization. All the default reports are, by default, organization-owned.

▶ Individual-owned reports are visible just to the owner of the report. Just like other records in Microsoft Dynamics CRM, the owner can share individual-owned reports with specific other users or teams.

Properties of a Report

Each report is stored as a record in Microsoft Dynamics CRM, and has properties that define how it can be used. If you plan to add reports using the Report Wizard, you'll use these properties to hook up your report to the user interface so that you can run it from where you want.

First, let's look at the General tab (see Figure 21.8) for the Account Overview report.

FIGURE 21.8
General tab.

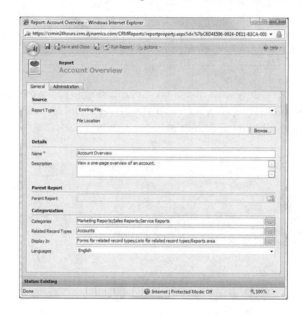

The Source area defines the source for the report. There are three options: an Existing File, a Link to a Web Page, or a Report Wizard report.

The Details area provides a name and description.

The third area, Parent Report, is only used by some default reports and by report customizers using On-Premise installations of Dynamics CRM. Some complex reports have subreports, and this field keeps the subreport and parent report connected.

The most interesting area is the Categorization area. This is where you determine where in the user interface a report will be visible:

- ▶ You can select which forms and lists should include the new report on the Reports menu. If you put a value in Related Record Types, the report will be available on the Reports menu in that area of Dynamics CRM.

- ▶ The Display In selection controls whether the reports are available in forms, records, or the main Reports list. In Figure 21.8, the report will show up in the

Reports area, on the Report menu in the Accounts area, and in the Report menu on an Account form.

The Administration tab defines ownership settings for the report (see Figure 21.9). If you create a great report that everyone might benefit from, you can ask your system administrator or system customizer to make it organization owned.

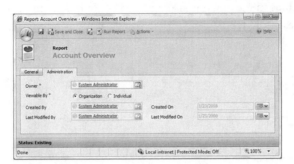

FIGURE 21.9
Administration tab.

Creating Your Own Report with the Report Wizard

The Report Wizard lets you create charts and tables that summarize your data. In this example, we'll use the wizard to create a chart of Opportunities by State.

To start the wizard, from the Reports area, click New, Report Wizard.

On the first page of the wizard (see Figure 21.10), select that you want to start a new report.

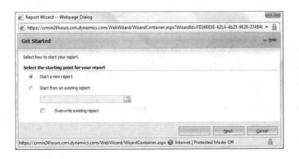

FIGURE 21.10
Getting Started page of the Report Wizard.

You can also use the wizard to modify a report that was created with the Report Wizard.

Watch
Out!

Default Report Exception

You cannot use the Report Wizard to modify a default report.

On the next page of the wizard, after specifying a name and description, you select which records to include in the report (see Figure 21.11). For this example, we'll just use the Opportunities record type.

FIGURE 21.11
Specifying the record types to include in a report wizard report.

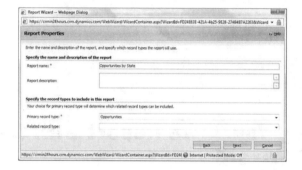

The next page of the wizard (see Figure 21.12) prompts you to define the default filter for the report. We've added the filter of opportunities that close in the next six months.

The next page, Layout Fields, is the most important page of the Report Wizard. This is where you select what data to put in your report and how to organize the data. The first step is deciding the big buckets for the report: how to group the information. In Figure 21.13, we'll group the report by state.

As part of selecting the field to group the records by, we can also select the properties for the grouping. In Figure 21.14, we specify an ascending sort order, and that we want to see a count of records in each group.

Then, you need to select the fields to display in the report.

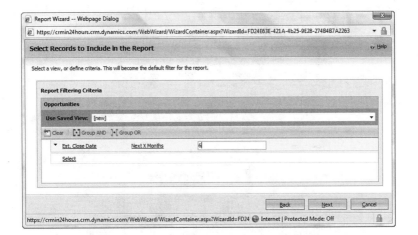

FIGURE 21.12
Selecting records to include in a report wizard report.

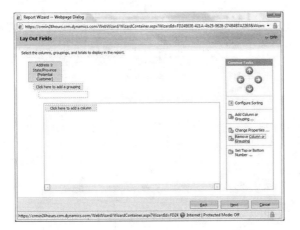

FIGURE 21.13
Selecting grouping and specifying columns.

Numeric Field Needed

If you want to create a graph or chart, you need a field that is numeric, and you need to select a summary option for it. Otherwise, the Report Wizard creates only a tabular format report.

In Figure 21.15, we'll select the potential customer name and the estimated revenue fields. Because we want a chart, we'll group the data in the Estimated Revenue column.

Figure 21.16 shows the completed Lay Out Fields page with one level of grouping, and two columns in the report.

FIGURE 21.14
Defining the group properties.

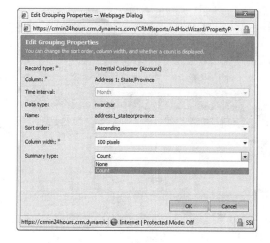

FIGURE 21.15
Defining the properties for a column.

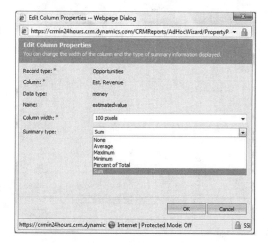

After the grouping and fields for the report are set, the remaining wizard choices are straightforward: defining whether you want a chart in the report, and if so, defining the text for the axes for the report.

When you complete the wizard, you run the report to see the results. If you selected to create a chart, the chart is on the first page, and the table is on the second page.

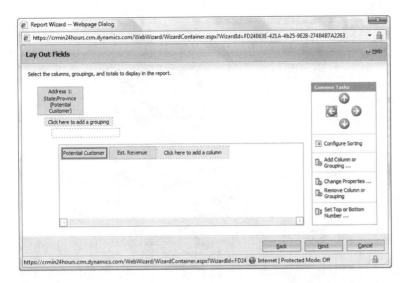

FIGURE 21.16
Completed specification for the report layout.

Figure 21.17 shows our Opportunities by State report.

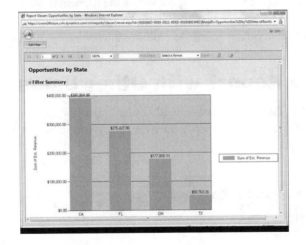

FIGURE 21.17
Page 1 of the Opportunities by State report created with the Report Wizard.

Note that charts created with the Report Wizard do not let you drill down to see the table behind the chart. Instead, go to the next page of the report to see the details (see Figure 21.18).

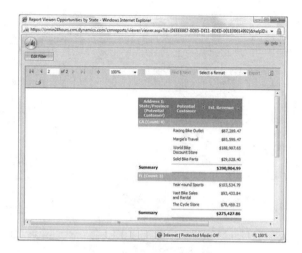

If you don't get the report exactly right on the first try, just restart the Report Wizard and go back through the wizard, changing whatever is needed.

After the report is doing what you expect, define the properties to make sure it shows up in the user interface where you need it, and if you want, share it with other users or convert it to an organization-owned report so that everyone can use it.

Share a Report with Other Users

To share a report that you created with other users, select the Sharing option on the More Actions menu, and then specify the teams or users who need to use this report (see Figure 21.19).

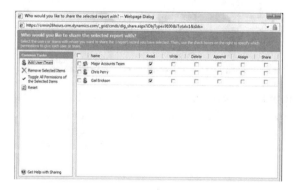

Add a File or Web Page as a Report

Any type of file can be added as a report and made available to users through the Microsoft Dynamics CRM user interface. This helps users stay within the Microsoft Dynamics CRM application.

From the Reports area, click New. In the Report Type box, click Existing File. See Figure 21.20.

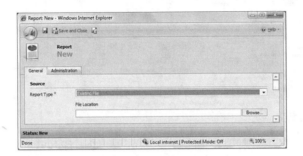

FIGURE 21.20
Adding an existing file.

For Microsoft Dynamics CRM Online, you can add static files and dynamic Excel files that read data from the Microsoft Dynamics CRM database.

For On-Premise versions, you can add any type of dynamic files that read data directly from the Microsoft Dynamics CRM database, including custom reports.

To add a link to a web page as a report, click Link to Web page. Notice in Figure 21.21 that the next box changes, giving you a place to specify the URL of the page.

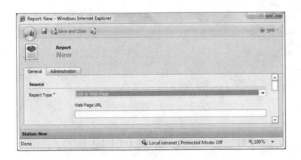

FIGURE 21.21
Linking to a web page.

You'll need to set the rest of the properties to specify where in the user interface this new web page or file should be displayed. For example, suppose you create a dynamic PivotTable to help analyze data related to large accounts. Figure 21.22

FIGURE 21.22
Specifying where
the new report
will be visible.

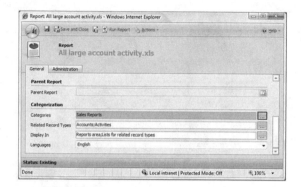

shows the Display In options necessary to view this report so that in the Reports list, and in the Accounts and Activities areas, but not from any Account forms.

After you save the new report, the Actions menu will be available (see Figure 21.23). Depending on your security role, you may see one or both of Sharing and Make Report Available to Organization, so you can make the web page or file you added available to those who need it.

FIGURE 21.23
Actions menu for
a report.

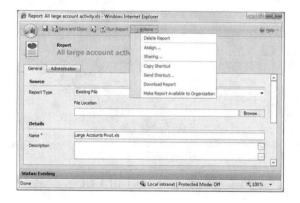

Create Report Snapshots (On-Premise Only)

Report snapshots let you save the data in a report at a particular moment in time. This is useful for measuring end-of-time period results. Snapshots can be run on demand or scheduled to run regularly. Figure 21.24 shows the page for scheduling the frequency for creating a snapshot of the Account Distribution report.

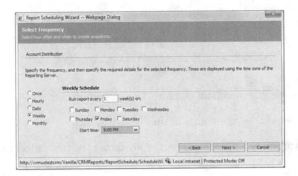

FIGURE 21.24
Report Scheduling Wizard.

The scheduled report shows up right in the user interface as a new report, and you can edit its properties to determine where it is available.

Watch Out!

Scheduled Reports

Scheduled reports are individual owned by default. If you need these to be visible to other users, be sure to share them or change them to organization owned.

Scheduled reports can be set up to be emailed to other people. This must be set up in Microsoft SQL Server Reporting Services. For more information, see the Microsoft Dynamics CRM Team Blog at http://blogs.msdn.com/crm/archive/2009/08/05/creating-report-subscriptions-in-microsoft-dynamics-crm-4.aspx.

Tips for Keeping Reports Organized

If your organization does a lot of custom reporting, whether with the Report Wizard or other tools, the list of records in the Reports area can get large. There are default views for this area set up for four categories of reports: Sales, Marketing, Service, and Administration. You can customize these categories for your organization.

Click Settings, and then click System Settings. The Report tab provides a place to define and organize the categories (see Figure 21.25).

FIGURE 21.25
Defining cate-
gories for organ-
izing reports.

After the categories are modified, there are two more steps:

1. For each report, set the values in the Categories field.

2. Customize the views for the Report entity to use the new category names.

Custom Reports That Don't Use the Report Wizard

You can also create custom reports, such as dashboards, reports with other layouts, or reports with more complex drill-downs into the data reports.

Microsoft Dynamics CRM provides filtered views that make it easy for report writers to use the Microsoft Dynamics security roles. Therefore, even custom reports only show data that a user has permission to see. However, creating custom reports requires a more technical skill set. (Many solution providers specialize in creating custom reports.)

On-Premise

For On-Premise Microsoft Dynamics CRM, if you need custom reports beyond what the Report Wizard can create, anyone with the System Customizer or System Administrator security role can modify the default reports or create new reports and upload them to Microsoft Dynamics CRM.

Because the default reports are written using Microsoft SQL Reporting Services, modifying them requires the following report-development environment:

▶ Microsoft Visual Studio or any product that uses the Visual Studio .NET integrated development environment, such as Microsoft Visual Basic .NET

▶ Microsoft SQL Reporting Services Report Designer

Modifying default reports is usually done by someone who specializes in report design or a programmer, not by a regular user. This is an area where a solution provider can come in handy.

New reports can also be created in any ODBC-compliant application, including Microsoft Access, Microsoft Excel, Microsoft SQL Server Reporting Services, and a wide range of business intelligence tools. These new reports can be added in as a new report.

Microsoft Dynamics CRM Online

For Microsoft Dynamics CRM Online, there are several options for custom reports, each of which requires developer and or report-writing skills:

▶ If you subscribe to the Microsoft Dynamics CRM Online Professional Plus edition, you can use offline data synchronization to synchronize data locally. Then, you can use any ODBC-compliant tool to write reports against the local data store.

▶ You can use an integration tool to integrate Microsoft Dynamics CRM data with a local database and write reports based on the local data.

▶ You can use the Microsoft Dynamics CRM Software Development Kit (SDK) to develop a custom .NET application. This is usually done by experienced developers or solution providers.

Hours 22, "Integration to the Other Applications," and 24, "Microsoft Dynamics CRM as a Development Framework," go into more depth for options for extending Microsoft Dynamics CRM.

Workshop

Joyous Fitness is a chain of exercise studios that uses Microsoft Dynamics CRM Online to track members and class attendees. It has made some customizations to Microsoft Dynamics CRM, renaming the Accounts entity to Members, and editing the values of all the drop-down lists to match their terminology. It uses the Product entity to track memberships and has created a new entity to track class attendance.

The studio uses the marketing module of Microsoft Dynamics CRM as is to track mailings to customers and radio advertisements.

Q&A

Q. *We do not use the Service module in Microsoft Dynamics CRM. Can we make it so that those reports are not visible?*

A. Yes. Anyone with the System Administrator or System Customizer security role can modify the properties for those reports and change them so that they are not displayed.

Q. *Can we rename the default reports and change the default filters?*

A. Yes. These changes can be made in both Microsoft Dynamics CRM Online and the On-Premise version.

Q. *Will the default reports work for us; or do we have to create our own?*

A. Because Joyous Fitness is using the Microsoft Dynamics CRM marketing module without customization, the marketing default reports will work. The sales reports will also work as is, although renaming the reports to use the word *Member versus* Account would make it easier for employees to identify the proper report.

There are some custom reports that are needed for class attendance. These can be created using the Report Wizard or by exporting data to Microsoft Excel.

Q. *Do we need to hire someone to write these custom reports, or can we do them ourselves?*

A. You can use the Report Wizard or Microsoft Excel to generate the reports, so no special knowledge or expertise is required.

Quiz

1. When I share a report with my manager, why does she see different numbers than I do?

2. What's the best way to save a report that captures data for a specific time period?

3. Are there any best practices I should follow when I create new reports?

4. How many record types can be included in a Report Wizard report?

5. Can I change the layout of a report?

Answers

1. Each person who opens the report sees data that matches records that he or she has permission to view in Microsoft Dynamics CRM. For example, you may only be able to see data for accounts that are owned by you, but your manager may be able to see data for accounts owned by anyone in your group.

2. Run the report and export it to a format, such as PDF, that can be easily archived. In the On-Premise edition, the report can be scheduled to run at the end of a time period and can be stored as a snapshot in Microsoft Dynamics CRM. Because the number of snapshots that can be saved for a report is limited, you'll also want to export the snapshots.

3. Because a report will take longer to run if it includes large numbers of records, default filters are recommended for every report.

4. In an On-Premise version, if you have a report that runs on large datasets, use the Report Scheduling Wizard to run it at times when the system is less heavily loaded.

5. When you create the report, you select the two main record types to include in the report. Because data from related record types can be included, you can pull in information from other record types, too.

   Regular users cannot change the layout of a report. The layout of reports is fixed. If you are using Microsoft Dynamics CRM On-Premise, a person with a full report development environment and the appropriate security role can change the layout of the default reports.

   If you need complete layout flexibility, create your report in Excel.

Exercise

To do the basic setup required for Joyous Fitness, complete these steps:

1. Rename all account reports to use the terminology used by the organization.

2. Create a new report using the Report Wizard that shows campaign responses grouped by campaign, and sorted by ZIP code.

3. Modify the properties for the service reports so that they do not show up in the Reports list.

HOUR 22

Integration to the Other Applications

What You'll Learn in This Hour:

▶ What Is Bridge Software and When to Use It

▶ Integrating to ERP or Accounting Applications

▶ Introducing Some Independent Software Vendors

▶ Getting Data into the System: Data Migration

This hour looks at options and places to integrate Microsoft Dynamics CRM to other applications and how to best work with third-party independent software vendors (ISVs) and their offerings. We will also focus on integrating with some of the commonly available tools and using these tools to support data migrations.

Bridge Software

In between any two applications, there might be another application that translates information from one database to the next, from one application to the next, from one method to the next, from one service to the next or from one user interface to the next. As we integrate, extend, and expand Microsoft Dynamics CRM into environments where other software applications already reside and where integration is needed, we are faced with differences between designs and database structure.

How should we approach this situation? There exists the option to write custom software to tie multiple applications together, but this can be time-consuming, error-prone, and a long-term investment in updates and upgrades. We have another option.

This is where bridge, integration, middleware, or enterprise application integration (EAI) software comes into play. A bridge or integration software application offers a framework to support technology and business rules as data is translated between environments. Software and technologies in this space support the creation of accurate, consistent, and transparent information flows between different systems.

Given that Microsoft Dynamics CRM is built to connect, it is a great application to drop into the technology space of integration and bridge software.

Points of Connect

Microsoft Dynamics CRM has many different places where other applications can connect, but a few common points are as follows:

▶ Importing or synchronizing leads, accounts, or contact details from a web page

▶ Sharing accounting-oriented information, such as quotes, orders, and products with a back office accounting application

▶ Synchronizing account-specific financial information, such as invoice history, credit holds, and credit limits with an accounting application.

▶ Updating internal Microsoft Dynamics CRM data from industry standard information sources, such as Hoovers, OneSource, Harte Hanks, and others.

Each of these places for connection has a number of different solution, design and architectural approach options.

The following sections cover a couple of these points as they relate to the ISV offerings. For more detailed information about the ISV offerings, set aside an hour to listen in on one or more of the many vendor webinars available and ask questions; it is worth the time investment if connecting Microsoft Dynamics CRM to other applications is a business requirement. Of special note: You do not have to approach gathering more information from the vendors as a painful listening to sales presentations exercise. The world has changed, and the vendors have a wealth of consultative technical and industry niche expertise that is available to you.

Integration to External Web Sources

Extra external software is not necessarily needed to integrate Microsoft Dynamics CRM to an externally facing environment; however, the extra software can offer quick configuration for resolving business rules and regulations. It can also offer a quick ramp up and a space for a layer of validation.

Take, for instance, a need to filter out leads that have a name of Donald Duck or the need to validate and protect against data changes that impact existing information negatively. You might also have an interest in interacting with users who are not authenticated users of your CRM system prior to offering them access to change anything within your Microsoft Dynamics CRM environment.

Data can be cleansed through the website application software or through a piece of middleware software that sits between Microsoft Dynamics CRM and the externally facing website. Search and business rules that look for special characters or for commonly used bogus accounts can be added to this middleware layer and business validation and external interaction can also be a feature.

Now, shift gears and think about the more trusted audience perhaps with a customer portal: a website that empowers customers to reduce the need to pick up the phone or to send email when they have a problem or question. A customer portal site that offers a subset of information for validation and updating, or a site that offers the ability to submit and review the status of support cases. And consider this: Software that takes Microsoft Dynamics CRM data and displays it and that captures data and then turns around and updates Microsoft Dynamics CRM.

There are more reasons to share data with an externally facing website or an internal intranet that might be disconnected from the project, but the key point is that in the past this was always limited to an extensive and expensive custom solutions. This is not the case with Microsoft Dynamics CRM and the supporting offerings from the vendor community.

Integration to Accounting Applications

Integration to accounting applications has a technical and a business culture context.

Business Context

Many times, there is a cultural difference between the needs of the accounting or finance department and the needs of all the other departments within a company. A common request and resistance is to open up access to an accounting application to the entire firm, but what is really needed is visibility to a subset of key accounting data for those people who require certain parts of it. This includes the sales team working with prospects and existing clients who might need financial history to qualify leads and the service team working with existing customers who can use cutting off service to increase collections for those looking for support.

A salesperson can be empowered to do quotes and take orders, but there are many companies that then cross reference and check those incoming orders when invoicing occurs.

This is the same for service. Service contracts can be sold, hours and tickets against those contracts can be used, but generally, the invoicing remains in the finance role.

Technical Context

When setting technical context, it is all about what data needs to be accessed by what department and what person. It is also about what the business processes are around the data and the timing and flow of data between perhaps two or even three different applications.

It is not uncommon to have numerous salespeople entering orders and even doing invoicing, but the items often show up in a queue or batch for accounting to manage.

There is always choice.

Many companies might decide that real-time data from all the teams is not an issue and the ultimate control will be managed through balancing finances.

Either choice we can quickly drop into the thought of a middleware application—an application that translates data coming from Microsoft Dynamics CRM into a format that the accounting software is expecting and the same middleware software with functionality to translate data coming from the accounting software pushed to Microsoft Dynamics CRM.

Now that we have a general idea of where middleware, integration, or bridge software might fit, who are some of the vendors that have solutions in this space?

Some of the "Integration" Independent Software Vendors

There are a number of ISVs in the integration, middleware, data tools, and bridge software space and a number of Microsoft Partners specializing in Microsoft Dynamics CRM who have done numerous custom integration projects. I list a few of the ISVs whose names come up more than once in the Microsoft Dynamics CRM community.

The first sets of players are those that offer more options when it comes to integrating many different applications.

The second two ISVs are those vendors with a strong focus on DynamicsGP and who generally have a DynamicsGP background. They focus on application integration to DynamicsGP and have Dynamics CRM to DynamicsGP offerings.

ISVs that cover a wide variety of different database applications include the following:

- ▶ **CastIron** (www.castiron.com/integration-solutions/index.html), and its CastIron for Microsoft Dynamics CRM offering (www.castiron.com/integration-solutions/ms-dynamics/index.html)

- ▶ **Scribe** (www.scribesoft.com/) and the Scribe Insight product suite (www.scribesoft.com/DynamicsIntegration.asp)

- ▶ **Pervasive Software** (www.pervasivesoftware.com). and the Pervasive Data integrator (www.pervasiveintegration.com/data_connectors/Pages/microsoft_dynamics_integration.aspx)

- ▶ **Microsoft BizTalk** (www.microsoft.com/biztalk/en/us/default.aspx), and the Microsoft BizTalk CRM adapter (www.microsoft.com/downloads/details.aspx?familyid=ABD3BB9E-A59A-4EB6-8DE8-FB25B77926D7&displaylang=en)

- ▶ **Keelio Software** (www.keelio.com/Home/tabid/36/Default.aspx) and its Dynamics GP SSIS Toolkit and XML SSIS Toolkit (www.keelio.com/Products/tabid/87/Default.aspx)

ISVs that have an integration to DynamicsGP focus include the following:

- ▶ **eOne** (www.eonesolutions.com.au), and its SmartConnect products (www.eonesolutions.com.au/Content.aspx?page=SmartConnect)

- ▶ **Nolan** (www.nolancomputers.co.uk/dynamics/Home.aspx) and its integration bridge

There are so many different ways to provide the functionality that you almost need a specialist in the integration space to help translate. If you choose to work with any of these listed vendors and their partners, you will want to get direct information from the involved parties. Here are a few areas and questions that you might want to focus on and areas for deeper consideration:

▶ How has each of the ISVs architected their solution? Are they talking directly to the various databases? Are they using web services? Do they have a database in the middle that needs monitoring?

▶ When was the last time an update was released? What did it include? Is the ISV using modern tools or antiquated solutions? Just as Microsoft Dynamics CRM has had numerous releases and design updates over the past six years, has the ISV kept pace?

▶ How are translations handled (for instance, when data in one database does not map directly to data in the other database)? What about when field lengths are different? Is data truncated?

▶ What are the performance benchmarks for customers using the solution in a similar environment to your own? Performance is unique to each individual environment and is impacted by numerous variables; however, it is worth asking any references about any performance concerns that they have had.

▶ How are errors handled? This includes data errors such as one of the databases dropping offline in the middle of processing and business errors, such as a user conflict or a conflict between data entered in two different systems at the same time and the data integration toolkit needing to know which data source takes priority or is an authoritative source.

▶ How is the solution supported once it is up and running in your organization? Who do you call when you have a problem? If you are working with a partner, is there a backup in case something happens? Is it a solution that another partner or the vendor can support if needed?

We have talked a little bit about your options around ongoing data integration. Now, let's look into the world of data migration. Data migration is generally considered an occasional or one-time event.

Data Migration

Data migration is a world of risk, intrigue, housecleaning, and discovery. You really never know all that you will run into.

> ### Data Migration
> Never underestimate data migrations.

There are also a number of assumptions surrounding data migration. So, if you are a technical person reading this, ask a ton of questions and have solid deliverables and a change management process in place. If you are a businessperson reading this, understand that data migration can be very complex.

When you are starting with Microsoft Dynamics CRM and considering data migration, take a good hard look at the actual data that you want to migrate and convert. You also want to weigh whether it is worth it to migrate the data or if there is perhaps a different option.

> ### Think Hard About
> A solid and well-done data migration can make a *huge* difference in how you feel about the Microsoft Dynamics CRM software moving forward.

I have also seen many firms burden their users with data entry and the task of learning new software. Perhaps they think that users need the excuse to practice with the system and clean their contact details or perhaps there is no other way, but there is nothing more difficult than learning a new system and having to do excessive data entry at the same time—all, of course, while keeping up with the tasks of the job! The investment in a data migration is worth it, even if you save dollars in other ways, such as by migrating only account and contact data or only migrating data from the past six months and leaning on the old system for historical reference. If you have no other choice, the investment in some temporary help can also make a significant difference.

There are different tools available for data migrations that offer different functionality that might not be required when importing a list of contacts or leads.

It is also recommended that you consult with a Microsoft partner who is experienced with data migrations before moving forward, particularly if you are trying to convert from an existing line-of-business application with a database on the back end or from an existing customer relationship management software application that might have data organized differently.

If you do move forward with your own data migration, Microsoft offers a couple of different options.

Data Import/Data Migration Tools from Microsoft

Microsoft offers two tools for data import into Microsoft Dynamics CRM: the Data Import Wizard and the Data Migration Manager (DMM). Partners have also been known to build their own tools or to use mastery in third-party tools to handle more complex migrations.

Import Wizard

The Microsoft Dynamics CRM Import Wizard is designed to import a list of fairly structured, flat data. It can be used with a simple list of contacts or a separate list of accounts. It is recommended that if you are going to do a data import that you separate data into logical groups such as contacts, accounts, and so on. It is also a good idea to set up a test file of perhaps 10 records and import that until you are comfortable with the data format and your import design.

Watch Out!

> ### Import Wizard
>
> The Import Wizard is not designed to do full data migrations with multiple layers of data from different places. For full data migrations, there are other better-fitting tools to handle some of the more complex business rules that apply when moving data from one CRM system to another.

Data Migration Manager

The Data Migration Manager (DDM) works on the basis of data maps that define a mapping between the source data schema and Microsoft Dynamics CRM data schema. The data map is the core building block of the DMM. In general, a data map is an XML structured file built out of entities used for data mapping during data migration. Here are some of the key differences between the DMM and the Data Import Wizard built into Microsoft Dynamics CRM.

The DMM can

- Import multiple files and work with relational datasets
- Maintain the owner of the imported record
- Maintain the original create date supporting historical context
- Import record status and status reasons such as active and inactive
- Create custom entities during the import process (*not recommended*)
- Run a batch delete to delete records that were imported

Deleting Imported Records

Import can also delete imported records.

The Microsoft DMM is a powerful tool that is worth taking another look at if you currently do not have a solution for data migrations.

A few practical tips to keep in mind about the Data Migration Manager:

▶ It must be run by someone with the System Administrator security role.

▶ It must be installed on a separate computer.

▶ It includes tools for transforming data as part of the process.

▶ It has a wizard UI to guide you through it, although more complex migrations can be done by directly editing the data map.

Workshop

Silver Lining Steal Manufacturing has been using Microsoft Dynamics CRM for two years. It first rolled out the solution to its sales department with plans to further expand into the solution as it learned more about the product and after it switched the accounting software application. The company has now moved to Microsoft Dynamics NAV and is looking at integrating its Microsoft Dynamics CRM solution to the new Microsoft Dynamics NAV accounting software. It plans to share the details of the client accounts receivable history with the sales team, and it will be empowering their sales team to convert quotes directly into orders, as appropriate, which will then show up as unprocessed orders in Dynamics NAV.

Q&A

Q. *We are a small firm that is considering doing our own data migration. We hoped to have each salesperson enter his or her own leads, but this chapter indicates that might not be a good idea. Why is this so?*

A. It makes sense to encourage your salespeople to enter 2 to 10 of their own leads to get the hang of the software, but entering 50 to 200 leads is a poor use of valuable sales energy.

Q. *We want to migrate all our data from Sage ACT!, including email. Are either of these tools a perfect fit for that task?*

A. The best tool for migrating ACT!, including email, is either experienced partners with custom solutions for handling ACT! emails or an application built for the specific need. ACT! email storage is messy and difficult to migrate.

Q. *We are integrating to Microsoft Dynamics GP, and our partner recommends Scribe Software. Is there a similar package we can look at for comparison?*

A. You might want to look at eOne Software. It specializes in Microsoft Dynamics GP and competes with Scribe.

Quiz

1. What are two common places that people connect Microsoft Dynamics CRM with other applications?

2. Identify two ISVs that offer solutions in the integration and middleware software space?

3. Would the Data Import Wizard built in to Microsoft Dynamics CRM be a good choice for a data migration?

Answers

1. Synchronizing leads and sharing accounting information.

2. Scribe and CastIron.

3. No. There are better tools for data migration.

Exercise

What are some of the key variables that Silver Lining Steel Manufacturing need to consider as it looks to integrating its solutions?

Given that it is integrating Microsoft Dynamics CRM with Microsoft Dynamics NAV, which three vendors should the company talk with about possible solutions?

Does Silver Lining Steel manufacturing need to consider data migration?

HOUR 23

Microsoft Dynamics CRM Utilities You Can Add

What You'll Learn in This Hour:

- ▶ Enhancing Contact Information
- ▶ Business Intelligence in CRM
- ▶ Enabling Microsoft Dynamics CRM for Mobile Devices
- ▶ Database Tools and Utilities
- ▶ Compliance and Auditing Tools

In this hour, we examine specific tools and utilities that increase your productivity with Microsoft Dynamics CRM On-Premise. Part of the power of Microsoft Dynamics CRM On-Premise is the number of ways that it can be expanded, enhanced, customized, and upgraded. From simple informational tools that retrieve additional contact information online, to tools that help build reports, to database performance enhancements—if there is a tool that you are looking for, chances are it can be found and integrated into your Microsoft Dynamics CRM On-Premise system.

Enhancing Contact Information

With Microsoft Dynamics CRM's extensible interface, there have been many solutions built to enhance the functionality around Accounts, Contacts, Leads, and Opportunities. There are tools such as enhanced email solutions that streamline Microsoft Dynamics CRM processes and bridge the gaps in functionality. In addition, tools can be used to augment the existing information that you have in your database, such as connections to online databases of contacts (for example, ExxactTarget). The current tools are impressive, and the industry is dynamic. A passion for discovering and adopting new trends, new searchable data, new technologies, and changes in traditional business process, such as social marketing and online networks, is highly recommended and something that the expansive offerings of complementary products can offer.

Sending HTML Emails

Microsoft Dynamics CRM provides built-in capabilities to send emails to contacts in a number of different ways (email templates, mail merge templates, and marketing campaigns, for example), but these tools don't always meet the more complex needs of HTML emails. Complementary tools can help expand Microsoft Dynamics CRM so that it is even easier to send HTML emails in a marketing campaign or for any other reason.

One such email enhancement tool is provided by ExactTarget (www.exacttarget. com). After the installation of the email tool provided by ExactTarget, it is a simple matter of selecting a campaign and pressing the custom Send ExactTarget Email button. This will allow you to create and send a sophisticated customized HTML email to all those being targeted in the campaign. Beyond initially sending HTML emails, there is also an interface that can be used after the emails have been sent. This interface enables you to view some detailed statistics that have been collected on what happened when the e-mail was received. For example, you can see the number of emails that were not only sent but also opened, and you can see the number of links followed, and all this information allows you to assess the impact of your campaign.

Extending Contact Information

Online networks extend far and wide, so it is more than likely that your customers will be registered in one of the many online databases on the market. There are tools out there that connect Microsoft Dynamics CRM to online databases, like Hoovers or LinkedIn, and provide more in-depth knowledge regarding customers that exist in those services. Sales and marketing campaigns can be improved and targets can be refined when you can add more comprehensive contact information to CRM, including the internal and external connections of your contacts. Products such as Hoovers and LinkedIn provide these capabilities.

Hoovers is a "global database of more than 28 million public and private companies and 36 million executives" according to its website (www.hoovers.com/business-information/—pageid__16781—/global-mktg-index.xhtml). Connecting your Microsoft Dynamics CRM deployment to the Hoovers database will expand your ability to communicate with your contacts and can potentially fill in missing data that would be invaluable to your users. After you purchase the product, it is a simple matter of installing and connecting to Hoovers so that your current customer information will become a wealth of knowledge about what the customer does, the company they work for, and the connections that they have to others. If you start out with just a name and a phone number, the Hoovers database can completely fill in the rest of the information in Microsoft Dynamics CRM for almost any contact, and then follow up by providing information about people linked to your original contact who might be of interest to you. The information that can be gathered allows for targeted campaigns and possible growth opportunities.

Another online service that provides similar capabilities is LinkedIn (www.linkedin.com). This online database provides publicly available information about contacts. Currently, no products connect LinkedIn to CRM, but the steps required to customize Microsoft Dynamics CRM and link it to LinkedIn are relatively straightforward. In fact, the Microsoft Dynamics CRM team has provided steps to connect Microsoft Dynamics CRM to LinkedIn on their team blog. You can find that information at http://blogs.msdn.com/crm/archive/2008/07/16/linkedin-to-microsoft-dynamics-crm.aspx. This simple connection can increase your knowledge about a contact and enable you to see current records as updated by the contacts themselves.

Business Intelligence in Microsoft Dynamics CRM

Business intelligence (BI) is becoming increasingly more important to well-functioning companies, and depending on whom you are talking with about BI, it can vary in its definition. Wikipedia comes close in its definition, but it is also fairly generic, as follows: "Business intelligence (BI) refers to skills, technologies, applications and practices used to help a business acquire a better understanding of its commercial context. Business intelligence may also refer to the collected information itself."

BI in the following descriptions means gathering and presenting relevant data on current processes, structure, and organization, including business analysis and planning.

With the right customizations and additions, Microsoft Dynamics CRM can provide executives with summary reports, sales managers with sales-rep statistics, and Microsoft Dynamics CRM can also provide sales representatives with reports on locales and key performance indicators (KPIs). Microsoft Dynamics CRM is often considered the right tool for the extraction and the presentation of BI data because of how it is structured and because it is extensible and customizable.

If you already have Microsoft Dynamics CRM or are planning on deploying it, any savvy user can capitalize on some immediate benefits. The most immediate benefit is being able to run queries and reports that give the current status of a set of sales and marketing campaigns. When retrieving this information inside CRM, further drill down on the results can be done quickly by linking to specific cases of interest. Beyond these initial reports, other benefits include being able to get an accurate picture of the sales pipeline with reports on leads and opportunities, being able to see the current rank of sales representatives against specific criteria, and being able to see the history of all those sales representatives. Reports and queries such as these can either be created internally by customizing Microsoft Dynamics CRM or purchased from any number of third-party vendors with BI packages for CRM.

Basic BI Internal to Microsoft Dynamics CRM

Some basic BI tools can be used right away with any Microsoft Dynamics CRM deployment, including Advanced Find and Reporting, which provide internal tools that can be used immediately to gather data for BI. As you learned in Hour 21, "Reporting and Query Basics," Advanced Find is a quick and easy tool for any Microsoft Dynamics CRM user to produce simple BI. Reports are also a great tool that can be used by any user with the time and technical knowledge to produce meaningful results. Both of these approaches have drawbacks, though, because they do not scale for large amounts of data and the time it takes to customize and build these BI tools yourself can be prohibitive.

Beyond the tools built in to Microsoft Dynamics CRM, there is the Microsoft jump start accelerator toolkit, which includes the Analytics Accelerator. The Analytics Accelerator has been created by the Microsoft Dynamics CRM team and is a toolset that provides your organization with additional reports, dashboards, and database enhancements that can be used to increase the BI functionality in CRM. There are three planned releases for the Analytics Accelerator and, at the time of this writing, they have released only the first two: R1 and R2. R1 provides Microsoft Dynamics CRM users with a set of SQL Reporting Service (SRS) dashboards for SQL Server 2005, as well as an Analysis Service cube that provides an OLAP cube that will extract data from Microsoft Dynamics CRM. Releases 2 and 3 are intended to provide more powerful and technical tools for those users who need to leverage a high degree of BI. See the Analytics Accelerator website for more information about the features and dates of the next release.

By the Way

OLAP Cube

OLAP (Online Analytics Processing) cubes were developed to provide an efficient analysis and presentation of structured data. OLAP cubes are an alternative to standard relational databases, which have limits on analyzing and displaying large amounts of data quickly.

The Microsoft SQL Reporting Services dashboards available in R1 include reports of Microsoft Dynamics CRM usage, report for sales manager, reports for support, and reports for account executives. They can be installed on any Microsoft Dynamics CRM deployment that uses SQL Server 2005 by going to the Reports section and creating a new report from an existing file. The Analytics Accelerator also provides a simple OLAP cube that can be loaded and used to extract data out of Microsoft Dynamics CRM for quick and easy presentation. Figure 23.1 shows the OLAP cube solution provided in the accelerator loaded within Visual Studio and connected the a Microsoft Dynamics CRM deployment.

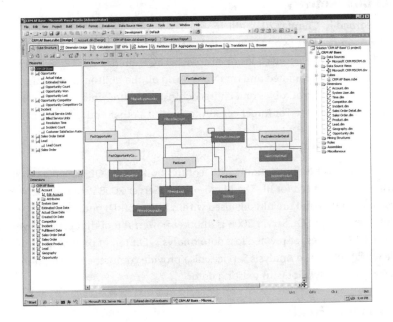

FIGURE 23.1
OLAP cube provided in Analytics Accelerator.

Plans for R2 and R3 include support for SQL Server 2008 dashboards, an enhanced OLAP cube, data mining, and PerformancePoint Server scorecards.

Microsoft Products That Help with BI

One of the best parts about working with Microsoft Dynamics CRM is the integration points with other Microsoft products. Several Microsoft applications integrate well with Microsoft Dynamics CRM to provide rich BI on top of what can be customized within CRM. Microsoft Excel and Microsoft Dynamics CRM link together through Microsoft Dynamics CRM Excel Connectivity. SQL Server 2008 has built-in support for BI. Microsoft PerformancePoint can be linked directly to CRM, or indirectly through an OLAP cube, to provide structured KPIs or ad hoc analysis. Having these options allows for Microsoft Dynamics CRM customers to evolve from simple BI tools into more sophisticated tools with software and services that are usually already being used within their current organization.

Excel Connectivity

As you learned in Chapter 20, "Utilizing the Power of Microsoft Excel with CRM Data," we can connect Excel to the data in Microsoft Dynamics CRM and download that data based on user selections or customized SQL queries. After the data is in Excel, it can be manipulated and analyzed using all the built-in capabilities of Excel, such as setting up pivot tables and charts against the data, which works well for a specific individual user. For larger corporate analysis, other options are a better fit.

SQL Server 2008

Among the rich set of functionality and features built in to SQL Server 2008, several key aspects can be used for BI. The Microsoft SQL Server 2008 Reporting Services are a large part of this and are already used within Microsoft Dynamics CRM itself. The Analysis Services in SQL Server 2008 is another powerful tool that can be leveraged to create OLAP cubes for pivoted fast data analysis. On top of providing the ability to create OLAP cubes, the Analysis Services also provide comprehensive data-mining tools for deep analysis of your existing data.

PerformancePoint

Microsoft Office SharePoint Server's PerformancePoint product is a comprehensive organization and analysis system that can attach directly to Microsoft Dynamics CRM or an OLAP cube. It provides a sophisticated feature set that includes structured reports, reports and notifications for KPIs, and even ad hoc reporting depending on the setup and configuration of the server. An entire business can be managed from a PerformancePoint Server when it is fully integrated into products like Microsoft Dynamics CRM.

BI Software from Vendors and ISVs

There are other BI solutions outside of the set of Microsoft applications, some of which include ZAP Technology's Business Analytics and customizations provided by companies such as Power Objects.

Dundas Data Visualization

Dundas Charts provides a general solution that connects to all those applications that support Microsoft Dynamics CRM to provide charting, dashboards, and graphical reporting. With advanced extensions for SQL Server Reporting Services, as well as solutions for OLAP services, Dundas can provide powerful external charting capabilities. This allows users to gain in-depth BI after it has been configured to interact with Microsoft Dynamics CRM through their easy-to-use interface.

PowerObjects Solution

PowerObjects is a Microsoft Dynamics CRM partner that provides a host of services and solutions, from email tracking to integration of Microsoft Dynamics CRM with Live Maps. One of the BI solutions that they provide is the ability to create custom dashboards inside a Microsoft Dynamics CRM deployment. The dashboards can be created with a number of charts, which are populated from saved queries that are already defined and stored in the system. These dashboards give Microsoft Dynamics CRM users a broader picture of what is going on in the system and provide a limited amount of BI.

ZAP Technology

The product provided by ZAP Technology is called Business Analytics, which provides a web-based application that contains a set of prepackaged analytics for sales, marketing, and services. The application provides dashboards, scorecards, KPIs, as well as reports and drill-down capabilities that link back into Microsoft Dynamics CRM for the full view of any record in question. Business Analytics is relatively easy to deploy because it recognizes customizations in Microsoft Dynamics CRM and imports them into a structured cube for fast analysis and reporting. Custom reports and summary reports are quickly and easily created and run, allowing for targeted dashboards and KPIs that can be viewed and updated regularly. Further features include the ability to import user security privileges from Microsoft Dynamics CRM so that Business Analytics only allows access to those records that a user is allowed to view. With such a full-featured product, ZAP Technology has provided an excellent BI product for almost any Microsoft Dynamics CRM system.

Enabling Microsoft Dynamics CRM for Mobile Devices

It is increasingly familiar to see a sales and marketing staff with mobile devices, such as a BlackBerries and Windows Mobile devices. It is possible to tap into that existing resource and allow access to your Microsoft Dynamics CRM data through these devices. Providing access to Microsoft Dynamics CRM through mobile devices becomes a logical and natural extension of the Microsoft Dynamics CRM system that will save time and make your organization more effective.

There are several scenarios where enabling Microsoft Dynamics CRM on mobile devices might help. Quickly browsing Microsoft Dynamics CRM data before a face-to-face sales meeting can make the encounter more productive. It can make a conversation at a conference more personal and focused. Having Microsoft Dynamics CRM data available at an opportune time during a lunch meeting can provide a crucial bit of information necessary to turn a lead into an account. All these scenarios would benefit from mobile access.

If enabling mobile Microsoft Dynamics CRM sounds like something your organization might benefit from, there are several options from which to choose. The Microsoft Dynamics CRM team currently provides the Microsoft Mobile Express solution that can be customized on your system. Companies such as TenDigits and CWR Mobility provide integrated solutions for Windows Mobile and BlackBerry devices that are fully functional and customizable. iPhone users will have to turn to the solution provided by SoftBridge for access to CRM. Picking a mobile Microsoft Dynamics CRM solution requires more than knowing what device your users will have, though. You want to weigh all the different aspects:

- ▶ Feature set provided

- ▶ Customizability

- ▶ Security

- ▶ Cost

- ▶ Supported deployments (Online versus On-Premise)

- ▶ Supported devices

Other considerations that might come into play are customer support, documentation, and future development plans. Most solutions provide a website outlining all the information on their products. See Table 23.1 for more information.

TABLE 23.1   Mobile Solutions

Product	Company	Website	Notes
MobileExpress	Microsoft	www.microsoft.com	Just released.
MobileAccess	TenDigits	http://tendigits.com/mobileaccess.html	Provides both online and offline access to Microsoft Dynamics CRM data.

TABLE 23.1 *Continued*

Product	Company	Website	Notes
CWR Mobile CRM 4.1	CWR Mobility	www.cwrmobility.com	Straightforward solution to enable mobile CRM.
Bridge2CRM	SoftBridge	www.softbridgeinc.com	Supports the iPhone.
Retail Management System	ADC Technologies	www.adctech.com	End-to-end solution that includes mobile CRM.
Mobile CRM+	SoftTrends	www.crmmobileplus.com	Supports Nokia, Windows Mobile, and BlackBerry devices.
Mobile Edge	iEnterprises	www.ienterprises.com/microsoft-crm-mobile	Highly configurable product for BlackBerry.
Mobile Connector	Logotec	www.logotecengineering.com/mscrm	Quick and easy solution.

We will look at two of the solutions in depth here and see what options they provide. I encourage you to research the benefits of all the solutions before selecting one for your custom deployment.

MobileExpress

MobileExpress is a beta solution that is provided by the Microsoft Dynamics CRM team. The product is installed on the Microsoft Dynamics CRM server and allows for online-only, web-based interaction with Microsoft Dynamics CRM on any mobile device that has a browser and a network connection. Because it uses the browser on the device, no installation or maintenance is necessary on the device itself, but it also means there is no access to records when there is no network connection. This cost-effective solution provides administrative configuration on the server, allowing a certain set of entities to be viewed on the device, and can even be configured down to the field level. The entities can be searched, accessed as read-only, and edited depending on how access was configured on the Microsoft Dynamics CRM server. Additional functionality includes a breadcrumb trail that allows instant access to previously viewed pages and the use of saved queries to filter results retrieved from the server. Downloading this solution from Microsoft allows almost any On-Premise Microsoft Dynamics CRM deployment to become mobile quickly and easily, although with limited functionality.

MobileAccess

MobileAccess is the mobile solution provided by TenDigits that extends Microsoft Dynamics CRM so that it can be accessed on BlackBerry and Windows Mobile devices. MobileAccess provides standard Microsoft Dynamics CRM functionality, such as searching and lookup, creating, editing, deleting, and assigning records from your mobile device. It has also been built with automatic synchronization capabilities so that records can be accessed both when connected to the Microsoft Dynamics CRM server and when there is no network connection. Advanced functionality includes notifications/alters when new records have been created or assigned, integration with mobile capabilities so that initiating a call or email can occur from within CRM, and then tracking of those activities after they have been completed. With all this functionality, MobileAccess is a good choice for mobile integration with Microsoft Dynamics CRM.

Database Tools and Utilities

Supporting and maintaining Microsoft Dynamics CRM is important, but it is also important to do the same for the engine that drives CRM: SQL Server. Microsoft SQL Server is the heart of CRM, and it provides a stable base to build anything from a moderately sized application, to a multiserver, large-scale, high-use system. It is important to keep your SQL Server well tuned so that you can fully benefit from the infrastructure that it provides. There are tools provided with SQL Server to tune and maintain the databases, and other products can be purchased that help support SQL Server with more specialized tools and user-friendly interfaces.

The original platform that Microsoft Dynamics CRM was built to run on was Microsoft SQL Server 2005. SQL Server 2005 is a solid platform that provides all the basic needs of a Microsoft Dynamics CRM system, but it is a bare-bones product when used on its own. It does provide the commands and infrastructure for maintenance, but the user interfaces are not necessarily the easiest things to use. To get everything out of SQL Server 2005, it is necessary to have a high degree of technical knowledge about the product and the commands used to control it. This is not a feasible option for many organizations using Microsoft Dynamics CRM, and the database can slowly become inefficient if not maintained correctly.

Another option provided for consumers of Microsoft Dynamics CRM is Microsoft's most recently released database engine, Microsoft SQL Server 2008. SQL Server 2008 vastly improves upon the functionality in SQL Server 2005, but the tools included with SQL Server 2008 are not much different from the ones included with SQL Server 2005. The interfaces are similar and provide performance analysis, database backup, and maintenance, but only to those with the technical skill to configure and control SQL Server. An obvious drawback to only having SQL Server 2005 or 2008 is that none of the tools provide automation through the user interface, so they all have to be set up and run either manually through the interface provided or through complicated automation scripts.

After weighing the initial options for supporting the database, we can find ourselves looking externally for tools that will be able to tune, manage, and maintain SQL Server. Several options on the market support SQL Server, and one of the more comprehensive ones is the solution provided by Idera. Idera's applications wrap around Microsoft SQL Server to provide user-friendly interfaces that enable database administrators to easily tune for performance and to maintain and back up their databases. Their products are easy to set up and provide automation for most tasks, including backup and defragmentation. Figures 23.2 and 23.3 show examples of the functionality in the defragmentation interfaces. Figure 23.2 shows the defragment manager with the Microsoft Dynamics CRM database loaded, and Figure 23.3 shows how easy it is to initiate the defragmentation.

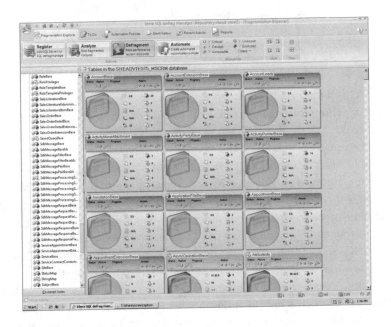

FIGURE 23.2
Idera Defrag Manager interface with Dynamics CRM loaded.

In addition to the backup and defragmentation support, Idera's products can set up notifications so that when tasks are completed those people who need to track a job's success or failure can be informed. The notifications can also be set up on diagnostic triggers so that if something were to go wrong on the server, like a sudden sustained spike in CPU, the support staff can know about it quickly and deal with the problem in a timely manner. Any complex organization or deployment requires tools such as these to properly manage and maintain their system.

FIGURE 23.3
Initiating defragmentation in the Idera defrag manager.

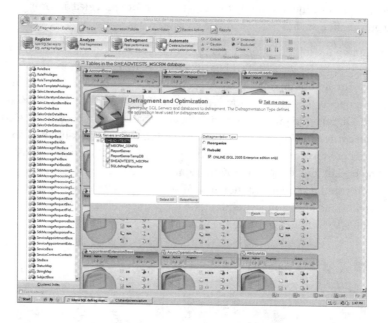

So, what does all this actually mean to your instance of Microsoft Dynamics CRM? The most important things to remember about your deployment are that the data has to be backed up, the database has to be regularly defragmented, and you need plenty of resources (such as disk space) for the SQL Server to run properly. Because the data and structure of Microsoft Dynamics CRM is completely contained within the database instances underlying the application, Microsoft Dynamics CRM can be restored from any point both at which the organization database and the configuration databases are backed up. So whether you have nightly, weekly, or monthly backups of your database, make sure you capture both the organization database (or databases, if you are using a multitenant deployment) and the configuration database. After regular backups, the next most pressing concern to keep the SQL Server in peak running order is to defragment the database so that the indexes will do their job and speed up queries instead of slowing them down. Indexes on highly used tables—those with the most insertions, updates, and deletions—can become fragmented across a hard drive and slow down queries on those tables. It is important to regularly check and defragment these indexes if appropriate. And finally, the last thing that can cause trouble for a SQL Server is not having enough resources. Whether it is CPU cycles, memory available, or disk space, the SQL Server generally requires a good deal of it to run at peak performance. That is why it is important to know when one of these resources is running low and take the appropriate action to fix the situation. If all these things are done, your SQL Server will be supporting your instance of Microsoft Dynamics CRM the way it was meant to.

Compliance and Auditing Tools

Microsoft Dynamics CRM is used for many different types of applications. Some of those applications have highly sensitive data that requires tracking and analysis. That is, it is common to need to know what fields were changed when, and also who changed those fields. Microsoft Dynamics CRM provides auditing capabilities for scenarios such as these in several different forms. There are built-in auditing options, simple customizations that can be done to perform auditing, and plug-ins that can be installed to provide more comprehensive auditing solutions. With a moderate amount of effort and understanding of the extensible nature of Microsoft Dynamics CRM, your application can have an auditing trail installed and running.

The first and simplest form of auditing is built right in to the entity definitions in Microsoft Dynamics CRM. Any system customizer can turn on auditing for a customizable system entity, or any new entity. When this flag is enabled, the entity acquires four attributes that track who created a record (CreatedOn and CreatedBy) and who was the last to change the record (ModifiedOn and ModifiedBy). These fields do not keep a full list of who changed the record and at what time, but they do provide the means to see where the most recent changes came from and who is responsible for creating the given record. This simplistic auditing trail often is not enough, though.

If a more complete list of changes needs to be kept, through the addition of a few custom entities that mirror those needing to be audited and the definition of complementary workflows for each entity, you can track all relevant fields. The basic idea is that every time the entity changes, the workflow is triggered and stores the new values in a new instance of the mirror entity so that a record is kept of all the changes. The eService accelerator provides this basic auditing for the Account, Contact, and Case entities, and the example can be followed to provide auditing for any other entities that require it. If simplistic auditing is required, this will be enough; but it is often the case that other functionality is required for auditing, such as "before and after" snapshots for changes, full-featured search capabilities, and analysis services. For these things, we have to look toward plug-ins that can be added to CRM.

Microsoft provides a basic auditing plug-in called Microsoft CRM 4.0 Audit Plugin for its customers and partners that can be used to increase the auditing capabilities in Microsoft Dynamics CRM to track field-level changes. The plug-in is available on

CodePlex and is distributed under open source licensing for all who have the knowledge and capabilities to program and customize Microsoft Dynamics CRM plug-ins. The plug-in can be extended to cover almost all of CRM, except it cannot track the customization of entities (metadata).

Customers will have to turn to vendors for a full auditing solution product, with field-level tracking, before and after snapshots of the entities, as well as search and analysis of entity changes. Vendors such as c360 provide the full functionality of a comprehensive auditing solution with tools such as their Audit Tracker. These tools capture changes to standard entities, but more important, they track changes to custom fields and custom entities. They enable you to gain a full picture of what has changed in the system and when it happened. They also provide tools such as the Audit Analyzer, which lets you search and analyze past Microsoft Dynamics CRM data for specific changes or trends in the system. With tools like these, auditing and compliance can be built in to any Microsoft Dynamics CRM system.

Workshop

Adventure Works Cycle is a mid-sized company that makes and distributes bicycles across the United States in a number of locally owned bike shops. It has a small sales force that is constantly traveling and needs to remain connected at all times. It has a Microsoft Dynamics CRM deployment on which it has installed TenDigit's MobileAccess solution so that all of its sales agents can access records anywhere, whether they can get a network connection or not, and retrieve and enter data. Opportunities and sales orders can be tracked immediately by entering information on the mobile device or by gathering orders and entering them at the end of the day from their laptops. Sales managers back in the head office keep track of how the different agents are doing through the use of a dashboard that they have installed from Business Analytics, a product provided by ZAP Technology. Simple auditing is necessary for the opportunity records and the order records, so analogous auditing records have been set up and connected to two workflows that trigger whenever an order or opportunity is updated to save the new values of the sale and who entered the information. Thanks to the Business Analytics product, quarterly and year-end reports are easily generated and presented to keep executives abreast of the current sales, as well as of the sales pipeline that is being developed.

Q&A

Q. *We are considering moving into a mobile solution. What things should we should consider?*

A. One of the first things to consider is if you need offline capability. Offline adds a significant layer of complexity to any offering.

Q. *As a small company, is it necessary to invest in Microsoft SQL Server management tools?*

A. Not necessarily. Microsoft SQL Server is a robust and powerful database that usually does not need any extensive care in a small firm.

Q. *Are there other offerings available? You mentioned so many.*

A. Yes. There are many other offerings available, and a personal apology to all that were not mentioned.

Quiz

1. What are two Microsoft products that can be used for gathering business intelligence? What are two non-Microsoft products that can be used for gathering business intelligence?

2. What are the three things that have to be done to ensure Microsoft SQL Server supports you Microsoft Dynamics CRM deployment properly?

3. Which Microsoft Dynamics CRM Accelerator provides basic auditing capabilities for the Account, Contact, and Case entities?

4. What are the benefits of using MobileExpress? What are the drawbacks?

Answers

1. Advanced Find and Reporting and ZAP Technology's Business Analytics and Dundas Charts.

2. Tune, manage, and maintain the Microsoft SQL Server by backing up the database, defragmenting, and indexing.

3. The eService Accelerator.

4. MobileExpress allows for online-only, web-based interaction with Microsoft Dynamics CRM on any mobile device that has a browser and a network connection. This is both an advantage and disadvantage.

Exercise

Using the blog post provided by the Microsoft Dynamics CRM Online team, http://blogs.msdn.com/dynamicscrmonline/archive/2009/04/07/adding-linkedin-contact-searches.aspx, add a LinkedIn contact search to your Microsoft Dynamics CRM deployment. The post can be followed for both standard and online deployments, so don't worry if you have one or the other. As can be seen from the post, the Name fields can be connected to an action and a button that triggers a search to be performed of all the LinkedIn contacts to see whether a match can be found and their information is displayed.

Microsoft Dynamics CRM as a Development Framework

What You'll Learn in This Hour:

▶ Options: What Can Be Changed?

▶ When to Consider Microsoft Dynamics CRM as a Development Platform and When Not To

▶ Skills Required: Microsoft Dynamic CRM Certifications and Who Can Make the Changes

Microsoft Dynamics CRM is a product that is as much *xRM* (where *x* can be any relationship-oriented line-of-business application) as it is CRM (where *C* is focused on customer relationship management). Microsoft Dynamics CRM On-Premise is fully functional and, yet, the expectation in many situations is that it will be expanded, configured, connected, and enhanced. It is also designed to offer control and best practice around this extending so that when a new major upgrade is released from Microsoft it will not break a partner or customer's development efforts and customizations. Microsoft Dynamics CRM Online can also be significantly enhanced through customizations, but this hour focuses primarily on the On-Premise version and where to focus so that it can morph into many other areas.

Options: What Can Be Changed?

Developers who want to fully exploit Microsoft Dynamics CRM need to learn to "Think CRM" and they also need to master a number of significantly different development skill sets. Each skillset discussed in this hour is benefit to the CRM development platform as standalone expertise, but a deep understanding of all does make a significant difference.

Extending the Core Microsoft Dynamics CRM code

Microsoft Dynamics CRM is a .NET application that can be extended with more .NET code or enhanced with scripts, workflow or other complementary or modular coding. In addition, Microsoft Dynamics CRM is architected and designed to include a methodology and development framework that wraps the application and any new customizations in a way to reduce the need to rewrite code with each major release. Microsoft also provides a complete Software Development Kit (SDK). This SDK has tools, samples, documentation, and a methodology for extending the core Microsoft Dynamics CRM code. The following sections look at each area of extension. For those using Microsoft Dynamics CRM Online, comments have been added where this applies.

Plug-Ins

Microsoft Dynamics CRM offers synchronous and asynchronous plug-in models that are based on .NET 2.0. Plug-ins are registered for a single organization and they are stored in the database. This enables automatic deployment across a cluster as well as other things. Plug-ins must be signed.

> ### Trusted Code
> Plug-ins are trusted code and must be reviewed for security.

Creating and Adding Workflow Using the Windows Workflow Foundation

Built in to Microsoft Dynamics CRM On-Premise and Online is the Microsoft Windows Workflow Foundation, which is a core component of the development framework. The foundation is also extended with a user-friendly interface to enable end users with limited or no development experience to add workflows.

Extending Forms with Scripts

Form OnLoad, OnSave, and Attribute (Field) OnChange

Every entity within Microsoft Dynamics CRM On-Premise and Online has one form. Each of these forms has an editable OnLoad event option where JScript can be embedded. This JScript is client-side code run when the user opens and uses the form. In addition, each attribute (field) within the form can have an OnChange event where JScript can be embedded offering the ability for some fancy footwork on specific changes to attributes (fields).

> ### Form Behavior
>
> A lot of form behavior will depend on whether the record already exists in the database.

Figure 24.1 shows an example of the form properties OnLoad or OnSave. To get there, do the following:

1. Choose Settings.

2. Choose Customization.

3. Choose Customize Entities.

4. Choose an entity (in our example, we chose Account).

5. Choose Forms and Views.

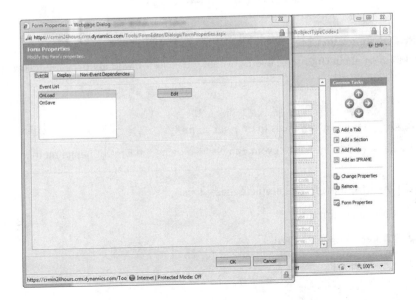

FIGURE 24.1
Form properties.

6. Choose Form.

7. Choose Form Properties.

You can also add an OnChange event to a specific attribute (field). Figure 24.2 shows an example of the area where you would add OnChange event script.

FIGURE 24.2
Attribute proper-
ties.

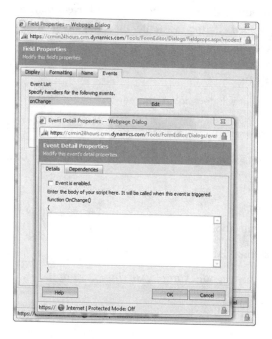

OnChange Events

A key thing about OnChange events is that they only fire when both of the following conditions are true:

1. The value changed.

2. The user has given focus to another control.

Alternatively, the OnChange event can be fired using the FireOnChange method.

To get there from the form, complete these steps:

1. Choose an attribute.

2. Choose Change Properties.

3. Choose Events.

4. Choose OnChange.

5. Choose Edit.

Adding iFrames to Forms

An iFrame option is available for both Microsoft Dynamics CRM On-Premise and Online and is hosted within the form or on the left navigation pane of a form. Within the world of the iFrame, Microsoft Dynamics CRM will optionally pass the object type code and object ID (GUID) to the provided external URL.

iFrame Interaction

iFrames display web pages within a form and generally do not interact with the data within Microsoft Dynamics CRM.

Figure 24.3 shows an example of setting up an iFrame. To get there, do the following:

1. Choose Settings.

2. Choose Customization.

3. Choose Customize Entities.

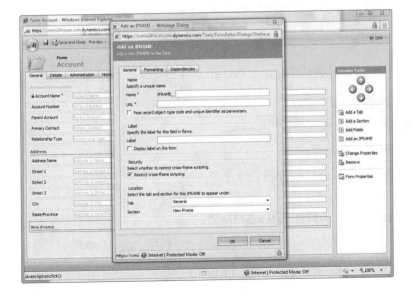

FIGURE 24.3
Add an iFrame property.

4. Choose an entity (in our example, we chose Account).

5. Choose Forms and Views.

6. Choose Form.

7. Choose or create the tab where you want your iFrame to appear.

8. Add a new section.

9. Add an iFrame to this section.

Changing or Adding to the User Interface Menus and Buttons

The drop-down items on the menus and the buttons within the main left navigation pane can be changed in Microsoft Dynamics CRM On-Premise. So, you can add new menu items, replace existing menu items, or add or replace buttons (such as the Sales button or Service button). These changes to the user interface menus are made within the SiteMap and ISV.Config XML files, as follows:

1. Select Settings.

2. Select Customization.

3. Select Export Customizations.

4. Select ISV.Config. (You can alternatively select sitemap.)

5. Choose Export Selected Customizations from the drop-down menu.

The saved zip file can be extracted so that you can edit the XML file inside it.

When your edits are complete, import the modified ISV.Config file as follows:

1. Choosing Settings.

2. Choose Customization.

3. Choose Import Customizations.

Enhancing with Silverlight

Silverlight is a fairly new option within the world of Microsoft Dynamics CRM (although some might argue that point). Silverlight is based on Microsoft Windows

Presentation Foundation (WPF) and is all about graphics, animation, and rich media interfaces. Silverlight is a browser plug-in and is an interesting complement to Microsoft Dynamics CRM extendibility. Silverlight includes items such as skinning and styling, deep zoom, and shadowing, all of which can be used to explode the Microsoft Dynamics user interface into a rich media experience.

Integrating to SharePoint (WSS/MOSS) for Support of Unstructured Data

Many Microsoft Dynamics CRM projects require unstructured data. Unstructured data includes large blocks of text, Word documents, PowerPoint files, and other undefined data that lends itself to organization and enterprise search. Some of this data can be structured into entities (record types) and attributes (fields), but other items are much better suited to organization and collaboration software (such as copies of documents). SharePoint meets this need and naturally connects to Microsoft Dynamics CRM. SharePoint can also be highly integrated to Microsoft Dynamics CRM as a dynamic or static component.

As a dynamic component, SharePoint can bring up and down pages on demand, and as a static component SharePoint can have a permanent two-way connection to Microsoft Dynamics CRM. Integrating to Microsoft SharePoint is not currently offered to Microsoft Dynamics CRM Online users; however, it is an option if you are using Microsoft Dynamics CRM hosted by some of the hosting providers.

Integrating to the World of Finance and ERP Using a Bridge Application (Custom or Third Party)

Just as unstructured data is best managed with technology designed for unstructured data such as SharePoint, financial information for accounting departments is best managed with a well-loved and established accounting software or enterprise resource planning application. Accounting software is focused on tight auditing and control within a smaller audience and has well vetted software offerings focus around flexible General Ledgers, Accounts Payable, Payroll and other accounting specific modules. Microsoft Dynamics CRM never had the intention of being an Accounting or General Ledger package.

Integrating to a robust Accounting application; however can be a beneficial and seamless offering. Core company accounting data can be pushed to a wide audience of users (such as everyone in the company) while the interactive and delicate finances within an accounting application are controlled and maintained within a company's financial department and financial information audit processes.

External Access: Web Page Integrations

When managing prospect and client information, there is an interest in allowing specific external contacts the ability to interact directly with their contact information and there is also a need to control and retain data quality around that incoming information. The interaction between an external web interface of prospect and client information is part of many Microsoft Dynamics CRM projects.

Some examples of core areas where this applies including capturing leads from a company's website, interacting with possible attendees to hosted events, and working with contacts and company's on support related issues.

Accelerators

Microsoft Dynamics CRM is so fun to extend that it lends itself to shared and Microsoft-vetted libraries of source code, configurations, and customizations. The Microsoft Dynamics CRM accelerators offer building blocks of source code, configurations, and customizations that empower a Microsoft partner or customer to quickly add features and functionalities. The library of accelerators continues to grow. Some examples include the Sales Forecasting Accelerator, which offers configurations for tracking sales goals and the Analytics Accelerator, which offers a set of custom dashboards and reports. Some accelerators work with Microsoft Dynamics CRM Online and others require that you have full access and security to the programs in the Microsoft Dynamics CRM On-Premise environment.

Dashboards

You have numerous dashboard options with Microsoft Dynamics CRM, including building your own dashboards with Windows Presentation Foundation and Visual Studio, using the Microsoft Dynamics CRM analytics accelerator, integrating to Windows SharePoint Services WSS/MOSS or adding in Microsoft Dynamics CRM third-party add-in products, such as the numerous options available from Zap Technology (www.zaptechnology.com/).

Reporting

Microsoft SQL Server Reporting Services can be used with Microsoft Dynamics CRM On-Premise to create various reports that you can integrate into the reporting menus within Microsoft Dynamics CRM.

In addition, you can create reports via the Microsoft Dynamics CRM Report Wizards or numerous views. If you want to stretch reporting into other areas of presentation, there are also independent software vendor (ISV) solutions available.

Microsoft Excel Dynamic Spreadsheets

As you learned in earlier hours, the power of Microsoft Excel dynamic spreadsheets is almost beyond imagination. You can tie an Excel spreadsheet to Microsoft Dynamics CRM, and every time this spreadsheet is opened, it will automatically be updated with new CRM data. In addition, the dynamic Excel spreadsheet retains and serves up the correct security so that each person who opens the spreadsheet gets the data that applies to him. You can add your own columns and formulas to these spreadsheets, and one way you can share these spreadsheets is by emailing them to other Microsoft Dynamics CRM users.

Microsoft Excel Static Spreadsheets

Microsoft Excel static spreadsheets do not get updated with any new Microsoft Dynamics CRM data when opened again and again. Data in static spreadsheets is structured and unchanging and, as such, a static spreadsheet offers a saved version of a data report. In addition, static spreadsheets can be shared with other people who are not Microsoft Dynamics CRM users.

Business Intelligence Analysis (BI Extensions and Tools)

You can pull out slices or cubes of data and do financial analysis, intense statistics, analytics, and more. Adding in third-party business intelligence agents, cubes, and tools allows for functionality not traditionally found in relationship management applications. The third-party tools can come from companies specializing in business intelligence or you can tap into other products and offerings from Microsoft.

Modifying the Outlook Client for Microsoft Dynamics CRM

Just as the Microsoft Dynamics CRM core application can be modified and extended, so can the Microsoft Dynamics CRM Outlook client. Enhancements to Microsoft

Outlook can add usability and allow you to take better advantage of the web-enabled Microsoft Dynamics CRM. For instance, you can set up special folders to access other areas of Microsoft Dynamics CRM, and you can change some of the default folders to favorites. Another way to customize the CRM client for Outlook is to extend or fine-tune the synchronization functionality between Microsoft Dynamics CRM and Microsoft Outlook e-mail, contacts, tasks, and the calendar.

Mobility

Microsoft has just released the Microsoft Dynamics CRM Mobile Express software. It has been built for customization, and the source code is available to partners who can create additional customer specific rich mobile extensions and complementary applications specifically to suit unique needs.

A key feature of CRM Mobile Express is that it enables you to use a mobile device's Internet connection to access critical Microsoft Dynamics CRM data.

In addition, mobility lends itself to offerings from many third-party ISVs, including the following:

▶ CWR Mobility, http://online.cwrmobility.com/

▶ iEnterprises, http://www.ienterprises.com/microsoft-crm-mobile

▶ Logotec, http://www.logotecengineering.com/mscrm/default.aspx

▶ Microsoft, http://blogs.msdn.com/crm/archive/2009/02/16/preview-mobile-express-for-microsoft-dynamics-crm-4-0.aspx

▶ softBRIDGE, www.softbridgeinc.com/

▶ Softtrends, www.crmmobileplus.com/

▶ TenDigits, www.tendigits.com

Now that we covered a number of areas where Microsoft Dynamics CRM On-Premise and Online can be extended and enhanced, let's look at when using Microsoft Dynamics CRM On Premise as a development platform makes sense.

When Microsoft Dynamics CRM Is a Good Fit

If you are looking at a development project and you are considering Microsoft Dynamics CRM, you might want to consider the following big-picture questions:

▶ Does your project require you to track any type of relationships?

If yes, the Microsoft Dynamics CRM framework is definitely something to consider. These relationships can include relationships between two people, relationships between companies, relationships between a person and a company, relationships between things, relationships between animals, relationships between parts and a final product, and basically the relationships between any two nouns.

▶ Does your project require you to automate/document process?

If yes, the Microsoft Dynamics CRM framework is definitely something to consider. These automated processes can include standardizing the steps that need to happen to get a project done. Scheduling and completing specific activities, historical reference to the completed activities, the association of specific activities to specific people. The tracking of specific activities with a specific person or the automation of alerts and notices and more.

▶ Does your project require role-based feature and functionality security and user-specific or office-specific limited data access?

Built in to the Microsoft Dynamics CRM framework is a multilayered configurable security system that helps you control who can do what and who can access what. In addition, the Microsoft Dynamics CRM security is tied to Microsoft Server authentication. (Features your developers would otherwise have to write and keep updated.)

▶ Does your project require long-term updates, upgrades and support?

The Microsoft Dynamics CRM release methodology includes small rollups every two months and a major upgrade every two years. These upgrades are built to recognize existing customizations and modifications. You also have the long-term upgrade and update support, the development control and the CRM SDK and the added features that you might not have time to write, such as duplicate checking, user-friendly reporting, integration to Microsoft Office, and layers of data import options.

▶ Does the project lend itself to a design of parallel asynchronous processes that could otherwise cause software bottlenecks and performance issues?

If yes, mastery and access to the Microsoft Workflow Foundation within a user-friendly interface within Microsoft Dynamics CRM might make sense.

Now that we have looked at a few areas where Microsoft Dynamics CRM as a development platform makes sense, let's look at areas where further architecture needs to be added to enhance the core system.

When the Core of Microsoft Dynamics CRM v4 Might Need Additional Architecture and Design

If you are looking at a development project and you think that Microsoft Dynamics CRM is not a good option, you might want to consider the following big-picture questions.

▶ Does your project require a layered rollback option?

With the introduction of Microsoft SQL 2005, we were offered a much more robust and sophisticated option in the world of the core backend database and for database maintenance. Microsoft SQL 2005 introduced the ability to take part of a Microsoft SQL Server database offline for maintenance, while the rest of the database was still up and running with a ton of data pouring in. These sophisticated features were not new to the world of huge databases, but were new to the world of Microsoft SQL Server. Microsoft Dynamics CRM v4 did not have these features available to it during design. Future versions of Microsoft Dynamics CRM will continue to take advantage of new technologies within their base toolsets, such as the new embedded features within Microsoft SQL Server.

If your project requires a layered rollback option, Microsoft Dynamics CRM v4 will most likely require additional architecture.

▶ Does your project require extensive financial analysis, balancing, data-driven statistical analysis, and accounting information?

Microsoft Dynamics CRM is not a statistical oriented programming language set). If your project depends heavily on financial information, various formulas, data from mathematical equations that creates data for other mathematical equations that all result in telling the system to do something at a certain time, you most likely will need further architectural design to use Microsoft Dynamics CRM as the base application.

It is not that Microsoft Dynamics CRM can't handle this. Instead, it's just that you will find that the core features in this area need additional architecture for you to potentially do all that you want to do.

▶ Does your project require extensive interaction with users who are not licensed Microsoft Dynamics CRM users (for instance, integration to the Internet for data collection)?

Microsoft actually falls in the gray area on this topic. Numerous accelerators are available to support your efforts to do event management and extensive marketing;

however, potential exists in this area that your project might need enhanced architecture to do what you want to do.

Now that we have an idea of which projects are a good fit and which projects should be assigned a Microsoft Dynamics CRM architect, let's look at what skills are required to make some of the previously mentioned changes.

Skills Required: Who Can Make the Changes

Microsoft Dynamics CRM can be modified and extended in different ways all of which require different levels of skill and different skill sets. A user without much training can add data to the system and use the application; a user with a little more training can create his own workflows; and a user with configuration training can change the look and feel of the forms, add new entities, and new attributes. However, even with the easiest features, it is wise to understand the training requirements and the experience that can make such a critical difference to the success of a project.

A number of Microsoft Dynamics CRM exams lead to various certifications that encompass four core skill sets: installation, application, customization, and extending. Each skill set maps to people with a background in four core areas: development/programming, network architecture/infrastructure, CRM consulting/training and application architecture. These are high-level categories, but are important to keep in mind. Take, for instance, a senior developer/software programmer. Developers can have many specialties, from the development languages that they are proficient in to their chosen focus for continued training and mastery. Two different developers can be so different that they are more like comparing apples and oranges than apples to apples.

To get a better idea about how Microsoft organizes certification, let's look at some requirements. The core Microsoft Dynamics CRM Business Management Solutions Professional exams are as follows:

- ▶ Extending Microsoft Dynamics CRM

- ▶ Applications for Microsoft Dynamics CRM

- ▶ Installation and Deployment for Microsoft Dynamics CRM

- ▶ Customization and Configuration for Microsoft Dynamics CRM

And the certifications require you to pass a core exam and certain electives. The list of exams and electives can be found within CustomerSource or PartnerSource.

Workshop

Radical Rail and Roofing is a company that installs metal roofs and decorative iron porch rails. It has a team of ten people who work all around a local area replacing old roofs with new, colored roofs and replacing wooden banisters and small fences with decorative iron rails. It also has a sales team, a marketing group, and a number of subcontractors and internal artists whom it tracks. Radical Rail and Roofing takes pride it its creative, one-of-a-kind railings and the largest selection of colors in their area of metal standing seam roofs. Radical Rail and Roofing is working with a Microsoft Dynamics CRM partner, who is installing Microsoft Dynamics CRM so that Radical Rail and Roofing can keep track of the team schedules and all the choices that its prospects and clients make (from its wide selection of offerings). Radical Rail and Roofing also subcontracts some of its services to local artists who come up with some of the unique design offerings for its railings, which internal craftsmen then produce.

Radical Rail and Roofing is also extending Microsoft Dynamics CRM to integrate with its Microsoft Dynamics GP accounting software. It will do quotes, orders, and invoicing through Microsoft Dynamics CRM integrated with Microsoft Outlook, and after the invoice has been generated, it will appear in Microsoft Dynamics GP as an unposted invoice for accounting to review and process. In addition, if accounting places a client on credit hold, the sales team, using Microsoft Dynamics CRM, will be notified and will not be able to create a quote or order until the credit hold is resolved.

Q&A

Q. Are there accounting applications that are a better fit with Microsoft Dynamics CRM, or can we integrate with our existing accounting software?

A. Some applications are more integration friendly. Just as Microsoft Dynamics CRM is built to be extended and integrated, your accounting application needs to have the necessary hooks to allow outside applications to communicate with it.

Q. We have internal resources that are going to focus on gaining additional skills in the Microsoft Dynamics CRM area. Where should we focus their efforts?

A. Depending on their background, you might want to divide and conquer. A developer is a good fit for extending the application and understanding the Microsoft SQL Server database environment. A network administrator can master all the little details of the installation and the long-term maintenance of checking the server logs and dealing with any environment errors. A technical user or manager who understands the business needs can be trained to do many customizations of the user interface, such as revising views, editing drop-down lists, and so on.

Q. *Reporting and business intelligence options are important to us. Is Microsoft Dynamics CRM a good platform for capturing all the data that we might need for sophisticated analysis?*

A. Yes. Microsoft Dynamics CRM is an excellent repository area for layers of data, including data that might be of interest to a specific report, to a Microsoft Excel CRM user, or to some of the more advanced business intelligence tools.

Quiz

1. Name four areas where the Microsoft Dynamics CRM software can be enhanced through the skills of a developer.

2. How many tests are required to become a Microsoft Certified Business Management Solutions Professional - Developer for Microsoft Dynamics CRM?

3. Name one reason why Microsoft Dynamics CRM is a good choice for a new custom development project.

4. Name one custom development project area where more advanced application architecture might be required.

Answers

1. Microsoft Dynamics CRM .NET Plug-Ins, iFrames, Microsoft Dynamics CRM Workflow, and Form OnSave/OnLoad.

2. Four.

3. The development teams would not have to write code to support security and user authentication.

4. The need to support hour-by-hour or minute-by-minute instantaneous database rollback.

Exercise

Think about the people who work within your organization and the resources you have access to through a Microsoft partner. As you consider these individuals, who would be a perfect fit to take on the role for your company of Microsoft Dynamics CRM infrastructure expert, Microsoft Dynamics CRM application expert, and Microsoft Dynamics CRM extending and developing expert? What about some of the other categories where you might want to expand into, such as an expert on the available third-party or ISV offerings or an expert on reporting and business analysis? List these people and interview them regarding their interest and their backgrounds.

Index

properties of, 209-211

sections

  adding, 201-203

  changing columns within, 204-205

  tabs, 203-204

FTC (Federal Trade Commission), Canned Spam Act, 255

G

General tab

  Account forms, 119-120

  Contacts, 224-227, 232

  leads

    Currency field, 106-107

    Rating field, 107

    Topic field, 107-106

  reports, 388

gift certificate templates (Mail Merge templates), 277-279

grouping

  report records, 390

  reports, 386

GUID (globally unique identifiers), Accounts, 127

H

Hoovers, 414-415

HTML email, 414

I

iFrames, adding to forms, 206-209, 433

importing

  Campaign Responses, 172

  Import Wizard, 410

  leads, 96-105

    Data Import Wizard, 98-99

    data maps, 99, 101

individual-owned reports, 387

Industry Data fields, Account forms, 121-122

installing CRM

  email router software, 49-50

  Microsoft Dynamics CRM Application Software, 46-47

  Microsoft Dynamics CRM Hosted, 45

  Microsoft Dynamics CRM Online, 44-45

  Microsoft Dynamics CRM On-Premise, 41-44

  Microsoft Dynamics CRM SQL Server Databases, 47

  Microsoft SQL Reporting Services, 48

  Microsoft Windows Server, 48-49

  MobileExpress, 44

  multitenants, 48

  Outlook clients, 44

integration

  accounting applications, 405-406

  bridge software, 402-404

  CRM, 52

  data migration, 408-409

  DMM (Data Migration Manager), 410-411

  external web sources, 405

  Import Wizard, 410

  ISV (Independent Software Vendors), 407-408

  points of connect, 404

intellectual capital, retaining, 7

Internet, adding to forms, 206-209, 433

investment, ROI (Returns on Investment), 7

ISV (Independent Software Vendors), integration, 407-408

J

job roles, tailoring security roles to match job roles, 62

Job Title field (Contacts General tab), 225

K

KBA (knowledge base articles), support management, 325-328

FREE Online Edition

Your purchase of **Sams Teach Yourself Microsoft Dynamics CRM 4 in 24 Hours** includes access to a free online edition for 45 days through the Safari Books Online subscription service. Nearly every Sams book is available online through Safari Books Online, along with more than 5,000 other technical books and videos from publishers such as Addison-Wesley Professional, Cisco Press, Exam Cram, IBM Press, O'Reilly, Prentice Hall, and Que.

SAFARI BOOKS ONLINE allows you to search for a specific answer, cut and paste code, download chapters, and stay current with emerging technologies.

Activate your FREE Online Edition at www.informit.com/safarifree

> **STEP 1:** Enter the coupon code: OICEGDB.

> **STEP 2:** New Safari users, complete the brief registration form. Safari subscribers, just log in.

If you have difficulty registering on Safari or accessing the online edition, please e-mail customer-service@safaribooksonline.com